THE
SOCIAL
SOURCES OF
FINANCIAL
POWER

A volume in the series

Cornell Studies in Political Economy

EDITED BY PETER J. KATZENSTEIN

A full list of titles in the series appears at the end of the book.

THE SOCIAL SOURCES OF FINANCIAL POWER

Domestic Legitimacy and International Financial Orders

Leonard Seabrooke

Cornell University Press

ITHACA AND LONDON

First published 2006 by Cornell University Press

Printed in the United States of America

Library of Congress Cataloging-in-Publication Data

Seabrooke, Leonard.
    The social sources of financial power : domestic legitimacy and international financial orders / Leonard Seabrooke.
      p. cm. — (Cornell studies in political economy)
    Includes bibliographical references and index.
    ISBN-13: 978-0-8014-4380-0 (cloth : alk. paper)
    ISBN-10: 0-8014-4380-6 (cloth : alk. paper)
    1. International finance—Social aspects.   2. International finance—Political aspects. 3. Economic policy—Social aspects.   4. Legitimacy of governments.   5. Economic assistance, Domestic—Political aspects.   6. Economics—Sociological aspects.   I. Title.
II. Series.
  HG3881.S395   2006
  332'.042—dc22
                                            2005027432

Cloth printing   10 9 8 7 6 5 4 3 2 1

Till min jordgubbe, Anna

Contents

Figures

Preface

How do states generate the power to shape their international financial order? Explanations invariably concentrate on relationships at the "big end of town": those between financial institutions, regulators, and financial elites. These relationships are undoubtedly of vital importance, but existing studies neglect how states can generate financial power from people earning below median income. To overlook the potential contribution of people in lower-income groupings does a disservice to understanding historical change in the international political economy, because it favors a story of continuity among financial institutions and elites, which, in turn, de-emphasizes how non-elites can transform their political and economic environment. By including lower-income groupings we can expose discontinuities in the story of how states generate financial power and provide a better means to differentiate the domestic origins of international financial orders.

This book turns the spotlight away from the big end of town. It investigates how a state's legitimation of credit, property, and tax politics for lower-income groupings can generate a social source of financial power. This social source of financial power then helps the state's capacity to influence the international financial order of the day. My chief aim is to highlight how state intervention in the economy for people in lower-income groupings builds a social source of financial power—a point largely overlooked in studies of "state capacity," "varieties of capitalism," and the like. To remedy this omission I suggest that questioning the legitimacy of state intervention in the economy for lower-income groupings requires us to disaggregate that intervention into positive and negative forms. This is the case because the conferral of legitimacy relies on consent from non-elites that emerges from a contestation of power between state and society. People in lower-income groupings believe that they have a right to positive state intervention in accordance with their economic social norms. If the state then intervenes to help them achieve their belief-driven wants, they will confer legitimacy on the state and provide greater stability to the financial system in general. From this I posit an ideal type that positive state intervention for lower-income groupings on tax burdens, credit, and property access deepens and broadens the domestic pool of capital and propagates financial practices that bring capital flowing back to the state. Conversely, negative state intervention permits greater room for rentier interests and undermines a state's international financial capacity. These dynamics provide the subject matter of this book.

This book also responds to a concern that the literature in institutional theory, comparative political economy, and international political economy have all excluded or downplayed the concept of legitimacy. Even the growing literature on "economic constructivism" has a poor understanding of how legitimacy is required between state and society, and instead has viewed the proclamation of ideas from contests between ideational entrepreneurs as auto-legitimating. This will not do. As a remedy this book seeks to augment economic constructivism with Weberian economic sociology. The pay-off from this marriage, I contend, is a better understanding of how legitimation contests between state and society generate a sustainable social source of financial power.

I have incurred intellectual debts while writing this book, and good manners dictate that I must publicly honor my creditors. I thank, first and foremost, John M. Hobson, whom I first came to know through a mutual respect for Max Weber's work, and with whom I have built a tremendous friendship. I thank John for his enthusiasm and questioning, and for countless splendid academic debates conducted over Sydney billiard tables. My special thanks to Mark Blyth, whose extensive feedback was vitally important in revising the manuscript. My gratitude also goes to Mlada Bukovansky for her criticisms and suggestions on draft manuscripts. Thanks also to those who responded to various chapters and papers. They are Mark Beeson, Stephen Bell, Jacqueline Best, Brett Bowden, Michael J. Boyle, Peter Breiner, Eric Helleiner, Randall Germain, Patricia Goff, Geoffrey K. Ingham, Patrick Thaddeus Jackson, Paul Langley, Ian Marsh, Adam David Morton, Herman M. Schwartz, Ole Jacob Sending, Jason Sharman, and Tianbiao Zhu. I am also grateful to Richard Leaver for his inestimable intellectual support over the last decade.

A range of academics, policy makers, and archivists contributed to the development of the case studies investigated in this book. In particular I thank Jennifer Amyx, Lance Davis, Richard Deeg, Oliver Wavell Grant, Timothy Guinnane, Avner Offer, and Frances Rosenbluth for their advice. My thanks also go to Sarah Millard, archivist at the Bank of England, and Martin Müller, archivist at the Historical Institute of the Deutsche Bank Archive. Staff from the National Community Reinvestment Coalition, the Federal Reserve, and the Office of Thrift Supervision generously afforded me time for interviews.

Working with Cornell University Press has been an absolute joy. Peter Katzenstein provided immensely helpful feedback on the original manuscript and encouraged me to demonstrate how tools from economic sociology can revise standard understandings of change in political economy. I am grateful to Roger Haydon for pushing me to make the prose clear and for his support. I also thank Teresa Jesionowski for her patience.

The book was extensively rewritten and then further revised while I was a Research Fellow in the Department of International Relations in the Research School of Pacific and Asian Studies at the Australian National University—and where I now hold a position as Adjunct Senior Fellow. My gratitude goes to Chris Reus-Smit for his intellectual support over the past few years. I also thank my ANU colleagues for fostering a happy and productive research environment. I am deeply indebted to John Ravenhill for his intellectual counsel, in general, and insightful comments on draft chapters in particular. Mary-Louise Hickey proofread drafts and provided feedback on the manuscript in general. I also thank Barry Hindess, Ben Kerkvliet, Andrew MacIntyre, and Ben Reilly for their advice and collegiality. A band of hard-working and hard-playing graduate students at ANU provided important feedback on the manuscript and also made social life in Canberra enjoyable. I tip my cap, in particular, to André Broome, Taylor Speed, and Shogo Suzuki.

My thanks go to old friends and scholars, Jessica Ellis, Carmen Huckel, Justine Hugo, Maryanne Kelton, Chris Lumsden, David Scott Mathieson, Philip J. Radford, and Ween Thompson. My deepest gratitude goes to my parents, Len and Betty, and sister Natalie, who have encouraged me through my eternal studentism (perhaps Mum's childhood book subsidies should take the blame for this). Thanks also to the Carnerup family, with whom life in Øresund has kicked off personally and professionally. Tusind tak to Ove Kaj Pedersen, John L. Campbell, and all my colleagues at the International Center for Business and Politics at the Copenhagen Business School for their intellectual encouragement and support.

This book is dedicated to my bride, Anna Carnerup, whose passion for science, food, wine, and merrymaking keeps life fun. *Tack för din kärlek och ditt stöd. Du är som solen på mitt ansikte.*

LEONARD SEABROOKE

Copenhagen, Denmark

Abbreviations

ABA	American Bankers' Association (U.S.)
ACORN	Association of Community Organizations for Reform Now (U.S.)
AHP	Affordable Housing Program (U.S.)
AMF	Asian Monetary Fund
ASEAN	Association of Southeast Asian Nations
BIS	Bank for International Settlements
Bodenkreditinstitute	Public Land Credit Institutes (Germany)
BoE	Bank of England
BoJ	Bank of Japan
CCPC	Cooperative Credit Purchasing Company (Japan)
CDC	Community Development Corporations (U.S.)
CFI	Community Financial Institutions (U.S.)
CRA	Community Reinvestment Act 1977 (U.S.)
DIDMCA	Depository Institutions Deregulation and Monetary Control Act 1980 (U.S.)
Fannie Mae	Federal National Mortgage Association (U.S.)
FDIC	Federal Deposit Insurance Corporation (U.S.)
FDICIA	FDIC Improvement Act (U.S.)
Fed	Federal Reserve Bank (U.S.)
FHA	Federal Housing Administration (U.S.)
FHEFSSA	Federal Housing Enterprises Financial Safety and Soundness Act 1991 (U.S.)
FHLB	Federal Home Loan Bank (U.S.)
FHLBB	Federal Home Loan Bank Board (U.S.)
FHLBMA	Federal Home Loan Bank Modernization Act 1999 (U.S.)
FIRREA	Financial Institutions Reform, Recovery, and Enforcement Act 1989 (U.S.)
FMAs	Federal Mortgage Agencies (U.S.)

FRC	Financial Revitalization Commission (Japan)
Freddie Mac	Federal Home Loan Mortgage Corporation (U.S.)
FSA	Financial Supervisory Agency (Japan)
FSLIC	Federal Savings and Loan Insurance Corporation (U.S.)
G.St.GA	Garn-St. Germain Act 1982 (U.S.)
Ginnie Mae	Government National Mortgage Association (U.S.)
GLBA	Gramm-Leach-Bliley Act 1999 (U.S.)
Großbanken	Great Banks (Germany)
GSE	Government sponsored enterprise (U.S.)
HLC	Housing Loan Corporation (Japan)
HMDA	Home Mortgage Disclosure Act 1975 (U.S.)
HOEPA	Home Owner Equity Protection Act 1994 (U.S.)
HOLC	Homeowners' Loan Corporation (U.S.)
HUD	Department of Housing and Urban Development (U.S.)
Hypotheken	Mortgage banks (Germany)
IBA	Independent Bankers' Association (U.S.)
ILSA	International Lending Supervisory Act 1983 (U.S.)
IMF	International Monetary Fund
IPO	Initial public offering
IRAs	Individual Retirement Accounts (U.S.)
jūsen	Housing loan company (Japan)
Länder	Federal states (Germany)
Landschaften	Public agrarian large-landholder banks (Germany)
LDP	Liberal Democratic Party (Japan)
LIGs	Lower-income groupings
LSE	London Stock Exchange
LTCB	Long-Term Credit Banks (Japan)
MBS	Mortgage-backed security
MoA	Ministry of Agriculture, Forestry and Fisheries (Japan)
MoC	Ministry of Construction (Japan)
MoF	Ministry of Finance (Japan)
NBFIs	Non-bank financial intermediaries (U.S.)
NCRC	National Community Reinvestment Coalition (U.S.)
NFHA	National Fair Housing Alliance (U.S.)
NPA	National People's Action (U.S.)
Nōrinchūkin	Central Association for Agricultural Cooperatives
OCC	Office of the Comptroller of the Currrency (U.S.)
OECD	Organisation for Economic Co-operation and Development
OTS	Office of Thrift Supervision (U.S.)
Preußenkasse	Prussian Cooperative Central Bank (Germany)

RCDRIA	Riegle Community Development and Regulatory Improvement Act 1994 (U.S.)
REFCorp	Resolution Funding Corporation (U.S.)
RM	Reichsmark
RNIBEA	Riegle-Neal Interstate Banking Efficiency Act 1994 (U.S.)
RTC	Resolution Trust Corporation (U.S.)
S&L	Savings and loans association (U.S.)
Sparkassen	Public savings banks (Germany)
SPD	Social Democratic Party (Germany)
TRA	Tax Reform Act (U.S.)
VA	Veterans' Administration (U.S.)
yūcho	Postal savings system (Japan)
zaitō	Fiscal Investment and Loan Program (Japan)
Zenginkyō	All Japan Banking Federation (Japan)
Zenshinren	Central Association for Small Business Credit Cooperative Associations (Japan)

THE
SOCIAL
SOURCES OF
FINANCIAL
POWER

1

Legitimacy Is a Social Source
of Financial Power

"Financial wealth consists in promises and nothing else."[1] Credit and money are social constructions and can be generated only if we believe in their legitimacy, if we believe that others will honor their promises to lend or to pay their debts. Because legitimacy is necessary to sustain credit and money, actors' everyday belief-driven economic social actions have causal significance in shaping a financial system. This is all the more true because allocations of credit allow some actors to satisfy their material desires and not others. It is not surprising, then, that how credit and money are distributed within an economy breeds political struggles in ordinary economic life. These battles over everyday economic life are fought by actors whose actions are imbued with beliefs in what is legitimate according to economic social norms, and are waged with the hope that ideas and interests can be transformed through the daily grind.[2]

Everyday economic struggles can be seen in the most seemingly ordinary aspects of a state's financial and fiscal systems: who has access to credit, who can hold property, and who pays what kinds of taxes. State reforms to these systems concern not only financial elites and institutions, but the broader population. People in lower-income groupings (people with below median income, hereafter referred to as LIGs) are of particular importance here because they often find it difficult to access credit without state support yet, if they can, provide a potentially rich source of public and private capital to a financial system. Who LIGs are exactly is particular to the income distribution within the society under investigation. As such, we should not think of them as a class group like the working or middle classes, but as individuals

1. W. G. Langworthy Taylor, "The Source of Financial Power," *Journal of Political Economy* 13, 3 (1905): 369.
2. On "everyday" action in political economy see John M. Hobson and Leonard Seabrooke, eds., *Everyday International Political Economy: Non-Elite Actors and the Transformation of the World Economy* (forthcoming). On the interweaving of interests and ideas see Mark Blyth, *Great Transformations: Economic Ideas and Institutional Change in the Twentieth Century* (Cambridge: Cambridge University Press, 2002), 37.

whose income is below median, who do not live in poverty, and who associate with others in groups that are recombinant and based on more than one's bank balance but also specific social values and norms.[3] States often target people above the poverty line but below median income for positive intervention because they more readily provide policy success that can be used to strengthen the state's claims to legitimacy. As a consequence, those who are unable and unassisted in scraping together some savings do not play much of a role in my story.

LIGs share frustration about how the economy should be working for them. Their often-frustrated potential to access credit makes their relationship with the state on financial matters highly contested. LIGs therefore call for state intervention on taxes, credit, and property so that they may fulfill their wants. Such contestation from LIGs can then change how the state influences the international realm.[4] The aim of this book is to examine the mechanisms that link the state and social groups in broadening or narrowing a state's social source of financial power.[5] Understanding these mechanisms requires us to interpret how actors behave according to their economic social norms.

This book puts forward the proposition that if the state intervenes positively on behalf of LIGs, it can generate a social source of financial power by broadening and deepening the domestic pool of capital, which then bolsters the state's influence in the international financial order. Conversely, if the state intervenes against the interests of LIGs, it permits room for a "rentier shift" spurred on by economic elites. This shift diminishes the state's international influence by narrowing the domestic pool of capital and investing it in politically and economically reckless ways that foster discontent at home.[6] It follows, then, that contests over the legitimacy of everyday financial reforms leads to transformations in the function, role, and purpose of financial and fiscal institutions in the domestic economy, and also influence how a state engages in the international political economy. I call the latter international financial capacity, understood as the capacity to draw credit from and increase the generation of credit to the international financial order, as well as influencing this order's regulatory and normative structure.

---

3. Gary Runciman's term "systacts" for recombinant groups based on a multiple forms of identity and economic and social status is useful here. W. G. Runciman, *A Treatise on Social Theory*, Vol. 2 (Cambridge: Cambridge University Press, 1989), 20–27.
4. See the excellent study of how non-elite groups shape economic development in Diane E. Davis, *Discipline and Development: Middle Classes and Prosperity in East Asia and Latin America* (Cambridge: Cambridge University Press, 2004).
5. John L. Campbell, *Institutional Change and Globalization* (Princeton: Princeton University Press, 2004), Chapter 3.
6. A *rentier* can be understood as a person who substantially benefits from what may be socially perceived as "non-productive," "unearned," or "passive" investments, particularly debt securities and non-owner-occupier land. See, among others, John A. Hobson, *The Problem of the Unemployed* (London: Methuen & Co., 1896), 91, 99.

My concern is with the domestic social sources that permit international financial capacity. I study England and Germany in the turn from the late nineteenth to the early twentieth centuries, and the United States and Japan in the closing decades of the twentieth century. Under particular scrutiny is state legitimation of financial reforms to LIGs during two periods in which financial institutions became more concentrated under intense financial internationalization, and in which LIGs agitated for increased economic and political representation.

In contrast to most studies of financial power, I turn the spotlight away from the "big end of town" to focus on ordinary peoples' concerns, to understand the opportunities and constraints for LIGs to contest the legitimacy of state policy changes to what I call the "financial reform nexus": the interaction of credit, property, and tax politics. Taxation is studied because it is the primary means through which governments directly affect the private sector; property is studied because it provides the "institutional membrane that connects the state and economy"; and credit is studied because it shows the capacity to transform access to resources beyond existing monetary stores.[7] Credit access, property ownership, and tax burdens provide focal points for LIGs to contest the legitimacy of financial reforms and to call upon the state to intervene on their behalf and against the interests of rentiers. LIGs contest the legitimacy of changes to a financial reform nexus through their belief-driven actions on how the economy should work for them.

I therefore seek to answer the big question of how states create financial power, by analyzing small dynamics: how a state's legitimation of its financial reform nexus for LIGs bolsters or undermines its creation of a broad and deep domestic pool of capital that the state and private financial institutions may then employ internationally. Such a scenario requires positive state intervention to enable capital to flow up the chain from LIGs' pocketbooks to smaller financial institutions and, eventually, the global financial marketplace. This scenario represents an ideal type, an interpretive scheme with which to compare against the case material to "reveal the network of interrelations which distinguishes one social structure from another."[8] Importantly, the ideal type requires that we disaggregate state intervention into positive and negative forms, and discuss how domestic institutional and social change relies on dynamic relationships between the state and various

---

7. Campbell, *Institutional Change*, 132. See, in particular, Sven Steinmo, *Taxation and Democracy: Swedish, British, and American Approaches to Financing the Modern State* (New Haven: Yale University Press, 1993).
8. Reinhard Bendix, *Nation-Building and Citizenship* (Berkeley: University of California Press, 1977), 22. I follow Max Weber's understanding of an ideal type as "a purely limiting concept with which the real situation or action is *compared* and surveyed for the explication of certain of its significant components." See Max Weber, *The Methodology of the Social Sciences* (Glencoe, Ill.: Free Press, 1949), 93.

social groups. These dynamics, in turn, have important implications for how the state interacts with others in the international political economy. The ideal type also provides a logical sequence through which we can forge an understanding of how individual subjective belief-driven actions respond to institutional opportunities and constraints.

Readers might object: "You're getting carried away—people below median income don't have much money, and they certainly don't influence the international financial system." But they can. LIGs provide a potentially large source of capital for financial institutions that operate domestically and internationally, as well as contributing essential portions of state revenues. Private financial institutions know this; for example, in both periods under study here, they increasingly sought to gain access to the deposits of "small savers." They were less keen, however, to extend credit back to them.

The biggest obstacle to LIGs receiving credit is that financial institutions tend to be myopic in their assessment of the creditworthiness of people on below median income. They therefore require additional economic or regulatory incentives to lend, and only when the state intervenes positively will financial institutions extend credit to LIGs.[9] If such intervention occurs, then a "cumulative process" can happen, permitting an increase in general consumption, indebtedness, and productivity from the social construction of credit with state support.[10] This cumulative process opens up new fruitful avenues of credit extension that contribute to a state's international financial capacity as long as these promises to pay can be honored by holding legitimacy. Further, if permitted access to credit and property, LIGs are also more likely to borrow heavily and engage in financial innovations that send capital up the chain from the pocketbook to the global marketplace.

More often than not such a chance is blocked. The English case from 1890 to 1915 demonstrates that when LIGs are ignored, the strong and broad roots of a financial system can wither and leave the state vulnerable to financial shocks. The financial shock associated with the economic burden of mobilizing for World War I provides a case in point. LIGs' withdrawal of confidence in the financial system, as seen in street protests at the collapse of the National Penny Bank in 1914, exposed the waning legitimacy of the English financial reform nexus and its weakening international financial capacity. The German and Japanese cases provide even more grim but fundamentally different tales of how LIGs' access to credit, property, and tax relief was blocked by negative state intervention into the financial reform nexus in support of a rentier shift. In contrast, the U.S. case tells us that positive state intervention permits LIGs' mortgage repayments to be

---

9. Max Weber, *General Economic History* (New York: Collier Books, 1961), 172, 191–92.
10. This view is informed by Knut Wicksell's view of credit as a "cumulative process" that can raise aggregate demand as long as its value is intersubjectively held to be true, as well as John A. Hobson's theory of underconsumption. See Knut Wicksell, *Nationalekonomiska essäer* (Stockholm: City University Press, 1997), 96–110; John A. Hobson, "Underconsumption: An Exposition and a Reply," *Economica* 42 (1933).

channeled up the chain to global investment, while also encouraging financial innovations that further deepen and broaden the domestic pool of capital. This activity is now commonplace in the United States, undoubtedly today's greatest financial power. As such, it may lead us to wonder why LIGs are not normally considered a source of financial power.

The Sources of Financial Power

Most of our understandings of the sources of financial power come from economics and political economy literature that views actors as individual economic utility maximizers. Such studies view financial power as emerging from opportunities exploited by individuals and states-as-individuals, and also from the capacity of these actors to place constraints on others within the marketplace.

Within the literature on opportunity, financial growth emerges from the efficiencies of market competition and from the guiding role of institutions that can provide regulatory oversight. Typical here are quantitative studies that examine the relationship between the financial sector and the "real" economy over time by aggregating financial wealth and comparing it against conventional national economic accounts.[11] The aim is normally to assess whether or not intense financial intermediation contributes to national economic growth. This research details different kinds of financial systems over time, including whether states were more bank-intensive or capital market-intensive, the extent of credit available to non-financial enterprises, and the different types of financial assets. What we do not get from the literature, however, is the politics of why some groups within an economy are allocated credit and others are not. A state's capacity to generate financial power, therefore, is judged on the basis of a static assumption of its factor endowments and institutional logics.

Within the literature on constraint, political economists have emphasized how factor endowments are not natural but born from political struggles among rational economic actors.[12] The focus here is on the political constraints imposed by the financially powerful "veto players" who seek to maximize their economic utility by blocking others' access to credit and capital. Studies of different degrees of state centralization have been particularly important here in outlining why different state forms lead to different kinds of financial systems.[13]

---

11. For example, Raymond Goldsmith, *Financial Structure and Development* (New Haven: Yale University Press, 1969); Thorsten Beck, Norman Loayza, and Ross Levine, "Finance and the Sources of Growth," *Journal of Financial Economics* 58, 1 (2000).

12. The exemplar here is Daniel Verdier, *Moving Money: Banking and Finance in the Industrialized World* (Cambridge: Cambridge University Press, 2002).

13. Ibid.; Andrew MacIntyre, *The Power of Institutions: Political Architecture and Governance* (Ithaca: Cornell University Press, 2002); Kenneth Schultz and Barry R. Weingast, "The Dem-

Also included in the literature on constraint is work on how international financial markets are able to restrict states' domestic behavior or, as the case may have it, how they often permit states "room to move."[14] These studies provide a great service in breaking down aggregated financial data into political struggles between actors that tell us why State A is more bank-oriented and State B more oriented toward capital markets. As a consequence, this literature demonstrates that financial globalization is not producing convergence but divergence.[15] Scholars in this area have, understandably, focused on actors who are at the top end of the food chain: the international financial market trader and the national politician. These players act typically out of self-interest, and changes within states and within different international financial orders are primarily determined by the outcomes from such struggles. The study of outcomes can also be tested statistically because it is assumed that the actors' preferences are stable over time as they seek to maximize their economic utility.

Both the literatures on opportunity and constraint in the formation of financial power ignore the role of economic social norms that inform struggle over how the economy should work. They concentrate almost exclusively on elites and institutions, rather than LIGs and institutional and social change. The concept of legitimacy is also absent from such studies. They have some difficulty, therefore, understanding how financial orders are created and constructed from institutional and social change, because there is a thin conception of how economic relations are socially constructed.

In an attempt to address these shortcomings, I follow Max Weber's insight that "purely material interests and calculations of advantages do not form a sufficiently reliable basis for a system of imperative coordination."[16] Any order requires legitimacy to reproduce itself, because credit generation demands an intersubjective belief that promises to pay will be honored.[17] As

---

ocratic Advantage: Institutional Foundations of Financial Power in International Competition," *International Organization* 57, 1 (2003).

14. Layna Mosley, *Global Capital and National Governments* (Cambridge: Cambridge University Press, 2003); Michael Loriaux, Meredith Woo-Cumings, Kent E. Calder, Sylvia Maxfield, and Sofía Pérez, *Capital Ungoverned: Liberalizing Finance in Interventionist States* (Ithaca: Cornell University Press, 1997). See also Leonard Seabrooke, "Civilizing Global Capital Markets: Room to Groove?," in Brett Bowden and Leonard Seabrooke, eds., *Global Standards of Market Civilization* (London: Routledge/RIPE Series in Global Political Economy, forthcoming).

15. On convergence see Susanne Soederberg, Georg Menz, and Philip Cerny, eds., *Internalizing Globalization: The Rise of Neoliberalism and the Decline of National Varieties of Capitalism* (London: Palgrave, 2005); Susan Strange, *The Retreat of the State* (Cambridge: Cambridge University Press, 1996). On divergence see John L. Campbell and Ove K. Pedersen, eds., *The Rise of Neoliberalism and Institutional Analysis* (Princeton: Princeton University Press, 2001); Herbert Kitschelt, Peter Lange, Gary Marks, and John D. Stephens, eds., *Continuity and Change in Contemporary Capitalism* (Cambridge: Cambridge University Press, 1999).

16. Max Weber, *Theory of Social and Economic Organization* (New York: Free Press, 1964), 325.

17. On money as a social construction, see, most recently, Geoffrey Ingham, *The Nature of Money* (Cambridge: Polity, 2004).

such, economic social norms do matter for institutional and social change, and to understand them we need to specify how people and institutions behave in different states and periods of time. I contend that it is the contestation of legitimacy of power within states that is especially valuable in understanding the domestic social sources of financial power and, therefore, how international financial orders change over time.

Economic Social Norms and Institutional Change

I seek to enhance the emergent literature on economic constructivism with a strong conception of legitimacy and belief-driven action drawn from Weberian economic sociology.[18] In doing so, I cross over boundaries between comparative political economy, international political economy, the "new institutionalism," and economic sociology. While the next chapter deals with criticisms directed at economic constructivist and new institutionalist literatures, it is important to first provide some definitions in the understanding of institutional and social change put forward here. I also outline some of the major shortcomings of extant economic constructivist literature that provide space for this work to provide a theoretical as well as an empirical contribution.

I view norms as "collectively shared expectations" and, like all economic constructivists, see that ideational factors are important "all the way through" in informing interests.[19] Economic social norms include both shared expectations and conventions about the mechanics of economic transactions, as well as how economic behavior should change to meet new collective expectations and form new conventions.[20] Economic social norms saturate the determination of material interests and are also concerned with how strictly non-economic behavior influences economic utility (for example, should the law stop me from bashing an old lady and stealing her handbag?), as well as how economic behavior influences non-

18. While this is not an exhaustive list, and recognizing that "constructivism" is a broad church that ranges from "rationalist systemic" to "critical" or "postmodern" scholars, some of the principal works in economic constructivism are Blyth, *Great Transformations;* Kathleen R. McNamara, *The Currency of Ideas: Monetary Politics in the European Union* (Ithaca: Cornell University Press, 1998); Rawi Abdelal, *National Purpose in the World Economy: Post-Soviet States in Comparative Perspective* (Ithaca: Cornell University Press, 2001); and Craig Parsons, *A Certain Idea of Europe* (Ithaca: Cornell University Press, 2003). The canonical book here is Martha Finnemore, *National Interests in International Society* (Ithaca: Cornell University Press, 1996); her work has greatly influenced both security and political economy literatures.

19. First quote: Peter J. Katzenstein, "Introduction: Alternative Perspectives on National Security," in Peter J. Katzenstein, ed., *The Culture of National Security* (New York: Columbia University Press, 1996), 7. Second quote: Blyth, *Great Transformations,* 270.

20. Max Weber, *From Max Weber: Essays in Sociology* (New York: Oxford University Press, 1946), 301; Max Weber, *Economy and Society: An Outline of Interpretive Sociology,* Vols. 1 and 2 (Berkeley: University of California Press, 1978), 1:33.

economic life (for example, how can consumption tax increases be fair when it means my grandmother cannot afford her medicine anymore?).[21]

Economic social norms are not static but dynamic and are therefore poorly understood as radical shifts or within a punctuated equilibrium model. Nor can economic social norms fruitfully be discussed as only national aggregates or as the possessions of "ideational entrepreneurs." Rather, economic social norms are generated from an individual level and then become aggregates as individuals seek to form collectives according to their perception of their own "life-chances" to change the political and economic dynamics of their time (more on this below).[22] This conception allows us to not reduce one's position in society to "class" or a similarly "rump materialist" logic that separates ideas from material effects.[23]

Examining how economic social norms are different for groups with different life-chances allows us to acknowledge, as stressed by Norbert Elias, that norms are "double-edged" and "bind people to each other and at the same time turn people so bound against others."[24] Once we discuss different groups with economic social norms, we cannot simply collapse an aggregated economic social norm into an institutional form, because while the state may propagate an economic social norm that favors their interests, LIGs may reject this norm and contest it.

In discussing institutional change, there are compelling grounds to accept Douglass North's definition of an institution as "any form of constraint that human beings devise to shape action"—except that it includes too much and therefore explains little.[25] If we are open to the notion that institutional change does not follow a linear evolutionary logic or rely on exogenous shocks, then it is critical that we maintain a conception of society that exists separate from these institutions. Accordingly, institutions within this book are primarily formal: financial institutions, laws regarding property ownership, tax regimes, electoral and party systems, and agencies of state intervention.

Often social change, particularly change in economic social norms, does precede and inform institutional change. On other occasions institutional change will occur prior to a change in economic social norms. Either way, potential sequencing problems can emerge from differences in the pace of

---

21. Respectively: economically relevant phenomena and economically conditioned phenomena in Weber's schema. Richard Swedberg, *Max Weber and the Idea of Economic Sociology* (Princeton: Princeton University Press, 1998), 163.
22. Weber, *Economy and Society*, 1: 302, 927–29.
23. Karl Marx, *A Contribution to the Critique of Political Economy* (New York: International Publishers, 1976), 20–21. A defense of how "rump materialism" affects life in addition to ideas is provided in Alexander Wendt, *Social Theory of International Politics* (Cambridge: Cambridge University Press, 1999), 109–10.
24. Norbert Elias, *The Germans: Power Struggles and the Development of Habitus in the Nineteenth and Twentieth Centuries* (New York: Columbia University Press, 1996), 160.
25. Douglass C. North, *Institutions, Institutional Change and Economic Performance* (Cambridge: Cambridge University Press, 1990), 4.

institutional and social change, and we should be wary about lumping social change into the institutional basket.[26] We should be especially cautious of this problem because it can lead to a functionalist interpretation of institutional change that tells us about the persistence and purpose of institutions, but not the ideas that informed their development.

We can, however, go too far in the opposite direction. While we should applaud recent economic constructivists' attention to the use of ideas as weapons in struggles over institutional change, this literature undermines itself by confining its claims about the causal significance of ideas to moments of radical uncertainty, when ideational entrepreneurs can carry their ideas as weapons into the fray. As such, economic constructivists could be interpreted as producing ideational punctuated equilibrium models of how ideational entrepreneurs engender institutional change only in periods of radical uncertainty. Such moments are preferred because this is when "ideas' distinct effects are clearest," suggesting a selection bias problem.[27] Worse still, such analyses could be viewed as collapsing economic social norms into institutions with little discussion of society.

A further concern with economic constructivism is that its focus on ideational entrepreneurs leads to a top-down conception of legitimacy by proclamation. This is a serious problem for economic constructivism because it means that the focus is on claims to legitimacy, rather than analysis of the belief-driven actions that led to a conferral of legitimacy from actors subordinate to those doing the proclaiming.[28] Legitimacy is a two-way street.

I suggest that economic constructivism can be augmented with Weberian economic sociology, including the assertion of an idiographic rather than nomothetic methodological individualism.[29] An idiographic methodological individualism leads us to interpret the influences and motivations of individual choice that are particular to a social and historical context, while nomothetic methodological individualism identifies universal incentives and motivations upon individual choice to explain historical change. As is clear throughout the book, there is much work to be done on understanding how ideas, norms, and interest interact in everyday life. I rejoin this discussion at some length in the following chapter.

Legitimacy and Everyday Economic Social Action

My chief theoretical concern is to augment economic constructivism with Weberian economic sociology. However, Weberian economic sociology, and

26. Gérard Roland, "Understanding Institutional Change: Fast-Moving and Slow-Moving Institutions," *Studies in Comparative International Development* 38, 4 (2004).

27. Craig Parsons, "Showing Ideas as Causes: The Origins of the European Union," *International Organization* 56, 1 (2002): 78.

28. David Beetham, *The Legitimation of Power* (London: Macmillan, 1991), 31–35.

29. Weber, *Economy and Society*, 1: 4, 13.

scholars working within economic sociology in general, can also learn a few new tricks here as well. The same applies to rationalist and historical institutionalist scholarship, including the latter's range of "state capacity" and "varieties of capitalism" literature. It is noteworthy that the concept of legitimacy is excluded from nearly all of this literature. But this is perhaps not surprising. Legitimacy is a slippery concept to mull over, and a devil to prove if it is understood as simply one's profession of belief in another's right to rule.[30] From this view there is not enough materiality to legitimacy for us to treat the concept seriously within the social sciences. In other words, how can we possibly know if Actor A really believed in the legitimacy of Actor B or in *x*? Maybe his or her motives were different? Maybe his or her actions were different from the professed belief? Legitimacy, one could criticize, simply means imputing what we want to see into the case material because we cannot see into people's minds.[31]

A key problem here is one of studying the legitimation of power relations as only belief rather than belief-driven action. Beliefs do drive actions. They go beyond the mind and the mouth and lead one to pull out one's pocketbook, to sign petitions, to vote, to protest, and to alter one's financial relations with institutions that violate economic social norms. In seeking to explain how ideas influence interests, Weber's famous "switchman metaphor" is worth quoting:

> Not ideas, but material and ideal interests directly govern men's conduct. Yet, very frequently the "world images" that have been created by "ideas" have, like switchmen, determined the tracks along which action has been pushed by the dynamic of interest. "From what" and "for what" one wished to be redeemed and, let us not forget, "could be" redeemed, depended upon *one's image of the world.*[32]

This metaphor has often been used to convey the role of ideas in shaping interests, and also to suggest how institutional change is path dependent.[33] It is crucial to remember, however, that the ideas are not separated from the individual and his or her engagement with real world contingencies. The focus should be on the switchmen and the train's passage, not the tracks. Switchmen operate mechanisms that permit a train to change tracks, but they do

30. This view is often attributed to Max Weber. But for Weber it is not only belief, but actions that demonstrate belief that are important. Beetham, *Legitimation of Power,* 8–10, 219; Weber, *Economy and Society,* 1: 213–15.
31. Robert Grafstein, "The Failure of Weber's Conception of Legitimacy: Its Causes and Implications," *Journal of Politics* 43, 2 (1981).
32. Weber, *From Max Weber,* 280, my emphasis.
33. John Kurt Jacobsen "Much Ado About Ideas: The Cognitive Factor in Economic Policy," *World Politics* 47, 2 (1995). On path dependence and policy feedback see Paul Pierson, *Politics in Time: History, Institutions, and Social Analysis* (Princeton: Princeton University Press, 2004).

not independently determine its passage. Trains can be robbed, derailed, delinked, or run out of steam. If we follow the notion of the switchman as establishing a line of path dependence until the consequent institutional equilibrium is punctured by uncertainty and reset by the next switchman along the line, then our understanding of social change is diminished. We should follow the politics and the path, the agents and the structures.

For Weber, everyday economic struggle is more important than moments of crisis and uncertainty. While charismatic leaders can lead us down the garden path, it is the relationship between state and society on everyday matters that has the real capacity to transform environments.[34] Furthermore, once we look at the politics of the historical period in question, we are less likely to explain institutional and social change through the lens of the present or a path dependent "narrative."[35] We can also provide agents with more agency than historical institutionalists have allowed in discussing how structures constrain individuals through a logic of appropriateness.[36]

A focus on everyday economic struggle fueled by belief-driven action also makes us less likely to view norms as error terms impairing otherwise strategic behavior by individual self-interested utility maximizers, as suggested by rationalist institutionalists.[37] And, as suggested by historical sociologists, our present values should not be imposed on our understanding of the past.[38] Our theoretical ambitions must be tempered to ground social processes rather than produce general laws. In short, a study of legitimacy requests modesty.

Weberian economic sociology provides the means to reconcile the general aims of economic constructivism with a strong emphasis on legitimacy. For Weber, all actions that take into account the behavior of others are social, even when in self-interest, and are therefore imbued with meanings on how an individual believes he or she should behave.[39] I use the term *axio-*

---

34. Weber, *Economy and Society*, 1: 253; Swedberg, *Max Weber*, 65–66. On everyday politics see Benedict J. Tria Kerkvliet, *The Power of Everyday Politics: How Vietnamese Peasants Transformed National Policy* (Ithaca: Cornell University Press, 2005). On everyday resistance see James C. Scott, *Weapons of the Weak: Everyday Forms of Peasant Resistance* (New Haven: Yale University Press, 1985).

35. Reinhard Bendix, *Force, Fate, and Freedom: On Historical Sociology* (Berkeley: University of California Press, 1984), 56; Robert H. Bates, Avner Greif, Margaret Levi, Jean-Laurent Rosenthal, and Barry Weingast, *Analytic Narratives* (Princeton: Princeton University Press, 1999).

36. The key texts here are Sven Steinmo, Kathleen Thelen, and Frank Longstreth, eds., *Structuring Politics: Historical Institutionalism in Comparative Analysis* (New York: Cambridge University Press, 1992); James Mahoney and Dietrich Rueschemeyer, eds., *Comparative Historical Analysis in the Social Sciences* (Cambridge: Cambridge University Press, 2003); and James G. March and Johan P. Olsen, *Rediscovering Institutions: The Organizational Basis of Politics* (New York: Free Press, 1989).

37. North, *Institutions*, 140; James Coleman, *Foundations of Social Theory* (Cambridge, Mass.: Harvard University Press, 1990), 292.

38. John M. Hobson, *The Eastern Origins of Western Civilization* (Cambridge: Cambridge University Press, 2004).

39. Max Weber, *Roscher and Knies: The Logical Problems of Historical Economics* (New York: Free Press, 1975).

rational rather than rational to emphasize that people's decisions are strongly informed by the economic social norms of their time.[40] Actors rationalize their behavior according to what they find meaningful for their life-chances rather than according to an ahistorical profit/loss calculation.[41]

Thus while LIGs all share a below median income, their perception of their life-chances does not bind them to the boundaries of what their economic income group can do. LIGs' belief-driven actions may indicate that they reject such boundaries. Indeed, much of the contestation over what is a legitimate reform to a financial reform nexus is not reducible to profit/loss calculations (see, for example, the fight over the introduction of a relatively small consumption tax in the Japanese case) but to potential barriers that hinder LIGs from fulfilling what they view to be their life-chances: their capacity to transform their own environment by calling upon the state to intervene for institutional and social change. Thus while I treat the state, LIGs, rentiers, and private financial institutions as collective actors, these collectives are composed of individual choices about how to behave rationally in accordance with extant economic social norms, and how such norms should be transformed.[42]

Weber's work is useful to economic constructivism because it views processes of legitimation as both "top-down" and "bottom-up." This is the case because legitimacy is a process by which those with power claim that their actions are morally just and legally right, but where the conferral of legitimacy upon such actions can only come from the expressed consent of those subordinate within the power relationship.[43] As such, any act of legitimation should only be studied in relative degrees ("high," "moderate," or "low" legitimacy rather than "legitimate" or "illegitimate") rather than categorical absolutes.

Disaggregating State Intervention and Mechanisms, Not Variables

This book has a theoretically modest claim: that legitimacy should be recognized as a social source of financial power, and that states that use positive intervention into their financial reform nexuses on behalf of LIGs can enhance their international financial capacity. This proposition does not apply to all states. I provide not a general but a "middle range" theory that seeks to pay attention to the social mechanisms that link types of state intervention to a state's legitimation of its financial reform nexus, and the subsequent aiding/hindering of the broadening and deepening of a domestic pool of capital that may then be employed internationally.

40. Weber, *Economy and Society*, 1: 25, 69–70.
41. Liah Greenfeld, *The Spirit of Capitalism: Nationalism and Economic Growth* (Cambridge, Mass.: Harvard University Press, 2001), Chapter 1.
42. Blyth, *Great Transformations*, 14.
43. Bendix, *Nation-Building*, 20; Beetham, *Legitimation of Power*, 31.

Many of the findings in the case material will appear to be counterintuitive, not least the argument that England and the United States provided positive state intervention into financial reform nexuses whereas Germany and Japan did not. Thus while the standard monikers used for types of economies, such as "liberal" and "coordinated," are intended to help us understand state forms as aggregates, they should not blind us to the different mechanisms and behaviors within the aggregate.[44]

As such, I also contribute to the literature on "varieties of capitalism" and "state capacity" by challenging some well-established conceptions about how liberal and coordinated economies worked in different periods, and how states can obtain "state capacity" beyond mimicking institutions possessed by states already understood as "winners."[45] Typically, the role of pilot economic agencies in coordinated states allows the state to centralize its resources and better respond to exogenous shocks in the international political economy.[46] State fragmentation in liberal states, by contrast, inhibits a rapid response and diminishes national economic competitiveness.[47] However, greater disaggregation is needed to know how states not only respond to changes but enact change in the international political economy.[48] By studying both institutions and society it becomes possible to recognize that institutions not only need policy coherence, but must respond to contestation from other institutions *and* social groups. I disaggregate state intervention into positive and negative forms, where positive intervention enhances LIGs' life-chances, while negative intervention does the opposite.

44. As suggested in Peter J. Katzenstein, *Small States in World Markets: Industrial Policy in Europe* (Ithaca: Cornell University Press, 1985), 133–35. See also Peter A. Hall and David Soskice, "An Introduction to Varieties of Capitalism," in Peter A. Hall and David Soskice, eds., *Varieties of Capitalism: The Institutional Foundations of Comparative Advantage* (Oxford: Oxford University Press, 2001), 35.

45. On "state capacity" see Michael Mann, ed., *The Rise and Decline of the Nation State* (Oxford: Basil Blackwell, 1988); Peter B. Evans, *Embedded Autonomy: States and Industrial Transformation* (Princeton: Princeton University Press, 1995); John M. Hobson, *The Wealth of States: A Comparative Sociology of International Economic and Political Change* (Cambridge: Cambridge University Press, 1997); Linda Weiss, *The Myth of the Powerless State: Governing the Economy in a Global Era* (Cambridge: Polity Press, 1998); and Linda Weiss, ed., *States in the Global Economy: Bringing Domestic Institutions Back In* (Cambridge: Cambridge University Press, 2003).

46. Weiss, *Myth of the Powerless State;* Meredith Woo-Cumings, ed., *The Developmental State* (Ithaca: Cornell University Press, 1999). G. John Ikenberry provides an early example of how decentralization can enhance state power in *Reasons of State: Oil Politics and the Capacities of American Government* (Ithaca: Cornell University Press, 1988).

47. The most common example is the United States as fragmented liberal versus Japan as centralized coordinated, at least up to the mid-1990s Asian financial crisis. Robert Gilpin, "Economic Evolution of National Systems," *International Studies Quarterly* 40, 3 (1996); and much earlier, John S. Zysman, *Governments, Markets, and Growth: Financial Systems and the Politics of Industrial Change* (Oxford: Martin Robertson, 1983).

48. Typified by the analyses in Katzenstein, *Small States;* Peter A. Hall, *Governing the Economy: The Politics of State Intervention in Britain and France* (New York: Oxford University Press, 1986); Suzanne Berger and Ronald Dore, eds., *National Diversity and Global Capitalism* (Ithaca: Cornell University Press, 1996).

A state (and its institutions) that is kept in check by its public is more likely to have higher levels of legitimacy and be able to sustain its social source of financial power. To further this process I do not seek to demonstrate co-variation in abstracted key variables: forms of state intervention, the extent to which a financial reform nexus is legitimated, and the consequent form of a state's international financial capacity. Rather, I seek to understand the linking social mechanisms within what is best understood as a constellation of variables.[49]

I see the main linking mechanisms as contestation, redistribution, and propagation. Contestation between LIGs and the state over the legitimacy of the financial reform nexus leads the state to enact policy changes. These changes spur interventions in the economy that can be positive or negative for LIGs and lead, accordingly, to a redistribution of political and economic assets and opportunities. This redistribution, depending upon its positive or negative character, engenders or prevents a rentier shift, which then leads to a propagation of economic social norms from the state on how the economy should work. Such propagation provides feedback to LIGs, who on the basis of how they believe the economy should work for them will engage in further contestation, and the process begins anew. By detailing these mechanisms we establish some focal points to examine what is particular about each case, and what forms of intervention into a state's financial reform nexus for LIGs led to different outcomes in its international financial capacity.

Changes to credit access, property ownership, and tax burdens provide focal points for LIGs to contest the legitimacy of state action. Calls for positive state intervention will compel the state to change its ways, or lose more legitimacy. Positive state intervention will engender institutional change to provide LIGs with greater potential for credit access, property ownership, and lower tax burdens. Such institutions will typically provide credit guarantees and discounts, the surveillance of private financial institutions, and tax incentives to achieve the above. Such enabling institutions will require funding either directly from the state's revenue base and/or from domestic and international financial markets. They will therefore generate credit for LIGs by attracting investment to their debt, as well as channeling capital from payments on loans into investments in the international financial order. In doing so, they also provide an important means for private financial institutions to access a safe source of capital for their own investments in the international financial order. To achieve all this, financial innovations may be necessary. Financial innovations not only serve a regulatory and technical function, but can also provide an important tool for the propagation of new economic social norms on financial practices.

Importantly, social mechanisms are saturated with ideas and normative context. Rentiers also seek to contest state policy, calling for state interven-

49. Campbell, *Institutional Change*, Chapter 3.

tion that reflects their economic interests and affirms their worldview on how the economy should work for them. A rentier shift is therefore a period in which the state has negatively intervened according to the above social mechanisms.

As discussed in the ideal type at the beginning of this chapter, if these mechanisms are correctly aligned and in good working order, then the state's influence in the international financial order—its international financial capacity—will rest on a more sustainable basis because the domestic pool of capital will be both broader and deeper. In demonstrating the social sources of financial power I do not provide a quantitative statistical investigation of financial change beyond outlining the context within which contests over access to credit, property, and tax take place, as well as describing how the key financial institutions were positioned. Rather, I use a qualitative comparative historical analysis of the dynamics between the state LIGs and financial institutions.

The Cases

In investigating the social sources of financial power and how domestic legitimacy affects the character of international financial orders, I examine England and Germany in the late nineteenth and early twentieth centuries, and the United States and Japan in the late twentieth century. As Charles Tilly reminds us, any middle range theory's choice of periods must be "bounded by the playing out of certain well-defined processes."[50] There are good reasons to study the above periods rather than, for instance, any time between 1915 and 1985. These two eras represented similar international dynamics in that they both possessed very high capital mobility, and the external constraint of financial globalization, goes the conventional wisdom, encouraged private financial institutions within the states under study to concentrate and merge. Furthermore, they are both periods in which the state is either thought to have been built up (early twentieth century) or dismantled (late twentieth century). These eras are, therefore, critical for understanding different forms of state intervention during times in which private financial institutions transformed rapidly given the opportunities within the international realm. By comparing the two periods we can learn how different forms of state intervention occur in a materially similar international economic environment. In doing so we can also understand why the first era could be described as an "international rentier economy," while the latter is an "international creditor economy."[51] Rather than selecting

50. Charles Tilly, *Big Structures, Large Processes, Huge Comparisons* (New York: Russell Sage), 14.
51. "International rentier economy" was coined by Michael Mann, *The Sources of Social Power, Vol. 2: The Rise of Classes and Nation-States, 1760–1914* (Cambridge: Cambridge University Press, 1993), 292.

"winners" in each period and "reading back" international financial capacity and a highly legitimate financial reform nexus for LIGs *ex post facto,* the cases demonstrate the importance of specifying the mechanisms through which social sources of financial power are created, particularly by disaggregating forms of state intervention. These changes can only be understood through reference to material conditions and normative changes in the domestic environments of the leading financial powers, which I refer to as the principal and the rival.

I have selected England and Germany of the late nineteenth and early twentieth centuries because they represent both the most different and crucial cases for the period. England and Germany are most different because they possessed dissimilar forms of state intervention in their financial reform nexuses and because they are commonly thought to represent the most liberal and most coordinated economies of the period, with England rapidly developing into a social liberal polity while Germany pursued its autocratic "special path" (*Sonderweg*). These states are also considered to possess the most different kinds of financial systems, with England's London-centered capital market-intensive system and Germany run by the power of the Great Banks (*Großbanken*). England and Germany also represent crucial cases because switching who was principal and who was the rival among them would have dramatically changed the international financial order. Examining why Germany was unable to produce a sustainable social source of financial power and why England undermined its once strong source of social power is crucial to understanding the period. Moreover, as we will see, the common view on England and Germany needs some revising.

The selection of the United States and Japan in the late twentieth century follows the same logic as above. The United States and Japan are most different because they are commonly thought to represent the most liberal and most coordinated economies of the period. The United States represents the vanguard of neoliberalism, in part because of the absence of the state due to its fragmented character, while Japan's pilot economic agencies were able to bring the state to great international prominence in the mid-1980s only to have to reorganize themselves in the 1990s. These states are also considered to possess the most different kinds of financial systems, the U.S.'s capital market-intensive system and incoherent financial regulation contrasting strongly with Japan's bank-dominated system and "convoy" approach to regulating financial institutions, with financial reform paced to the slowest institution. Like the earlier period, the United States and Japan also represent crucial cases because exchanging who was principal and who was the rival would have had an inestimable impact on the international financial order of the day. Exploring how the United States was able to build a sustainable and strong social source of financial power, and why Japan quickly undermined its social source of financial power despite massive exporting of capital from the mid-1980s, is essential to understanding the period. We will also find out some counterintuitive dynamics in both the United States and Japanese cases, particularly in the forms of state intervention and the state's susceptibility to a rentier shift.

While most material within the case studies is empirical evidence, particularly primary source material, I also present counterfactuals to emphasize why states were not able to deepen and broaden their domestic pool of capital, and what may have occurred if they did have the capacity. The use of counterfactuals is appropriate given the small number of cases under examination, and to support reasonable arguments concerning why states deviated from the ideal typical pocketbook–to–global finance scenario outlined above.[52]

In discussing the link between the domestic and the international, I contend that if the principal state can legitimate its domestic financial reform nexus to a high degree, it has a more sustainable basis with which to influence the international financial order and encourage other states to "organize their domestic structures in a way as to coincide with the dominant legitimacy conceptions of the day."[53] The international financial order in the late nineteenth and early twentieth centuries was increasingly an "international rentier economy" because it reflected domestic dynamics in England that intensified in the years immediately prior to World War I. The massive increases in rentier investments from the City of London emerged from domestic fights between rentier groups, LIGs, and a lackluster Liberal government. The state's incapacity to intervene against England's rentier shift also led to diminished international financial capacity and increased England's vulnerability to financial shocks when the war arrived. Likewise, the international financial order of the late twentieth century was an "international creditor economy" because of changes in the domestic legitimation of the financial reform nexus within the United States. The difference between the U.S.'s exposure to the debt crisis of the early 1980s (which had some impact) and the Asian financial crisis of 1997–98 (which had little impact) can be seen as, in part, a consequence of the high legitimation of the U.S. financial reform nexus post-1985, the propagation of financial innovations within the United States following contestation over financial reforms, and the U.S.'s capacity to block a rentier shift.

The Plan of the Book

The following chapter is concerned with theoretical and methodological issues, and concentrates on the role of legitimacy in understanding institutional and social change within prevalent political economy and institu-

52. Blyth, *Great Transformations,* 13; James D. Fearon, "Counterfactuals and Hypothesis Testing in Political Science," *World Politics* 43, 2 (1991).

53. Mlada Bukovansky, *Legitimacy and Power Politics: The American and French Revolutions in International Political Culture* (Princeton: Princeton University Press, 2002), 35.

tional approaches. The chapter critically reviews rationalist institutionalism, historical institutionalism, and the extant contributions from economic constructivism. I then seek to augment economic constructivism by drawing upon conceptual innovations in economic sociology, particularly Weberian economic sociology. I stress the importance of legitimacy for understanding belief-driven economic social actions.

Chapters 3–6 provide case studies of the legitimation of financial reform nexuses (if one wishes to race ahead, I summarize the cases in Figures 7.1 and 7.2). In Chapters 3 and 4 I analyze the English and German cases from 1890 to 1915, providing context before focusing on intense changes from 1900 to 1915 that created an "international rentier economy" (which is why the data run from 1900). I find that while England provided the most legitimate system of its time and expanded a social source of financial power from 1840 to 1890, a post-1890 rentier shift was not tackled with positive state intervention. This shift included the construction of "gentlemanly capitalism" in the 1890s that led to the concentration of assets to move away from the provinces and into the City of London, as well as the Bank of England's financial "crowding out" of capital generation in its provincial bank branches. Compounding this problem, the English state's positive interventionist success—the Post Office Savings Bank system—was utilized to supplement government revenue (thus effectively taxing LIGs twice) rather than enabling LIGs to access credit to fulfill social wants. In England, LIGs' contestation of state financial reforms led to symbolic changes on tax burdens, but did not provide significant redistribution on credit access or property ownership. The consequent propagation of rentier norms increased the frustration of English LIGs and weakened the legitimacy of the financial reform nexus and international financial capacity. Had England been able to legitimate the financial reform nexus, one could speculate that its financial depth would have been great enough to maintain its international financial capacity and role as principal in the international financial order after the financial shock of World War I. I provide a counterfactual that makes this case.

The German system provides an oddity. Despite persistent depictions of the German financial system as driven by *Großbanken* and the insistence on a socially progressive savings system, I find neither. Rather, the German financial reform nexus reflected the interests of landed and local rentiers and was embroiled in ongoing fiscal conflict between the Reich and the *Länder* over who should be burdened with taxes. As a consequence, the largest of German depository financial institutions, the savings banks system (*Sparkassen*), was used to prop up a socially regressive political system. The German financial system isolated LIGs and reflected both their lack of actual enfranchisement and the state's rejection of German social liberalism. In Germany, LIGs' contestation fell on deaf ears, and state-supported redistribution strongly supported a rentier shift that further propagated economic social norms of extraction of rents from LIGs across the financial reform nexus. As a consequence the legitimation of the financial reform nexus was very weak and the German state was unable to build a social source of financial power. This weakness was reflected in Germany's international financial capacity and problems in coping with the financial shock of World War I.

At first blush it may appear futile to compare two cases of ultimate failure. However, the important point here is that English international financial capacity came from a legitimate source in the 1840–90 period and declined thereafter. Germany, in my view, was a "non-starter" to act as principal in the international financial order, even though it was perceived by many as the main rival. It is important to understand the loss of the *social* sources of financial power in the English and German cases, especially in light of Japan's problems in consolidating international financial capacity during the 1985–2000 period.

In Chapters 5 and 6 I analyze the United States and Japan in the late twentieth century "international creditor economy." I demonstrate the extent of legitimate positive state intervention in the U.S. case, which compares favorably with the failure of the Japanese state to intervene positively to respond to LIGs' social wants, or to rescue the stagnating Japanese financial system.

The U.S. case provides an example of a state responding to the social wants of LIGs to legitimate its financial reform nexus, and therefore to enhance its international financial capacity, compared to the other cases and to the ideal typical scenario. Significant positive state intervention through financial re-regulation (particularly with support from the Democratic Party) illustrates the oft-ignored extent of U.S. government intervention in the private financial system. I argue that positive state intervention through institutional forms such as the emboldened role of federal mortgage agencies, the establishment of protective financial regulation to prevent "redlining," and tax relief reforms enhanced the domestic legitimation of the U.S. financial reform nexus and directly fed into its international financial capacity. In the U.S. case, after 1985, LIGs' contestation led to policy change that was positive, including the redistribution of tax burdens, credit access, and property ownership in their favor. This blocked a rentier shift and propagated norms of entrepreneurship and access to property ownership that helped legitimate the U.S. financial reform nexus and boosted U.S. international financial capacity.

In Chapter 6 I argue that the Japanese state and financial community ignored changing social norms and that the state actively supported a rentier shift after 1985. The Japanese state's incapacity to reform the financial system post-1992 was due to its centralization away from society, and its ties to rentier interests that encouraged the extraction of rents from LIGs. This problem pervaded the financial reform nexus from the use of the Postal Savings system to supplement government revenue—then spend it on extensive public works "extrastructure"—to publicly opposed regressive consumption taxes, to a failure to address the Japanese housing crisis. Moreover, Japan's significant international rentier investments, including a post-1995 strategy of banks seeking to speculate their way out of their financial woes, only weakened the legitimacy of the Japanese financial reform nexus. In the Japanese case, LIGs' contestation was largely ignored, redistribution further encouraged a rentier shift, and the propagation of economic social norms that sought to justify the extraction of rents from LIGs weakened the legitimation of the Japanese financial reform nexus and with it the state's international financial capacity.

Chapter 7 briefly analyzes how the legitimation of domestic financial reform nexuses in the two periods led to changes in the character of the international financial order over time. The international financial order reflects the legitimation of the financial reform nexus within the principal state. I argue that England's post-1890 rentier shift led to an "international rentier economy" that led massive volumes of capital to leave into types of investments that reflected England's increasingly shaky domestic foundations from conflict between the state, rentiers, and LIGs. For the modern period I argue that U.S. positive state intervention has led to an "international creditor economy" based on assessments of creditworthiness. While I detail how domestic legitimacy logically leads to changes in the character of the international financial order, I provide no analysis of whether or not other states accepted the legitimacy of the influence of the principal or rival. Such a study is beyond the scope of this book.

In Chapter 8 I emphasize the importance of legitimacy and everyday actions for economic constructivism. Finally, the Epilogue discusses changes to the U.S. financial reform nexus under the George W. Bush administration from 2001 to 2005—changes that are actively undermining the U.S.'s social source of financial power.

2

Legitimacy in Political Economy

The concept of legitimacy is important to political and economic life because it reminds us that we have some chance to transform our own environment by calling upon the shared expectations of our fellow citizens. In the past, political economy scholarship has ignored or downplayed the concept on the grounds that it reflects people's intersubjective beliefs and is beyond the purview of serious social science research. Recently, however, political economists have become interested in how actors influence institutional change through the use of ideas and economic social norms within intersubjective environments. Particularly important within this literature is the development of "economic constructivism," which seeks to understand the role of ideational and normative influences upon institutional change.

Given this emphasis, we need to be reminded that the nascent literature on economic constructivism has not attempted to develop a substantive conception of legitimacy. In remedying this failing, this chapter examines the role of legitimacy within political economy and the "new institutionalist" literature. While this presents an especially broad range of literature to examine, the chief grounds for doing so are that approaches within the literature have all borrowed and learned from one another, particularly in "bringing things back in."

To begin with, rationalist institutionalist scholarship borrowed from microeconomic theories of market failure to argue that institutional structures maintain an equilibrium that is then disturbed by an exogenous shock that produces uncertainty, and therefore information asymmetries, and requires self-interested maximizing actors to work out a new institutional equilibrium. The common criticism of this approach is that it can explain the endurance of institutions but not their creation.

The development of historical institutionalism sought to differentiate itself from rationalist institutionalism by understanding the political and social processes that inform institutional change rather than focusing on transactions costs. The key problem here was not "rationality," since all "soft" rationalist and historical institutionalist scholars agree that the sticking point is to identify how rationality is constructed from a mix of self-interest and social norms. Rather, historical institutionalism sought to specify why institutions were different and detail how different domestic systems informed institutional and social change. As such, there was a move away from the rationalist institutionalist notion of punctuated equilibrium and path dependence to discussing evolution and path dependence, with the actors involved going through a process of reflexive social learning. The dialogue between historical institutionalists and political economists also generated an array of literature on "state capacity" and "varieties of capitalism" that argued that states were taking divergent strategies in response to similar forces of economic globalization according to national systems.

Developing parallel to historical institutionalists, organizational institutionalists argued that the missing element within the broader literature was an understanding of the endogenous sources of institutional change. To this end, organizational institutionalists sought to provide a cultural understanding of how institutions change and, in doing so, directly informed constructivist scholarship in international relations.[1]

Within political economy the nascent literature on economic constructivism has emerged directly from the conversation between the above approaches and schools of thought. The primary aim of economic constructivism, thus far, has been to argue that institutional change cannot be studied by exogenous shocks but should, instead, concentrate on endogenous actors that are informed by norms and that use ideas to transform institutions. There is much to admire in the extant economic constructivist scholarship, but it is dogged by some hang-ups of the literature from which it borrows to make its case. Economic constructivism has attempted to "out-explain" earlier institutionalist approaches by asserting the autonomous transformative capacity of ideas. It also maintains, like other approaches, a focus on moments of uncertainty as crucial periods for institutional change. Finally, economic constructivism has a view of *legitimacy by proclamation*—that is, the assumption that an ideational entrepreneur's proclamation of a "winning" idea automatically generates legitimacy.

As a remedy I suggest that economic constructivism requires a strong conception of legitimacy and can borrow from economic sociology, particularly Weberian economic sociology, to produce an analysis of everyday institutional and social change. For Max Weber, individuals act according to their "life-chances" and not only according to their economic interests or class position.[2] One's understanding of life-chances is drawn from a perception of

1. Particularly Martha Finnemore, *National Interests in International Society* (Ithaca: Cornell University Press, 1996).
2. Max Weber, *Economy and Society: An Outline of Interpretive Sociology*, vols. 1 and 2 (Berkeley: University of California Press, 1978), 302, 927–29.

how the world works at a macro level and how to then act according to instrumental and value-oriented beliefs. Of particular importance here, then, is the notion that rationality is thoroughly saturated by economic social norms. Rationality may be instrumental but cannot help but be *axiological;* that is, that economic social norms and conventions inform one's actions. (To save a few syllables I refer to this as *axiorational* behavior.)

Weber's work provides a solid foundation for studying legitimacy by seeing it as relative and temporal, as a dynamic that emerges from contestation between the state and various social groups who seek to fulfill their life-chances. In this conception those in power may claim legitimacy for their actions, but the actions do not become legitimated unless actors subordinate within the polity provide consent. Legitimacy is not drawn in absolutes but relative changes within policy areas, social perceptions, and the violation or confirmation of existing economic social norms. Following Weber I assert that an *idiographic* rather than *nomothetic* methodological individualism is best suited to understand how actors behave in relation to other social actors and according to their normatively informed interests (these terms are defined in the previous chapter). This chapter outlines why legitimacy and economic social norms are important to belief-driven action.

There are three key reasons for why bringing legitimacy back in should be encouraged:

i)   Legitimacy encourages us to focus on contestation between the state and social groups rather than view the state as a functional space.

ii) Legitimacy encourages us to understand how economic social norms inform how individuals understand their life-chances, and how they act to transform their own environment with strong implications for institutional and social change.

iii) Legitimacy encourages a historicist approach to institutional and social change that emphasizes contingent mechanisms of change rather than applying linear evolutionary or punctuated equilibrium models.

It is important to recognize that as individuals work toward their life-chances, the accumulation of individual actions matter for the state in the domestic political economy, and for how the state engages the international political economy. The following sections discuss the role of legitimacy in the conventional approaches to political economy and institutional change, before making the case for augmenting economic constructivism with a strong conception of legitimacy and tools from Weberian economic sociology.

Legitimacy in Rationalist Institutionalism

Before getting started on rationalist institutionalism, we should first separate "hard" rationalist scholars who insist on universal theories of political behavior based on an atomized self-interested individual or state-as-individual,[3] and "soft" rationalists who insist that considering institutional change requires explaining "culturally derived norms of behavior."[4] While soft rationalist institutionalists still aim to model political behavior according to a microeconomic logic, they restrict themselves to general hypotheses that have predictive power within select cases rather than across all time and space.[5] The issue here is not the presence of culture and norms, but their prevalence—to what extent culture, ideology, norms, and ideas, however these terms are defined, matter. The key problem for such theorists is that there is no means to scientifically interrogate such concepts and, as a consequence, rationalist institutionalists prefer "transaction cost" and punctuated equilibrium models of institutional change that tell us about institutional persistence, but very little about institutional and social change. My view here is that rationalist institutionalists, despite their efforts to incorporate economic social norms into explanations of institutional change, fundamentally view *norms as error terms*.

The key elements of rationalist institutionalism are as follows: a theory of individual choice derived from neoclassical microeconomic theory; that relative price changes affect the structure of institutions; and, following the first two, that actors will seek to lower transaction costs and information asymmetries to maximize efficiency and improve their lot.[6] In doing so actors will form a strategic institutional equilibrium, where no individual would unilaterally alter his/her behavior given the available alternatives. Self-interest and utility maximization, either from material goods or from well-being, defines the individual's constant aim through time. As such, tracking changes to institutions according to their transactions costs and information asymmetries is thought to provide insight on how individuals and states-as-individuals can cooperate, or why they have grown faster or more productively than others (by enabling more efficient institutions).[7] The key

3. Gary Becker, *The Economic Approach to Human Behavior* (Chicago: University of Chicago Press, 1976). In international relations, most famously, Kenneth N. Waltz, Theory of International Politics (Reading, Mass.: Addison Wesley, 1979).

4. Douglass C. North, *Institutions, Institutional Change and Economic Performance* (Cambridge: Cambridge University Press, 1990), 140. This section hereafter deals with the "soft" variety of rationalist institutionalism.

5. Robert H. Bates, Avner Greif, Margaret Levi, Jean-Laurent Rosenthal, and Barry Weingast, *Analytic Narratives* (Princeton: Princeton University Press, 1999).

6. Douglass C. North and Robert P. Thomas, *The Rise of the Western World: A New Economic History* (Cambridge: Cambridge University Press, 1973); Oliver E. Williamson, *The Economic Institutions of Capitalism* (Cambridge: Cambridge University Press, 1985).

7. North, *Institutions;* Robert O. Keohane, *After Hegemony: Cooperation and Discord in the World Political Economy* (Princeton: Princeton University Press, 1984).

force generating institutional change is an exogenous shock that punctures the static equilibrium and generates a period of uncertainty in which the battle between self-interested individuals, with different resource capabilities, will then determine the next equilibrium.[8]

The typical criticism of rationalist institutionalism is that it mistakenly views individuals as having a stable set of preferences according to an *a priori* utility function. So while methodological individualism is given lip service as the starting position for rationalist institutions, individuals actually do very little other than respond to incentive structures provided by institutions *and* which generate institutional change. Given that individuals' preferences are fundamentally viewed as fixed, "institutions" are left doing all the heavy lifting by representing both the "rules of the game" obeyed by individuals *and* the strategic equilibrium that emerges from battles between individuals. We know only that the institutions change in retrospect by identifying punctures in equilibriums or by *ex post* assessments of the cost/benefit of the institution.[9] As such, rationalist institutionalism is criticized for being incoherent in conflating independent and dependent variables, and for analyzing "comparative statics." Rationalist institutionalists are therefore criticized for pilfering historical cases that demonstrate the predictability of their models.[10]

By assuming that individual's interests are primarily concerned with economic utility maximization across time, rationalist institutionalism provides little room for understanding how individuals give meaning to their institutional and social environments within particular historical periods. Understanding such meaning is important because new institutional "structures do not come with an instruction sheet" and the approach has no endogenous mechanism of institutional supply beyond lowering transaction costs.[11] After all, we need to know why actors do not defect from institutions other than from the fear of facing uncertainty.[12] Actors' binds to institutions are derived from normative commitments as much as they are from their calculation of costs and benefits.

For rationalist institutionalists, material "brute facts" are typically thought to oust normative concerns and also inform a "bounded rationality" on what choices are available to individuals.[13] Rationality is bound by the institu-

8. Margaret Levi, "A Model, a Method, and a Map: Rational Choice in Comparative Politics," in Mark I. Lichbach and Alan Zuckerman, eds., *Comparative Politics: Rationality, Culture, and Structure* (Cambridge: Cambridge University Press, 1997), 23–28.

9. Stephen D. Krasner, "Approaches to the State: Alternative Conceptions and Historical Dynamics," *Comparative Politics* 16, 2 (1984).

10. Jon Elster, "Rational Choice History: A Case of Excessive Ambition," *American Political Science Review* 94, 3 (2000).

11. Mark Blyth, *Great Transformations: Economic Ideas and Institutional Change in the Twentieth Century* (Cambridge: Cambridge University Press, 2002), 7, 19.

12. North, *Institutions*, 17–19, 84. See also Mark Blyth, "Any More Bright Ideas? The Ideational Turn in Comparative Political Economy," *Comparative Politics* 29, 2 (1997).

13. Robert Grafstein, "Thick Rationality and the Missing 'Brute Fact': The Limits of Rationalist Incorporations of Norms and Ideas: Comment," *Journal of Politics* 59, 4 (1997): 1040–47.

tional context from which actors can adapt in selecting goals, and by cognitive "processing limits" that blinker the options available.[14] These processing limits are understood by rationalist institutionalists as distortions introduced by culture, ideology, and norms to otherwise rational utility-maximizing behavior.

Avner Greif's work on business organization in the late medieval period, for example, compares the behavior of Genoese and Maghribi traders with the overall aim of discovering why some societies do not emulate the organization and institutions of more economically successful ones. Greif finds that Genoese behavior centered on an individualist equilibrium that permitted a vertical social structure and the use of law as the primary means of enforcement in trade. In contrast, Maghribi behavior centered on a collectivist equilibrium that determined a horizontal social structure and required the use of moral suasion in trade. As a consequence, the Genoese cut their trading costs through an impersonal bill of lading system, while the Maghribi had to pay for a trusted person to accompany their trading cargo to ensure its safe passage. For Greif, such culturally derived differences must be self-reinforcing (path dependent) to merit study and, in the end, what separates societies from one another is how "individuals attempt to find moral justifications for their behavior through cognitive dissonance."[15] Similarly, for Douglass North, individuals who exercise beliefs that are contrary to market expectations will soon find their actions too costly and, therefore, conform to institutionally sanctioned behaviors. Otherwise deviant behavior can also be explained by "rational ignorance" among actors who did not know any better about their potential opportunities and costs.[16] Brute facts therefore trump norms in decision-making processes, and while ideas and norms can provide "focal points" for institutional change, their explanatory power is only considered once interest-based material explanations have been exhausted.[17]

A further complication for rationalist institutionalists' study of how ideas and norms shape institutions relates back to the finding of general laws from which to build predictive models. There has been, for example, an insistence that norms should be *naturalistic*—that is, pertaining to properties in-

14. Bryan D. Jones, "Bounded Rationality," *Annual Review of Political Science* 2, 1 (1999).

15. Avner Greif, "Cultural Beliefs and the Organization of Society: A Historical and Theoretical Reflection on Collectivist and Individualist Societies," *Journal of Political Economy* 102, 5 (1994): 916–17. See also Avner Greif, *Institutions and the Path to the Modern Economy: Lessons from Medieval Trade* (Cambridge: Cambridge University Press, 2006).

16. North, *Institutions*, 22, 51, 135. See also Daniel Verdier, *Democracy and International Trade: Britain, France and the United States, 1860–1990* (Princeton: Princeton University Press, 1994), 9–12.

17. Geoffrey Garrett and Barry R. Weingast, "Ideas, Interests, and Institutions: Constructing the European Community's Internal Market," in Judith Goldstein and Robert O. Keohane, eds., *Ideas and Foreign Policy: Beliefs, Institutions and Political Change* (Ithaca: Cornell University Press, 1993), 176.

trinsic to all human behavior—to have great explanatory power to permit general modeling.[18] As such, rationalist institutionalism has no genuine notion of *economic social norms* because economic rationality is seen to be natural and timeless while norms are recognized as culturally specific. Furthermore, by invoking path dependence to "narrow conceptually the choice set and link decision making through time," and relying on exogenous shocks to institutional equilibria, rationalist institutionalists smooth out the politics from the path they seek to explain.[19]

It is not difficult then to see why rationalist institutionalists have not engaged with the concept of legitimacy, even if they recognize that it cannot explain historical change without it.[20] This is chiefly because, despite the emphasis on methodological individualism, most rationalist institutionalists are concerned with explaining institutional persistence through economic structuralism and conformity with institutional procedures.

Margaret Levi's work on "bringing people back into the state" is particularly instructive on this point. Levi "eschews the word *legitimate,* at least until the term acquires a consensual meaning," and in her earlier work relied on the concept of "quasi-voluntary compliance" to explain how rational actors strategically bargain over taxation according to a "perception of the bargain *rather than ideas about what a good or fair contract is.*"[21] In her latter work on why actors choose to conform to military conscription she argues that "in most cases citizens are willing to go along with a policy *they do not prefer* as long as it is made according to *a process they deem legitimate.*"[22] Only a thin procedural legitimacy is therefore important to sustain an institution since there is no substantive discussion of the political wrangling over the normative purpose of the institutions involved other than they hold a conception of fairness.[23] So how then do we know what is fair? By the institutions people conform to. This view does not help us understand any of the politics in processes of legitimation that precede the formation of institutions and their procedures.

Finally, rational institutionalists have shown a growing interest in identi-

18. Robert Sugden, "Normative Expectations: The Simultaneous Evolution of Institutions and Norms," in Avner Ben-Ner and Louis Putterman, eds., *Economics, Values, and Organizations* (Cambridge: Cambridge University Press, 1998), 77–79.

19. North, *Institutions,* 98–100. Similarly, but with greater emphasis on individual cognition and intentionality in institutions' adaptive efficiency, see Douglass C. North, *Understanding the Process of Economic Change* (Princeton: Princeton University Press, 2005).

20. North, *Institutions,* 24.

21. Margaret Levi, *Of Rule and Revenue* (Berkeley: University of California Press, 1988), 1 n. 1; 54, my emphasis.

22. Margaret Levi, *Consent, Dissent, and Patriotism* (Cambridge: Cambridge University Press, 1997), 23.

23. This criticism mirrors that of Chris Reus-Smit's on Thomas Franck's conception of international legitimacy. Christian Reus-Smit, "Politics and International Legal Obligation," *European Journal of International Relations* 9, 3 (2003): 601–2; Thomas Franck, *The Power of Legitimacy Among Nations* (Oxford: Oxford University Press, 1990).

fying causal mechanisms as a "meaningful connection between events as the basic tool of description and analysis."[24] But once again the aims here have been to produce a general deductive theory of a social process between periods of exogenous shocks "regardless of the specific case or the outcome being problematized."[25] Actors are still viewed as "self-propelling" entities following their utility maximization and norms are still considered to be error terms rather than as saturating rational individual choice.[26] As such, there is little room for studying processes of legitimation in understanding institutional change because society is reduced to being an external force rather than a source of input and feedback.

Legitimacy in Historical Institutionalism

Historical institutionalism cuts across political economy, institutional theory, international relations, and political and economic and historical sociology. Most scholars within this broad school of thought have derived their view of comparative historical studies, and of the state, from Max Weber. Accordingly, much of the early literature emerged from a need to "bring the state back in" as a conceptual variable.[27] Pioneering work by Peter Evans, Peter Katzenstein, Theda Skocpol, and others provided comparative analyses of how different types of states, with varied forms of intervention into their economy, informed a state's relationship with the international political economy and reflected historically informed domestic wrangling over political parties, economic groups, and national ideologies.[28] Historical sociological work, especially that of Michael Mann, sought to analyze the development of the state's institutional autonomy and relationship with social groups.[29] The key shared element among all of this work was that institu-

24. James S. Coleman, "Social Theory, Social Research, and a Theory of Action," *American Journal of Sociology* 91, 6 (1986): 1327. In international political economy see Layna Mosley, *Global Capital and National Governments* (Cambridge: Cambridge University Press, 2003), 14–16, 201–3.

25. Margaret R. Somers, "We're No Angels: Realism, Rational Choice, and Relationality in Social Science," *American Journal of Sociology* 104, 3 (1998): 752, in a debate with Edgar Kiser and Michael Hechter within the same journal.

26. Charles Tilly, "To Explain Political Processes," *American Journal of Sociology* 100, 6 (1995): 1595.

27. From the call made in J. P. Nettl, "The State as a Conceptual Variable," *World Politics* 20, 4 (1968): 562.

28. Peter J. Katzenstein, ed., *Between Power and Plenty: Foreign Economic Policies of Advanced Industrial States* (Madison: University of Wisconsin Press, 1978); Peter J. Katzenstein, *Small States in World Markets: Industrial Policy in Europe* (Ithaca: Cornell University Press, 1985); Peter B. Evans, Dietrich Rueschemeyer, and Theda Skocpol, eds., *Bringing the State Back in* (Cambridge: Cambridge University Press, 1985).

29. Michael Mann, *The Sources of Social Power, Vol. 1: A History of Power from the Beginning to AD 1760* (Cambridge: Cambridge University Press, 1986); Michael Mann, *The Sources of Social Power, Vol. 2: The Rise of Classes and Nation-States, 1760–1914* (Cambridge: Cambridge University Press, 1993).

tions were the site for conflict over ideas and interests that established historical paths and national frameworks, rather than simply the structures with which to test a general model.

Like rationalist institutionalists, historical institutionalists have used concepts such as path dependence, sequencing, and punctuated equilibrium, with the recognition that change should not be studied between "comparative statics" but can be viewed as incremental and evolutionary.[30] So while there is much discussion of how institutional structures face punctures alongside "critical junctures," "break points," and "triggers," these moments simply provide "windows of opportunity" for actors to change institutions.[31] Historical institutionalists therefore try to analyze both exogenous and endogenous factors that influence institutional change.

Historical institutionalists also argue that institutions are supported by both material and ideational foundations. The rub here, however, is that actors can only use ideas that have the right "fit" with the institution concerned, because institutions define the context within which individuals make their self-interested choices.[32] There is a strong attachment to the notion that institutions define *roles* through a "logic of appropriateness" that obliges actors to fall into line, rather than the standard rationalist institutionalist view of a "logic of consequences."[33] From this view institutions construct the "focal points" for action rather than by social groups. Accordingly, there is little notion of legitimacy and the role of contestation between social groups over how the economy should work that is separate from the institutional form under investigation.

Excellent reviews of the role of ideas and norms in historical institutionalism have been provided elsewhere,[34] so my aim here is to assess the role of legitimacy in the main political economy variants within historical institutionalism, namely the work on "state capacity" and "varieties of capitalism."

Legitimacy does not get much of a hearing in the literature on "state capacity," despite the fact that it is commonly seen as representing the Weberian view in political economy. State capacity can be understood to mean the extent to which the state can "actually penetrate civil society" with the aim of maximizing national economic and/or military competitive-

30. The two key collections here are Sven Steinmo, Kathleen Thelen, and Frank Longstreth, eds., *Structuring Politics: Historical Institutionalism in Comparative Analysis* (New York: Cambridge University Press, 1992); and James Mahoney and Dietrich Rueschemeyer, eds., *Comparative Historical Analysis in the Social Sciences* (Cambridge: Cambridge University Press, 2003).
31. Andrew P. Cortell and Susan Peterson, eds., *Altered States: International Relations, Domestic Politics, and Institutional Change* (Lanham, Md.: Lexington Books, 2002).
32. Peter A. Hall, "Conclusion: The Politics of Keynesian Ideas," in *The Political Power of Economic Ideas: Keynesianism Across Nations* (Princeton: Princeton University Press, 1989).
33. James G. March and Johan P. Olsen, *Rediscovering Institutions: The Organizational Basis of Politics* (New York: Free Press, 1989), 23.
34. John Campbell, *Institutional Change and Globalization* (Princeton: Princeton University Press, 2004), Chapter 4; Ellen M. Immergut, "The Theoretical Core of the New Institutionalism," *Politics & Society* 26, 1 (1998).

ness.[35] This aim was first thought to be best achieved by states with "isolated autonomy" from social groups, so that they had more room to organize to meet external international threats.[36] The early state capacity literature explicitly rejected the heuristic value of studying processes of legitimation on the grounds that a failure of legitimacy does not necessarily lead to a loss of organizational capacities.[37] While this view of state isolation became popular with scholars seeking to assert how external geopolitical threats spurred states to coordinate and grow, it was criticized for being too structuralist and therefore "kicking society back out."[38]

In response to these criticisms, scholars such as Peter Evans, Linda Weiss, and others developed the idea of "embedded autonomy" and "governed interdependence"; that states which make alliances with particular social groups are better able to boost their state capacity.[39] For Evans, economically successful states are ideally able to combine "Weberian bureaucratic insulation with intense connection to the surrounding social structure," particularly with rigorous connection to capitalist entrepreneurial social groups.[40] The trick here was for states to not be too isolated, or "under-embedded," from economic groups and also not to become "over-embedded" and allow dominant economic groups to transform their connectedness into capture.[41] For Weiss this "gravedigger" scenario can be avoided by states that maintain "governed interdependence" with dominant economic groups, particularly through the role of "pilot economic agencies."[42] Governed interdependence, however, relies upon the presence of the "right" institutional structures for it to continue to bolster state capacity.

How then do we know that the state has the right kinds of institutions? We know only that institutions performed well because they endure in some states and collapse or fail to appear in others in response to the key pressure upon state capacity: the anarchical external forces of international competition—either economic or geopolitical. This literature therefore retains some functionalist elements in finding strong state capacity only in states with strong economic performance and centralized pilot economic agencies. Moreover, there is also a strong element of path dependence in that building state capacity is reliant on the historical development of cultural

35. Michael Mann, *States, War and Capitalism: Studies in Political Sociology* (Oxford: Basil Blackwell, 1988), 5.
36. Theda Skocpol, *States and Social Revolutions: A Comparative Analysis of France, Russia, and China* (Cambridge: Cambridge University Press, 1979).
37. Ibid., 31–32.
38. John M. Hobson, *The State and International Relations* (Cambridge: Cambridge University Press, 2000), 184–91.
39. Peter B. Evans, *Embedded Autonomy: States and Industrial Transformation* (Princeton: Princeton University Press, 1995); Linda Weiss, *The Myth of the Powerless State: Governing the Economy in a Global Era* (Cambridge: Polity, 1998).
40. Evans, *Embedded Autonomy*, 17, 50, 248.
41. Ibid., 57–59.
42. Weiss, *Myth of the Powerless State*, 37–39.

traits on how the economy should be managed. Weiss, for example, argues that strong state capacity can be found in Taiwan and Japan, where there are prominent pilot economic agencies, but absent in Southeast Asian states due to cultural traits and, perversely, in the United States due to a lack of centralization among regulatory and legislative bodies. These outcomes are "shaped by the pre-existing constellation of ideas and institutions regarding the state-market relationship."[43]

Given such path dependence, this literature on state capacity has a limited engagement with the concept of legitimacy. Evans, for example, recognizes that a lack of legitimacy can undermine state capacity, but provides no means to analyze its presence or absence.[44] Legitimacy is viewed as a functional resource to get the public to fall into line, and this top-down focus also leads this literature to insufficiently disaggregate the value of pilot economic agencies for state capacity. Pilot economic agencies, as we shall see in the English and Japanese chapters, can intervene negatively against great sectors of their population. Nor is there any reason to suggest that state centralization is better for state capacity.[45] While state centralization may be more parsimonious, centralization does not necessarily breed legitimacy, and decentralized agencies may be better able to engage the public through greater "embeddedness."

Moving on from embedded autonomy, a third generation of literature on "social embeddedness" examines how conflicts between the state and dominant and subordinate economic groups informed state capacity.[46] An important break from the earlier literature is made here, because the state is viewed as a contested rather than functional space, in which the character of state-society relations is more important than state insulation from society or its connectedness with dominant economic groups. For example, according to John M. Hobson's study of domestic taxation and international trade in pre–World War I, Britain, Germany, and Russia demonstrated that conflict between domestic groups over taxation changed tariff levels and therefore a state's capacity to compete in the international political economy. His point here was to show that states which became embedded in the lower classes were able to avoid shifting to tariff protectionism. Thus in

43. Linda Weiss, "State Power and the Asian Crisis," *New Political Economy* 4, 3 (1999): 324–25, 328–29, 331.

44. Peter B. Evans, "Transferable Lessons? Re-examining the Institutional Prerequisites of East Asian Economic Policies," *Journal of Development Studies* 34, 6 (1998): 82.

45. As contended in Dietrich Rueschemeyer and Peter B. Evans, "The State and Economic Transformation: Toward an Analysis of the Conditions Underlying Effective Intervention," in Evans et al., eds., *Bringing the State Back in*, 55–56.

46. John M. Hobson, *The Wealth of States: A Comparative Sociology of International Economic and Political Change* (Cambridge: Cambridge University Press, 1997); Joel S. Migdal, *State in Society: Studying How States and Societies Transform and Constitute One Another* (Cambridge: Cambridge University Press, 2002); Leonard Seabrooke, *US Power in International Finance: The Victory of Dividends* (Basingstoke: Palgrave, 2001).

Britain the state was able to appeal to the lower classes by offering increases in progressive direct taxation, thereby maintaining free trade. Conversely, the German and Russian states were embedded only in the dominant economic classes. They therefore sought to increase regressive tariffs to enhance government revenues, thereby promoting a shift to protectionism after 1879 and 1877, respectively. Put simply, in Britain the state was able to "play off the dominant classes with the lower-middle and working classes" to win direct taxation and free trade, while Germany and Russia provided the opposite case because the state was too isolated from society.[47] Hobson's work helps us to understand how social liberal ideas and subsequent institutional changes provided a source of British dominance within the late nineteenth century and early twentieth century international political economy (as well as a reminder of the importance of social liberalism as a source of American dominance in our own era). A second, related, shift involved a different conception of the international system. Hobson argues that while the international system does indeed constrain states it is also a *"partial resource pool"* that states dip into to enhance their power and interests depending on the state's capacity to embed positive regenerative domestic state-society relations.[48]

The key problem with this literature on "social embeddedness" is that change is still explained through strategic pay-offs between rational actors and there is no substantive conception of legitimacy. We do not know why actors thought something was "embedded" other than that they gained from it materially. And we do not know how or if actors' perception of how the economy should work was important for institutional change. The state capacity literature undermines its understanding of institutional and social change by viewing state behavior as calculated by material interests rather than conducted with contested economic social norms that emerge from the bottom up. In short, embeddedness is an inadequate proxy for legitimacy (I discuss this at further length below in the section on legitimacy and economic constructivism).

Discussion of the embeddedness of institutions has also informed the literature on "varieties of capitalism," which seeks to account for institutional change by studying actions of firms and sectors within a national economic system. The concept of embeddedness is important here because actors will closely follow a logic of appropriateness when dealing with institutional change.[49] Earlier work in this literature by Robert Boyer, J. Rogers Hollings-

---

47. Hobson, *Wealth of States*, 236, Chapters 3 and 4. See also an excellent recent comparative investigation of taxation and state capacity, with a particular focus on identity politics, in Evan S. Lieberman, *Race and Regionalism in the Politics of Taxation in Brazil and South Africa* (Cambridge: Cambridge University Press, 2004).

48. Hobson, *The State and International Relations*, 192–93, 210–13, 229–30, Hobson's emphasis.

49. Peter A. Hall and David Soskice, "An Introduction to Varieties of Capitalism," in Peter A. Hall and David Soskice, eds., *Varieties of Capitalism: The Institutional Foundations of Comparative*

worth, and others asserted that domestic "social systems of production" lead to different types of capitalism, and the thesis that economic globalization is producing convergence toward one model of capitalism was overblown.[50] Although there was a transition from nationally embedded systems to "institutional nestedness," national, regional, and transnational types defied the notion of a homogenous globalization.

The work on "varieties of capitalism," typified by Peter A. Hall and David Soskice's collection of essays by the same name, emerged from this literature.[51] In contrast to nestedness, it seeks to provide a systematic account of national capitalist varieties according to regulatory, ideological, and economic differences, such as coordinated and liberal market economies. The aim is to identify the path-dependent historical evolution of institutional forms by paying attention to the role of the firm, which chooses complimentary institutions within a national context to maximize its efficiency. This literature pursues the notion that capitalist varieties follow "national trajectories," where a state's ability to transform itself is path dependent.[52] As such, the varieties of capitalism literature require exogenous shocks to explain institutional change, while also seeking to understand how actors innovate within institutions.

Accordingly, the literature on varieties of capitalism, like that of state capacity, relies too heavily on national traits, arguably obscuring important national subsystems that are counterintuitive to the given "liberal" or "coordinated" monikers.[53] For example, the role of U.S. public and quasi-public federal mortgages agencies detailed in Chapter 6, including their important redistributive mechanism in providing a social source of financial power, could easily be overlooked because it does not fit with our expectations about a "neoliberal" or "liberal market" United States.

The acknowledgment within the varieties of capitalism literature that ac-

Advantage (Oxford: Oxford University Press, 2001), 5–16; J. Rogers Hollingsworth and Robert Boyer, "Coordination of Economic Actors and Social Systems of Production," in J. Rogers Hollingsworth and Robert Boyer, eds., *Contemporary Capitalism: The Embeddedness of Institutions* (Cambridge: Cambridge University Press, 1997), 2, 11.

50. Hollingsworth and Boyer, eds., *Contemporary Capitalism;* Suzanne Berger and Ronald Dore, eds., *National Diversity and Global Capitalism* (Ithaca: Cornell University Press, 1996); J. Rogers Hollingsworth, Philippe Schmitter, and Wolfgang Streeck, eds., *Governing Capitalist Economies: Performance and Control of Economic Sectors* (Oxford: Oxford University Press, 1994).

51. Herbert Kitschelt, Peter Lange, Gary Marks, and John D. Stephens, eds., *Continuity and Change in Contemporary Capitalism* (Cambridge: Cambridge University Press, 1999); Hall and Soskice, eds., *Varieties of Capitalism.*

52. John S. Zysman, "How Institutions Create Historically Rooted Trajectories of Growth," *Industrial and Corporate Change* 3, 1 (1994).

53. Mark Blyth, "Same as It Never Was? Typology and Temporality in the Varieties of Capitalism," *Comparative European Politics* 1, 2 (2003): 219–22. See also Peer Hull Kristensen, "Modelling National Business Systems and the Civilizing Process," in Glenn Morgan, Richard Whitley, and Eli Moen, eds., *Changing Capitalism: Internationalism, Institutional Change and Systems of Economic Organization* (Oxford: Oxford University Press, 2005).

tors and institutions follow a logic of appropriateness should renew interest in the concept of legitimacy for historical institutionalists. But this has not been the case because ideas and norms are still separated from an explanation of institutional change. Ideas are powerful only when the existing institution can accommodate them, because the institution establishes a "system of ideas and standards which is comprehensive."[54] The emergence of new ideas for reforming institutions, such as the emergence of Keynesian economic management, is possible in times when powerful actors can use the uncertainty caused by an exogenous shock to create a quorum and justify new ideas and standards of appropriate behavior.[55] But, once again, we know this only in retrospect, and we have little idea of why actors agreed that x was just and appropriate and y or z were not. We do not know why the actors find it suitable, especially as utility maximization is still the prominent explanation for why actors choose one strategy over another.[56] There is therefore a great deal of circularity in explaining how actors work and much of the recent innovative work by historical institutionalists seeks to outline the casual mechanisms that will permit a "sequencing" of institutional change.[57] Still, there is a lack of understanding not only on how uncertainty forces actors to fall back upon their worldviews, but how their worldviews saturate understandings of what institutional and social change can be sufficiently legitimated according to contested ideas about how the economy should work.

Legitimacy in Economic Constructivism

Economic constructivism aims to understand the interrelation of ideas, norms, and interests to explain why actors adopt behaviors according to prevailing institutions, and what ideational resources they can draw upon to transform institutions. As such they argue that there is no such thing as a "pure" atomized and self-interested economic rationality because processes of rationalization are socially constructed. In exploring this construction, economic constructivism seeks to move away from a focus on exogenous structural shocks to explain institutional change, and instead study how agents relate to institutions to provide a more endogenous ex-

54. Peter A. Hall, "Policy Paradigms, Social Learning, and the State," *Comparative Politics* 25, 3 (1993): 277. It should be noted that Hall's earlier emphasis on socializing policy paradigms is later rejected within his work on varieties of capitalism, while an emphasis on international constraints links the two. My thanks to Mark Blyth for this point.
55. Hall, ed., *Political Power of Economic Ideas*. See also Blyth, *Great Transformations*, 20–21.
56. Blyth, *Great Transformations*, 27–29.
57. Paul Pierson, *Politics in Time: History, Institutions, and Social Analysis* (Princeton: Princeton University Press, 2004), Chapter 2.
58. On early constructivism see Peter J. Katzenstein, ed., *The Culture of National Security: Norms and Identity in World Politics* (New York: Columbia University Press, 1996).

planation.[58] To do so, economic constructivists have drawn heavily from organizational institutionalism within sociology, particularly the notion that institutions create logics of appropriateness that condition actors' behavior.[59] Unsurprisingly, then, earlier constructivist literature emphasized norms as social structures, and that norms could make "uniform behavioral claims upon dissimilar actors."[60] This early view of institutional change was therefore top-down from the institutional structures to the actors who should obey.

Earlier work that can broadly be considered to be "economic constructivist," such as that by Martha Finnemore, Eric Helleiner, Kathleen McNamara, and Kathryn Sikkink, demonstrated that ideas assist the construction of identities and social norms, which then inform how actors can behave to affect change.[61] And while ideas and norms provided symbolic weapons in informing institutional change, much of this work held similar traits to historical institutionalism discussed above, in that ideas and identities were recognized as powerful only when institutions could accommodate them. A good deal of this scholarship was concerned with policy emulation among elite policy makers within an international institutional context. In particular, the build-up of European monetary integration provided particularly fruitful ground for constructivists to fight it out with rationalists and historical institutionalists on why states would willingly cede their own sovereignty for a community ideal.[62]

It is important to note that earlier constructivist work was somewhat ambiguous on how important ideas and norms were in informing material life. Alexander Wendt, for example, famously maintained that there was a "rump materialism" that determined a hierarchy of needs in economic life and prevented the world from being "ideas all the way down."[63] So while the international system obliged actors to conform to norms held by international policy elites, economic self-interest was still very much at play. Seen this way,

59. Finnemore, *National Interests*, 29; March and Olsen, *Rediscovering Institutions;* Paul J. DiMaggio and Walter W. Powell, *The New Institutionalism in Organizational Analysis* (Chicago: University of Chicago Press, 1991); Friedrich Kratochwil, *Norms, Rules, and Decisions: On the Condition of Practical and Legal Reasoning in International Relations and Domestic Affairs* (Cambridge: Cambridge University Press, 1989).

60. Finnemore, *National Interests*, 22.

61. Finnemore, *National Interests;* Eric Helleiner, *States and the Reemergence of Global Finance: From Bretton Woods to the 1990s* (Ithaca: Cornell University Press, 1994); Kathleen R. McNamara, *The Currency of Ideas: Monetary Politics in the European Union* (Ithaca: Cornell University Press, 1998); Kathryn Sikkink, *Ideas and Institutions: Developmentalism in Brazil and Argentina* (Ithaca: Cornell University Press, 1991), 248–55.

62. McNamara, *Currency of Ideas*, 157. The key rationalist study in this area is Andrew Moravcsik, *The Choice for Europe: Social Purpose and State Power from Messina to Maastricht* (Ithaca: Cornell University Press, 1998). An alternative conception is provided in Ben Rosamond, "Imagining the European Economy: Competitiveness and the Social Construction of 'Europe' as an Economic Space," *New Political Economy* 7, 2 (2002).

63. Alexander Wendt, *Social Theory of International Politics* (Cambridge: Cambridge University Press, 1999), 109–10, 135.

ideas and norms provided means for cooperation between policy elites and, as Gramscians contended, a mask over a more material reality.[64]

Dissatisfaction with work on the *systemic* diffusion of norms upon states led constructivist scholars to place renewed emphasis on how states differed domestically in not only responding to international pressures, but in their engagement with society on domestic norms. Rather than a constructivism that argued that "norms, like genes, carry instructions," this approach to constructivism has sought to outline how ideas and economic social norms stray from an evolutionary path.[65] Katzenstein's work, for example, discussed how national domestic norms were split over issue areas and that the contestation of norms informed a state's relationship with the international order. From this view, norms were particularly "contested and contingent," and, as such, it was vital to understand not only how norms regulate behavior in outlining what is appropriate, but also how norms constitute the meaning of behavior.[66] As such, states not only responded to international normative dictates but were also instrumental in constructing the rationale for a state's "moral purpose" and the generation and reception of "moral authority" in the domestic and international realms.[67] For economic constructivists the key point here was that what societies want from the international political economy all depends upon who they think they are.[68] Accordingly, they became particularly interested in how transnational norms were translated into highly specific domestic contexts rather than homogenously diffused.[69]

Within economic constructivism the move away from an international systemic focus to a comparative domestic focus permitted greater discussion of how ideas and norms permeate material life. In particular, Mark Blyth chal-

64. Stephen Gill, *American Hegemony and the Trilateral Commission* (Cambridge: Cambridge University Press, 1990); and, more recently, Adam David Morton, *Unravelling Gramsci: Hegemony, Imperialism and Resistance in the Global Political Economy* (London: Pluto Press, 2005).
65. Ann Florini, "The Evolution of International Norms," *International Studies Quarterly* 40, 3 (1996): 374.
66. Peter J. Katzenstein, *Cultural Norms and National Security: Police and Military in Postwar Japan* (Ithaca: Cornell University Press, 1996), 3, 18–19; John Gerard Ruggie, "What Makes the World Hang Together? Neo-Utilitarianism and the Social Constructivist Challenge," *International Organization* 52, 4 (1998): 869–73.
67. Rodney Bruce Hall, "Moral Authority as a Power Resource," *International Organization* 51, 4 (1997); Christian Reus-Smit, *The Moral Purpose of the State: Culture, Social Identity, and Institutional Rationality in International Relations* (Princeton: Princeton University Press, 1999).
68. Rawi Abdelal, *National Purpose in the World Economy: Post-Soviet States in Comparative Perspective* (Ithaca: Cornell University Press, 2001); Sheri Berman, *The Social Democratic Movement: Ideas and Politics in the Making of Interwar Europe* (Cambridge: Cambridge University Press, 1998).
69. Peter Kjær and Ove K. Pedersen, "Translating Liberalization: Neoliberalism in the Danish Negotiated Economy," in John L. Campbell and Ove K. Pedersen, eds., *The Rise of Neoliberalism and Institutional Analysis* (Princeton: Princeton University Press, 2001); Margaret E. Keck and Kathryn Sikkink, *Activists Beyond Borders: Advocacy Networks in International Politics* (Ithaca: Cornell University Press, 1998); Thomas Risse, "'Let's Argue!': Communicative Action in World Politics," *International Organization* 54, 1 (2000).

lenged Wendt's view by asserting that it was "ideas all the way through" in contexts where economic social norms and economic ideas were richly contested.[70] The important break from the earlier literature here is an explicit focus on ideas as weapons, a focus that is common to all economic constructivists from those with more critical or postmodern inclinations, such as Jacqueline Best, to those developing a "constructivist-rationalist" approach like Craig Parsons.[71] The focus on *ideas as weapons* comes from a shared frustration with the existing work within constructivism on *why ideas matter* for political economy and institutional change.[72] At stake here is the question of whether ideas provide a useful supplement to interest-based explanations, or whether ideas can matter in their own right as a key explanatory variable.[73] Early work in economic constructivism was ambiguous in answering this question, deferring instead to the view, like historical institutionalists, that ideas are successful only when they fit, or that ideas are part of a "constitutive causality"—both answers were considered to be dodging the question at hand.[74]

For recent economic constructivists, providing a proper answer to the "why do ideas matter?" question requires an analysis of the contestation of ideas prior to institutional design, so that we cannot simply assume that ideas are selected on self-interest that is read *ex post facto* from institutional outcome into the actor designing the institution. Rather, actors carry ideas into their battles over institutional change from a socially constructed rather than merely instrumental basis.[75]

For example, Blyth argues that ideas provide "causal stories" that can cut across class and consumption boundaries to create new collectivities that are studied from struggles between ideas' key representatives.[76] In the building of Swedish "embedded liberalism," the Swedish Social Democratic Party shrugged off neoclassical economic ideas and, in a period of radical uncertainty (the depression), developed new economic ideas on underconsumption and the need to protect individual citizens from the excesses of market forces "regardless of his or her sectoral or class position."[77] In ideational battles over institutional change with trade unionists, employer representatives,

70. Blyth, *Great Transformations*, 29–30, n. 56.

71. Jacqueline Best, *The Limits of Transparency: Ambiguity and the History of International Finance* (Ithaca: Cornell University Press, 2005); Craig Parsons, *A Certain Idea of Europe* (Ithaca: Cornell University Press, 2003). On "relational social constructionism" see Patrick Thaddeus Jackson, *In the Name of the West: Language, Legitimation, and Postwar German Reconstruction* (Ann Arbor: University of Michigan Press, forthcoming).

72. John Kurt Jacobsen, "Much Ado about Ideas: The Cognitive Factor in Economic Policy," *World Politics* 47, 2 (1995).

73. See Rawi Abdelal, Mark Blyth, and Craig Parsons, "The Case for a Constructivist International Political Economy," in Rawi Abdelal, Mark Blyth, and Craig Parsons, eds., *Constructivist Political Economy* (forthcoming).

74. On constitutive causality see Alexander Wendt, "On Constitution and Causation in International Relations," *Review of International Studies* 24 (1998), special issue 5.

75. Blyth, *Great Transformations*, 17–19, 28; Parsons, *A Certain Idea*, 10.

and agriculturalists, the Social Democratic Party was able to build a new economic consensus that was positively redistributive for trade unions while also pro-productivity, pro-investment, and in favor of agricultural protections. Swedish embedded liberalism was, therefore, born from a battle over ideas and went on to spread through the broader population. In the United States, by contrast, a new ideational consensus on underconsumption brought together the state and industrial labor but excluded agriculture because agrarian labor was thought to be too small to provide a mass consumption base.[78]

Similarly, Parsons emphasizes contestation over ideas in his work on how French elites informed European integration. The main thrust here is that elites battled between themselves over ideas on how to handle uncertainty before "master frame" path dependence-inducing ideas become institutionalized. For Parsons, if one can separate the "ideational filter from its context" to view how actors compose their interests independently of direct responses to environmental conditions, an endogenous theory of ideas in institutional change can be created.[79]

This emphasis on contestation is most welcome because it permits more room to discuss the politics of how ideas and economic social norms are used by actors to create institutional change. A focus on contestation should, ideally, ignite interest in a substantive conception of legitimacy. Unfortunately this has not occurred. In my view there are two interrelated obstacles to a substantive conception of legitimacy: i) a persistent selection bias toward *moments of radical uncertainty* and *periods of embeddedness;* and ii) a view of *legitimacy by proclamation* due to an overwhelming focus on institutional and ideational entrepreneurs. I deal with each in turn, while maintaining a focus on the question of legitimacy.

The focus on periods of uncertainty has been constant throughout economic constructivism, particularly as it provides a fruitful avenue to discuss how actors construct their interests in contrast to the default position of self-interest in rationalist and historical institutionalist literature. For economic constructivists, uncertainty generates "highly fluid conceptions of interest," requiring actors to bring new ideas and normative commitments to the table to deal with new problems.[80] Uncertainty also spawns intersubjective ambiguities over technical problems that provide space for political actors to

---

76. Blyth, *Great Transformations*, 37–38. Gourevitch's work has long considered the politics of economic and ideational politics, albeit differently from economic constructivists. See Peter Gourevitch, *Politics in Hard Times: Comparative Responses to International Economic Crises* (Ithaca: Cornell University Press, 1986), Chapters 1 and 2.

77. Ibid., 112.

78. Ibid., Chapters 3 and 4.

79. Parsons, *A Certain Idea*, 13–15.

80. McNamara, *Currency of Ideas*, 7, 57–61; Parsons, *A Certain Idea*, 8–9.

bring normative considerations into battle to challenge fundamental questions about how the economy should work and for whom.[81]

Even more likely to induce change is "Knightian" or radical uncertainty where "agents have no idea what institutions to construct to reduce uncertainty."[82] Such environments compel actors to resort to "repertoires of action that resonate with their core identities" and transform their conceptions of self and others' interest.[83] The general relationship is as follows: there is consensus around a given set of political and economic ideas that is institutionally maintained until a seemingly unprecedented crisis generates radical uncertainty over what should happen next. At this point, ideational entrepreneurs grab onto ideas from the menu of available options at the time which fit with their normative commitments. A political struggle over interests then ensues until a new consensus is formed. Legitimation of this new consensus over an idea comes from the fact that it won out in the struggle. Because of a reliance on radical uncertainty this view of institutional change necessarily relies on the construction of exogenous shocks. We therefore end up with what could be interpreted as an *ideational punctuated equilibrium model* that flows like so: institutional and ideational equilibrium → radical uncertainty and battle over ideas → new institutional and ideational equilibrium.

The focus on radical uncertainty also brings questions about selection bias. Parsons, for example, attributes "causal effects to ideas only where their impact is most clearly demonstrable," that is, when he can make claim to the causal impact "only of certain ideas."[84] A harsh judgment would be that economic constructivists produce a theory of institutional change for what is arguably a minor subset of empirical cases: situations in which actors have no idea how to handle uncertainty. Worse still, one could allege that they have replicated the rationalist institutionalist mistake of selecting cases to conform to a prior model. In doing so, a strong claim concerning how legitimation contests over how the economy should work according to economic social norms held by different social groups has been forfeited for a much weaker claim.

Developing a substantive conception of legitimacy in economic constructivism has been further hindered by the marrying of a preference for moments of radical uncertainty with periods of "embeddedness" or "disem-

81. Best, *Limits of Transparency*, Chapter 2. On the use of "speech acts" by international organizations see Jason Sharman, "Rhetoric, Reputation and Regulation: Tax Havens, the OECD and the Struggle for Global Tax Standards," unpublished manuscript, University of Sydney, January 2005.

82. Blyth, *Great Transformations*, 36; see also Colin Hay, "The 'Crisis' of Keynesianism and the Rise of Neoliberalism in Britain: An Ideational Institutionalist Approach," in Campbell and Pedersen, eds., *Rise of Neoliberalism*.

83. Blyth, *Great Transformations*, 267.

84. Parsons, *A Certain Idea*, 12, 232.

beddedness." The use of embeddedness in economic constructivism, like its use in the "varieties of capitalism" literature discussed above, draws upon Karl Polanyi's notion of the market economy being embedded in society.[85] More embeddedness is generally considered to be good and its absence bad. As such, the embeddedness or disembeddedness of a society is often described statically. Polanyi's point, however, was to specify conflict between social groups within a dynamic *"always* embedded economy."[86] The notion of embeddedness also confronts us with the question of whose and what values are ideally embedded. As stated above, the concept of embeddedness is an inadequate proxy for legitimacy.

Studies of embeddedness often emphasize the state's need for broad social support of its policies in order to ensure their success. And such support only comes when the state's attempt to legitimate policy and institutional change gains sufficient consent from the broader population. As pointed out by Colin Hay, economic constructivism requires a prominent figure to provide an "ideational focus for the reconstitution of the perceived self-interests of the population at large."[87] Who can do so under radical uncertainty? The ideational entrepreneur, our modern charismatic leader, is the answer.

This brings us to our second obstacle within the extant economic constructivism: legitimacy by proclamation. While earlier constructivist work pointed to absence of the individual, and where organizational institutionalists argued that institutions were "resilient to the idiosyncratic preferences and expectations of individuals," recent economic constructivism has embraced a view of elite entrepreneurs as carriers of transformative ideas.[88]

Within extant economic constructivism, much work has discussed stagflation and the death of Keynesianism in the 1970s and the consequent institutional change to a "neoliberal" or monetarist consensus in the 1990s.[89] These studies detail how ideational entrepreneurs fight each other during

85. Karl Polanyi, *The Great Transformation: The Political and Economic Origins of Our Time* (Boston: Beacon Press, 1944); Blyth, *Great Transformations;* Hollingsworth and Boyer, eds., *Contemporary Capitalism.*

86. Fred Block, "Karl Polanyi and the Writing of the Great Transformation," *Theory and Society* 32, 3 (2003). A different use of "embedded" in economic constructivism is provided by Tim Sinclair's discussion of "embedded knowledge networks", where embedded refers to actors' internalization—and therefore legitimation—of the knowledge network. See Timothy J. Sinclair, *The New Masters of Capital: American Bond Rating Agencies and the Politics of Creditworthiness* (Ithaca: Cornell University Press, 2005), 15.

87. Colin Hay, "Ideas, Interests and Institutions in the Comparative Political Economy of Great Transformations," *Review of International Political Economy* 11, 1 (2004): 210.

88. Audie Klotz, *Norms in International Relations: The Struggle Against Apartheid* (Ithaca: Cornell University Press), 33–34; James G. March and Johan P. Olsen, "The New Institutionalism: Organizational Factors in Political Life," *American Political Science Review* 78, 3 (1984): 741.

89. Best, *Limits of Transparency;* Blyth, *Great Transformations;* McNamara, *Currency of Ideas;* Parsons, *A Certain Idea;* Wesley Widmaier, "The Social Construction of the 'Impossible Trinity': The Intersubjective Bases of Monetary Cooperation," *International Studies Quarterly* 48, 2 (2004).

periods of uncertainty to establish the next institutional form. So, for example, both McNamara and Parsons point to the crucial role of French president Valéry Giscard d'Estaing in the 1970s and early 1980s, as he was able to stand above the crowd, including electoral politics, and forge close links with West German chancellor Helmut Schmidt, and place France on a path-dependent track that pushed the European Monetary System forward. Giscard's unique foresight then permitted the leap from Keynesian to monetarist policies once the "overdraft economy" failed.[90] Likewise, in the building of Swedish embedded liberalism in the 1930s, Bertil Ohlin's posting of memos to interest groups led to "legitimating, and thereby empowering, one set of ideas over another."[91]

Great individuals therefore carry "master frames" which inform an "*institutional construction of interests*" that establishes a path-dependent logic of appropriateness. At his most extreme Parsons asserts that "given a heart attack or two and some plausible coalitional reshuffling," European integration might have proceeded significantly earlier than actually occurred.[92] We then end up with questions such as what might have happened if someone had chosen the chicken rather than the fish on the plane to Brussels. Furthermore, the focus on individuals asks us to consider if it is the quality of the idea or the charismatic and powerful leader that wins out in battle. After all, Parsons writes, in battle the "initial resources of each idea's initial proponents can decide the outcome."[93]

The economic constructivist view of legitimacy by proclamation, rather than contestation, comes not only from a focus on ideational entrepreneurs, but from the curiously thin conception of society that is separate from institutions. As such the legitimation of the ideas and economic social norms come down from on high, which is especially troubling if the key aim of constructivism is to understand norms as "collective social facts" contested between social groups engaged with the issue at hand.[94] So while ideational entrepreneurs can use ideas as weapons for their normative goals, if they are sufficiently powerful, in periods of radical uncertainty, the rest of us are "institutional dopes blindly following the institutionalized scripts and cues around them."[95]

To take an example, for Finnemore and Sikkink "domestic legitimacy is the *belief* that existing political institutions are better than other alternatives

90. McNamara, *Currency of Ideas*, 69, 123–26; Parsons, *A Certain Idea*, 175–76; see also Michael Loriaux, *France After Hegemony: International Change and Financial Reform* (Ithaca: Cornell University Press, 1991).
91. Blyth, *Great Transformations*, 108, 115. Blyth does recognize, however, that "agreement by elites does not necessarily translate into mass acceptance."
92. Parsons, *A Certain Idea*, 19, 32, 178, 235, emphasis in original.
93. Ibid., 20 n. 57.
94. Katzenstein, *Cultural Norms*, 17.
95. John L. Campbell, "Institutional Analysis and the Role of Ideas in Political Economy," *Theory and Society* 27, 3 (1998): 383.

and therefore deserve *obedience.*"[96] Or, more recently, Michael Barnett and Finnemore claim that international organizations' deployment of "intellectual technologies" provides them with *symbolic* legitimacy and encourages conformity to their ideas and norms. Here international organizations retain procedural legitimacy by following correct, proper, consistent rules and conventions, while substantive legitimacy comes from providing a good fit with the "values of the broader community" that are externally given.[97] *Legitimacy is therefore viewed as a condition rather than a process,* and takes us back to a logic of appropriateness argument.[98] As recently commented by Ole Jacob Sending, the use of such logic by constructivist scholars removes the notion of agency and a theory of individual action—two crucial elements in providing a substantive conception of legitimacy.[99] A major obstacle to the betterment of economic constructivist understandings of institutional change is, therefore, specifying the social mechanisms that link established norms to new ideas and norms beyond the role of powerful elites within a punctuated equilibrium model.[100]

We must augment the economic constructivist view of legitimacy by proclamation with a conception of legitimacy as a process in which social groups contest economic social norms within everyday life. To do so we can turn to Weberian economic sociology for assistance.

Legitimacy and Weberian Economic Sociology

While economic constructivism does have a few problems, it has much to offer in providing an approach to institutional and social change that stresses the importance of ideational and normative struggles between actors. My claim here is that Max Weber's conception of legitimacy can augment economic constructivism to provide a focus on everyday belief-driven actions that inform institutional and social change. Max Weber's work on *Wirtschafts-*

96. Martha Finnemore and Kathryn Sikkink, "International Norms Dynamics and Political Change," *International Organization* 52, 4 (1998): 903, my emphasis.

97. Michael Barnett and Martha Finnemore, *Rules for the World: International Organizations in Global Politics* (Ithaca: Cornell University Press, 2004), 166–70; Cf. Louis W. Pauly, *Who Elected the Bankers? Surveillance and Control in the World Economy* (Ithaca: Cornell University Press, 1997), 12–13.

98. Parsons, *A Certain Idea,* 14–15; Blyth, *Great Transformations,* 39; Finnemore and Sikkink, "International Norms," 895.

99. Ole Jacob Sending, "Constitution, Choice and Change: Problems with the 'Logic of Appropriateness' and Its Use in Constructivist Theory," *European Journal of International Relations* 8, 4 (2002).

100. Jeffrey T. Checkel, "Why Comply? Social Learning and European Identity Change," *International Organization* 55, 3 (2001). An excellent study of legitimation processes according to focus groups rather than elites is provided in Ted Hopf, "Making the Future Inevitable: Legitimizing, Naturalizing and Stabilizing: The Transition in Estonia, Ukraine and Uzbekistan," *European Journal of International Relations* 8, 2 (2002).

soziologie (economic sociology) and his interpretive *Verstehen* (understanding) approach to political economy and economic sociology provide fruitful avenues to explore in achieving this aim, as do works by political and economic sociologists such as Reinhard Bendix, Raymond Boudon, John Campbell, Richard Swedberg, and others.[101]

Max Weber's work is by no means alien to economic constructivism, particularly given Weber's emphasis on the understanding of how meaning is attributed to human action in political and economic life.[102] For Weber all economic activity, including the building of economic institutions, comes from historically contingent rationalizations undertaken by individuals. Here rationalization simply means making sense of the world in order to act in it, rather than the term's contemporary usage as a process of simplification and standardization to improve efficiency. Accordingly, Weber, and Weberian economic sociology in general, asks us to question how economic social norms inform legitimation processes that inform institutional and social change.[103] This aim is not restricted to analyzing economic phenomena, such as kinds of market relationships undertaken by corporate firms and networks (as is common in economic sociology),[104] but also how economic behavior is shaped by what we would normally consider to be non-economic behavior (what Weber calls "economically relevant phenomena"), and how economic behavior shapes non-economic behavior ("economically conditioned phenomena").[105]

For Weber, individuals put themselves through the wringer in searching for what meanings they wish to give, and rationalization they adopt (*not use*), in economic social life. For example, Weber's most famous study, *The Protestant Ethic and the Spirit of Capitalism,* demonstrates how individuals wrestled with ascetic Protestantism and changed their attitudes toward work and profit-making, which then provided the historically unique constellation that formed the "capitalist spirit."[106] Importantly, this macro-micro-macro

101. The key work here is Richard Swedberg, *Max Weber and the Idea of Economic Sociology* (Princeton: Princeton University Press, 1998). It should be noted that while the prominence of legitimacy in Weber's work is acknowledged by Weberian economic sociology, scholars in this area have not sufficiently engaged with the concept. See also, for example, Richard Swedberg, *Principles of Economic Sociology* (Princeton: Princeton University Press, 2003), 169–70.
102. Ruggie, "What Makes the World," 859; Ted Hopf, *Social Construction of International Politics: Identities and Foreign Policies, Moscow, 1955 and 1999* (Ithaca: Cornell University Press, 2002), 14–15.
103. Max Weber, *Gesammelte Aufsätze zur Religionssoziologie,* vol. 1 (Tübingen: J. C. B. Mohr [Paul Siebeck], 1972), 49; Weber, *Economy and Society,* 2: 953–54.
104. For example, Neil Fligstein, *The Architecture of Markets: An Economic Sociology of Twenty-First Century Capitalist Societies* (Princeton: Princeton University Press, 2002); Mark Granovetter, "Economic Action and Social Structure: The Problem of Embeddedness," *American Journal of Sociology* 91, 3 (1985).
105. Swedberg, *Max Weber,* 163; Max Weber, *Gesammelte Aufsätze zur Wissenschaftslehre* (Tübingen: J. C. B. Mohr, 1973), 163 (hereafter *GAW*). More generally, see Weber, *Economy and Society,* 1: Chapter 2.
106. Max Weber, *The Protestant Ethic and the Spirit of Capitalism* (London: George Allen and

transformation (from the environment to the individual to the environment) was not dependent on an individual responding to "natural" economic incentives, since there is nothing "natural" about either man or social life whatsoever.[107] To provide an analysis of similar dynamics we cannot posit a person who "naturally" seeks to maximize his or her utility, as rationalist institutionalists would have it. Nor can we privilege a normative structural explanation, such as a logic of appropriateness, or a general theory on how ideational entrepreneurs have their chance to transform their environment in periods of uncertainty, as historical institutionalists and economic constructivists contend. Rather we require *understanding* rather than *explaining* in specifying what is unique about a political and economic period and how actors attribute meaning to themselves and others within everyday life.[108] The bottom line here is that, when accompanied by an emphasis on legitimacy, conceptual tools from Weberian economic sociology can augment economic constructivism in three ways.

First, we can emphasize a conception of society that is separate from the institutions of analysis. Conflict is therefore not only between ideational entrepreneurs, but between individuals within social groups and the state. From this view the state is an arena for contestation. In short, we cannot produce a sociological understanding of how economic social norms influence institutional change by looking only at institutions and ignoring society.

Second, a focus on legitimacy requires that we produce an idiographic rather than nomothetic methodological individualism; that we seek to understand what is peculiar and particular to how individuals give meaning to their actions rather than seeing them as following universal or general laws.[109] Weberian economic sociology, I contend, provides us with a strong focus on how economic social norms saturate individual choice and provide customs, conventions, and norms within which economic life is conducted.[110] Following Weber and Boudon I refer to this as *axiorational* behavior.[111] In stressing axiorational behavior, Weberian economic sociology asks us to understand not only the constraints upon individuals provided by economic social norms, but *variations* in how individuals and groups of in-

Unwin, 1976); Swedberg, *Max Weber,* 130–31. See also Coleman, "Social Theory," and North, *Understanding,* 135.

107. Peter Ghosh, "Some Problems with Talcott Parsons' Version of the 'Protestant Ethic,'" *Archives Européennes De Sociologie* 35, 1 (1994): 115.

108. Hopf, *Social Construction of International Politics,* 13–14. See also Weber, *GAW,* 489–540; Mark I. Lichbach, "Social Theory and Comparative Politics," in Lichbach and Zuckerman, eds., *Comparative Politics.*

109. As contended in John S. Odell, "Bounded Rationality and the World Political Economy," in David M. Andrews, C. Randall Henning, and Louis W. Pauly, eds., *Governing the World's Money* (Ithaca: Cornell University Press, 2002), 168, 188.

110. Weber, *Economy and Society,* 1: 29.

111. Raymond Boudon, *The Origin of Values: Sociology and Philosophy of Beliefs* (New Brunswick, N.J.: Transaction Publishers, 2001), 93–110.

dividuals recombine elements of existing norms to *incrementally* generate new norms.[112]

Third, a focus on legitimacy demands that we make claims that are temporally limited and socially dynamic. An object or subject cannot be absolutely "legitimate" or "illegitimate" but, rather, has relative degrees of legitimacy that require historical specification.[113] As such the notion that institutional and social change is path dependent or follows a linear evolution must be problematized. We must, therefore, temper grand theoretical ambitions and turn to smaller claims that are more interested in outlining the mechanisms through which everyday legitimacy contests between the state and social groups occur and inform institutional and social change.

As discussed above, much of the literature in political economy and institutional theory ignores or downplays the concept of legitimacy, in part because of how the concept has been treated as a *condition* to be implemented by the state. We should not think, however, of legitimacy as a binary condition. The legitimacy of one's actions or the legitimacy of an institution can only be considered in relative degrees rather than absolutes. We should also dismiss the notion that legitimacy is *only* belief rather than *belief-driven actions*.[114] The idea of legitimacy as belief alone must be rejected on the grounds that people believe that something holds legitimacy because they can justify it in accordance with their experience of the world. Furthermore, any legitimation process demands not belief, but belief-driven actions between those who claim that their actions have sufficient legitimacy and those who can confer or withdraw their consent for the actions. From this view the process of legitimation requires "cumulative, individual acts of compliance or confidence" from actors who are subordinate to the system of power.[115] If dominant actors do not claim legitimacy for their policies and institutions by framing them within social "maxims," they may as well be talking to the wall.[116]

Processes of legitimation are informed by contests between individuals whose belief-driven actions represent and reflect economic social norms they *positively* embrace.[117] Weber's work on legitimacy stresses that moments

112. Max Weber, *Roscher and Knies: The Logical Problems of Historical Economics* (London: Free Press, 1975), 102–5.

113. Weber, *GAW,* 511.

114. Robert Grafstein, "The Failure of Weber's Conception of Legitimacy: Its Causes and Implications," *Journal of Politics* 43, 2 (1981): 466; cf. Max Weber, *Theory of Social and Economic Organization* (New York: Oxford University Press, 1964), 325–27; Weber, *Economy and Society,* 1: 32–33, 213–15.

115. Reinhard Bendix, *Nation-Building and Citizenship* (Berkeley: University of California Press, 1977), 21, 24. See also David Beetham, *The Legitimation of Power* (London: Macmillan, 1991), 11, 26.

116. Weber, *Economy and Society,* 1: 31; Rodney Barker, *Legitimating Identities: The Self-Presentation of Rulers and Subjects* (Cambridge: Cambridge University Press, 2001).

117. Liah Greenfeld, *The Spirit of Capitalism: Nationalism and Economic Growth* (Cambridge, Mass.: Harvard University Press, 2001), 16.

of charisma, such as the proclamation of legitimacy by an ideational entrepreneur, are not sufficient to sustain a political and economic order. Far more important is the everyday struggle between various actors and groups over how the economy should work.[118]

It is also imperative to understand that the concept of legitimacy is not synonymous with the concept of an economic social norm. Legitimacy involves struggle over what actors consider to be procedurally fair and morally and ethically "valid" behavior, while economic social norms represent the aggregates of conventional behavior that has been built up incrementally.[119] In this sense economic social norms impose a logic of appropriateness upon actors, but a reflexive one where actors can select conventions to influence change to economic social norms and, therefore, institutions. Economic social norms provide a menu of means individuals can use to deal with a problem. They do not necessarily prescribe the ends of actions.[120] Legitimacy contests provide the space for these means to be tested through struggle and selection.

Following this reasoning, the state has "no intrinsic value," but is "purely a technical instrument for the realization of other values."[121] The key, then, is to historically specify legitimacy contests between the state and social groups—and forms of state intervention—rather than assume continuity or path dependence.[122] Importantly, this suggests a conception of society that is separate from institutions, permitting a better understanding of how institutional change evolves from the "bottom-up." For example, the "shock therapy" economic reforms in Eastern Europe during the 1990s could be seen as conforming to a punctuated equilibrium model if we look only at the behavior of formal institutions. But if we look at how social groups fought for and anticipated the reforms, the process suggests more incremental change.[123] In short, we need to understand incremental social change because it provides the context for moments when important decisions are made.

The key protagonist in processes of legitimation is the individual.[124] We-

---

118. Weber, *GAW,* 486–87; Swedberg, *Max Weber,* 65–66.
119. Weber, *Economy and Society,* 1: 29–36. See also John Maynard Keynes, *The General Theory of Employment, Interest and Money* (London: Harcourt Brace and World, 1964), 147–65.
120. Peter J. Katzenstein, "Analyzing Change in International Politics: The New Institutionalism and the Interpretative Approach," MPIfG Working Paper 90/10 (Köln: Max-Planck Institut für Gesellschaftsforschung, 1990), 21. See also Weber, *Economy and Society,* 1: 65.
121. Max Weber, "The Meaning of Ethical Neutrality," in E. A. Shils and H. A. Finch, eds., *Sociology and Economics in the Methodology of the Social Sciences* (Chicago: Free Press, 1949), 47; see also Weber, *GAW,* 539–40.
122. Swedberg, *Max Weber,* 57.
123. John L. Campbell and Ove K. Pedersen, "The Evolutionary Nature of Revolutionary Change in Postcommunist Europe," in John L. Campbell and Ove K. Pedersen, eds., *Legacies of Change: Transformations of Post-Communist Europe* (New York: Aldine de Guyter, 1996).
124. Weber, *Economy and Society,* 1: 13.

ber argued that throughout history "the ordinary person [is] capable of taking thought of what he is doing" even if, *ex post facto,* he or she hurt their economic interests in the process.[125] Crucially important is that individuals are not socially atomized in their decision-making processes within political and economic life but, rather, their determination of interest is thoroughly saturated by economic social norms that are historically specific.[126] This view provides the basis for Weber's call for an *idiographic* rather than nomothetic form of methodological individualism to bring in a substantive conception of legitimacy and understand the motives behind belief-driven economic social action.[127] In *Economy and Society* Weber writes:

> It is a tremendous misunderstanding to think that an "individualistic" *method* should involve in any conceivable sense an individualistic system of *values.* It is as important to avoid this error as the related one which confuses the unavoidable tendency of sociological concepts to assume a rationalistic character with a belief in the predominance of rational motives, or even a positive valuation of rationalism.[128]

For Weber, rationality is a social construct that is imbued with values and produces an axiological rationality from which actors seek to act in ways they believe to hold greater legitimacy than the alternatives.[129]

Values, customs, and conventions therefore inform one's perception of life-chances and one's attitudes and actions on how the economy should work. The concept of axiorational behavior suggests that individuals do not simply choose to exercise an instrumental rationality abstracted from society. The influence of social life cannot be turned off like a tap. Rather, axiorational behavior calls us to understand how individual interest is saturated by economic social norms that, for Weber, are "liquid," permitting us to see them as both constraining and enabling, sink or swim.[130] An idiographic methodological individualism which includes axiorational behavior requires us to understand how actors draw upon "liquid" ideational societal resources to affect institutional change.

How then do individuals influence institutional change? The meanings individuals attribute to everyday economic life are necessarily intersubjective, and action is often expressed through "interest-driven regularities"

---

125. Reinhard Bendix, *Force, Fate and Freedom: On Historical Sociology* (London: University of California Press, 1984), 30.
126. Swedberg, *Max Weber,* 167–71.
127. Weber, *GAW,* 40–60; cf. Ruggie, "What Makes the World," 884–85.
128. Weber, *Economy and Society,* 1: 18.
129. Ibid., 24–25.
130. Weber, *GAW,* 579–80; see also Weber, *Economy and Society,* 1: 32. Sung Ho Kim, *Max Weber's Politics of Civil Society* (Cambridge: Cambridge University Press, 2004), 93, 117.

within groups of individuals who loosely share a conception of their life-chances, such as the LIGs in this study.[131] Through a group, actors incrementally select existing and new conventions as economic social norms to support their claims in assessing whether or not to provide or withdraw their consent for an institution and its policies.

It is here that Weber's often-neglected concept of *Auslese* (selection) is important in addition to his well-known emphasis on *Kampf* (struggle) through everyday political and economic life.[132] Weber's concept of selection is that as individuals struggle with one another and within themselves in political and economic life they call upon ideational, normative, and material resources to provide unique constellations that can improve their life-chances. Such struggle and selection is not, however, supported by instrumental reasoning or determined by a "fitness to survive."[133] Rather than following an evolutionary logic, Weber's notion of selection requires us to emphasize highly contingent incremental social change and limits the heuristic value of path dependence.[134] History is not a marching procession of rationalizations but, rather, a ramble.[135]

Weber's concept of selection shares some traits with John L. Campbell's recent clarification on how actors can generate institutional change by engaging in a process of *bricolage*. For Campbell, bricolage is a mechanism within which actors call upon extant institutional resources and recombine them in a way that can make new normative claims upon an institution.[136] In this light, institutions are both constraining and enabling, allowing the defiance of an otherwise daunting logic of appropriateness. For Campbell, agents use ideas drawn from social norms on what institutions *should* do and how institutions should behave to change what they actually do and how they view problems. Specific challenges on how an institution's legitimizing principles should be adjusted are then framed within broader social conceptions of that which the public is likely to confer their consent.[137]

131. The people within lower-income groupings vary, across the case studies, in race, age, gender, cultural heritage, and religion, but share a notion that the economy should provide more life-chances for people on below median income.

132. Peter Breiner, "'Unnatural Selection': Max Weber's Concept of Auslese and his Criticism of the Reduction of Political Conflict to Economics," *International Relations* 18, 3 (2004): 293–94. Cf. W. G. Runciman, "Was Max Weber a Selectionist in Spite of Himself?" *Journal of Classical Sociology* 1, 1 (2001).

133. Weber, *Economy and Society*, 1: 38–40.

134. As discussed by Collins, Parsons's work on Weber gave a path dependence that is out of line with Weber's intentions. Randall Collins, "Weber's Last Theory of Capitalism: A Systematization," in Mark Granovetter and Richard Swedberg, eds., *The Sociology of Economic Life* (Boulder, Colo.: Westview Press, 1992), 87.

135. Greenfeld, *The Spirit of Capitalism*, 20.

136. Campbell, *Institutional Change*, 65, 69–74. See also Mary Douglas, *How Institutions Think* (Syracuse: Syracuse University Press, 1986), 66–67; Mauro Guillén, *The Limits of Convergence: Globalization and Organizational Change in Argentina, South Korea, and Spain* (Princeton: Princeton University Press, 2001), 13–14.

137. Campbell, *Institutional Change*, 96–99. Campbell uses the term "frames" and "public

Weber's notion of selection and the recent work on bricolage by economic sociologists is important to understanding everyday actions because they do not rely on periods of radical uncertainty to open up opportunities for institutional change. Furthermore, both selection and bricolage suggest that while history matters in institutional and social change by providing an ideational and normative repertoire actors can draw upon, institutional logics are not overwhelmingly constraining and change is not evolutionarily linear.[138]

How can we study institutional and social change within political economy if we cannot posit path dependence or evolution? While much of the institutionalist literature discussed above seeks to map out systematic co-variation between causal variables, Weber insisted on interpretive "thick" narratives assessed against ideal types rather than an abstracted and reified causal analysis.[139] As such, an understanding of everyday legitimation processes requires a rejection of general theories and tempered, modest claims about social processes that do not naturalize the present, or see the past as simply a data farm for confirming the predictive capacities of general models.[140]

The best means of addressing this problem is to interpret institutional and social change through social mechanisms, an approach within the social sciences that economic constructivism has recently engaged in to specify input and output mechanisms by which to assess the role of ideas and norms in institutional change.[141] Mechanisms should not be seen as simply links between independent and dependent variables, but as "nuts and bolts, cogs and wheels," "small and medium-sized descriptions of ways in which things happen" within a complex social environment.[142] Mechanisms are constructs that help us understand a social process that has a repeated but indeterminate outcome and helps us understand the context for actors' belief-driven actions and therefore key processes of institutional and social change. Specifying social mechanisms permits us to avoid functionalist accounts where institutional outcomes are explained by their consequences,

sentiment" for the foreground and background. As Boudon has outlined, "frames" are often used as ad hoc explanations by rationalist institutionalists. By contrast, Campbell seeks to specify the mechanisms through which "framing" occurs. See Raymond Boudon, "Social Mechanisms without Black Boxes," in Peter Hedström and Richard Swedberg, eds., *Social Mechanisms: An Analytical Approach to Social Theory* (Cambridge: Cambridge University Press, 1997), 180, 183.

138. See also Colin Crouch and Henry Ferrell, "Breaking the Path of Institutional Development? Alternatives to the New Determinism," *Rationality and Society* 16, 1 (2004).

139. Andrew Abbott, *Chaos of Disciplines* (Chicago: University of Chicago Press, 2001), 117.

140. John M. Hobson, "What's at Stake in 'Bringing Historical Sociology Back into International Relations'? Transcending 'Chronofetishism' and 'Tempocentrism' in International Relations," in Steve Hobden and John M. Hobson, eds., *Historical Sociology of International Relations* (Cambridge: Cambridge University Press, 2002), 5–8.

141. Abdelal, Blyth, and Parsons, "The Case for a Constructivist International Political Economy."

as well as steering clear of mistaking correlation among variables as causation.

Within political and economic sociology discussion has generated a wide range of social mechanisms, most of which fall into structural, ideational, and social-relational categories.[143] What is important here is that mechanisms seek to tie down not only structures and institutions that provide constraints upon action, but also outline how actors can work toward their life-chances. Once more this view emphasizes contingent and incremental institutional and social change. Specification, however, does not completely eliminate modest generalizations of phenomena but only *universalizations* of phenomena. We can confidently generalize about how actors may behave across cases, but only within the boundaries of what can be justified from the empirical evidence and in light of our theoretical considerations and an ideal type.[144]

Understanding the Social Sources of Financial Power

This book is concerned with how a state's domestic legitimation of its financial reform nexus for lower-income groupings (LIGs) generates or hinders the development of a social source of financial power and its influence in the international financial order. How, then, does the above discussion of political economy and institutional theory assist us in studying processes of legitimation?

As stated in the previous chapter, LIGs are important to study because their frustrations over their lack of access to credit and property, as well as their relative tax burdens, can transform into significant political and economic influence. I stress here that their struggles with the state and with rentiers are important for disaggregating state intervention. Their struggles are also important for understanding not only how domestic financial systems differ, but key influences on the character of an international financial order. LIGs, as I have suggested, are not synonymous with a class group but are composed of individuals who select liquid conventions and who are satu-

142. Jon Elster, *Nuts and Bolts for the Social Sciences* (Cambridge: Cambridge University Press, 1989), 3; Interview with Jon Elster, in Richard Swedberg, *Economics and Sociology: Redefining Their Boundaries* (Princeton: Princeton University Press, 1990), 247. Cf. James Mahoney, "Beyond Correlational Analysis: Recent Innovations in Theory and Method," *Sociological Forum* 16, 3 (2001): 578–81. Mahoney outlines that there are well over twenty definitions of what a mechanism is. While I do not share Elster's approach, particularly his rejection of value rationality as meaningful, his definitions of a mechanism is wonderfully commonsensical.

143. For example, Doug McAdam, Sidney Tarrow, and Charles Tilly outline "environmental," "cognitive," and "relational" mechanisms, while Peter Hedström and Swedberg discuss "situational," "action-formation," and "transformational" mechanisms. Doug McAdam, Sidney Tarrow, and Charles Tilly, *Dynamics of Contention* (Cambridge: Cambridge University Press, 2001), 25–26; Peter Hedström and Richard Swedberg, "Social Mechanisms: An Introductory Essay," in Hedström and Swedberg, eds., *Social Mechanisms*, 21–23.

144. Hopf, *Social Construction*, 30–31.

rated by economic social norms. As such, norms cannot be understood as error terms in understanding how actors give meaning to their actions, but must be seen as historically contingent and central to everyday struggle. Nor can we discuss how states follow national trajectories, since this blinds us to social changes that background and inform institutional change. We also need a way to study legitimacy that does not view the proclamation of new ideas by elites as auto-legitimating.

As discussed above, Max Weber's work on legitimacy and Weberian economic sociology provides some answers to how we can study everyday institutional and social change. With application to understanding the social sources of financial power, I argue that we require an ideal type against which to compare cases, and social mechanisms to interpret the dynamics within them. This view of institutional and social change therefore tempers any pretensions to a universal theory of change and grounds our understanding to the empirical material.

I put forward three linked mechanisms that are involved in the legitimation of a financial reform nexus and involve LIGs, the state, and rentiers. First, in response to the existing institutional and social environment, LIGs and rentiers engage in contestation with the state over how the economy should work to meet their life-chances. In doing so, LIGs and rentiers call upon ideational and normative resources in putting forward public and private reasons that seek to sway the state's chosen form of intervention into the economy.

Following contestation, the state's choice to support either LIGs or rentiers (respectively, positive or negative state intervention) leads to a redistribution of political and economic assets and opportunities, including reforms to how formal public and private institutions interact with society at large. State intervention in favor of LIGs will broaden and deepen the domestic pool of capital, because LIGs will have greater access to credit and property and lower taxes, while state intervention against LIGs will do the opposite, narrowing the base and engendering what I term a "rentier shift." Of course, all of this is largely dependent on who is running the state.

Either way, the cumulative effect of contestation and redistribution will spark off a third mechanism, propagation, whereby the state will promote ideas on how the economy should work in an attempt to legitimate its previous actions and either encourage or discourage the use of financial innovations among LIGs. There is, of course, no guarantee that the state's claims to legitimacy will actually garner sufficient legitimacy for the state to continue its policies. Rather, propagation provides important feedback information for LIGs and rentiers to reflect upon as individuals prior to reengaging the first mechanism, contestation, and competing with other sources of ideas.

It is important to recognize that all the mechanisms above do not rely on exogenous shocks to institutions; nor do they rely on periods of radical uncertainty to kick ideational entrepreneurs into gear. Rather, these mechanisms are repeatedly played out in everyday life and require us to interpret struggles within social relationships. The case studies that follow this chapter compare how states, LIGs, and rentiers behaved in comparison to the ideal type detailed above. I also pay attention to how contestation, redistribution, and propagation mechanisms inform the legitimation of financial reform nexuses within discrete periods of time.

The three mechanisms described above are useful for comparing the cases against an ideal type of how states can generate a sustainable social source of financial power. While this is mentioned in the previous chapter, I would like to briefly restate it here.

The scenario is as follows: a state will intervene positively into its financial reform nexus for people in lower-income groupings in accordance with the latter's economic social norms. Positive state intervention would then create policy and institutional changes that the state could claim to have a high degree of legitimacy because of the good probability that LIGs would provide their consent for the changes, and because the intervention would also be against rentiers who would otherwise make the financial reform nexus worse for LIGs. As a consequence of the state intervening and sufficiently legitimizing the financial reform nexus, LIGs would receive greater access to credit and property, as well as lower tax burdens (relative to what they expect the state to do for them), thereby broadening and deepening the domestic pool of capital and propagating new economic social norms that encouraged the use of financial innovations as conventions. From this basis the state could permit capital to flow from LIGs' pocketbooks and pay packets through financial institutions and, eventually, to the global financial marketplace. If this ideal-typical scenario were possible, then the state could increase its international financial capacity and its influence on the regulatory and normative character of the international financial order through its increased capacity to access credit and to draw upon domestic innovations. There is a lot going on within this ideal-typical scenario and, as we shall see in the case studies, most states have great difficulty in producing a political and economic system that can do most of the above.

Finally, this discussion of legitimacy within a domestic context also has implications for our understanding of behavior between states and market actors within the international political economy. I claim that states that positively intervene into their financial reform nexus to support LIGs heighten their domestic legitimacy and their international financial capacity; that is their capacity to extract and export capital to the international financial order, as well as influence its normative and regulatory structure. I make no claims to legitimation processes *within* the international political economy, since this would require an investigation of how, for the case material in this book, England's and the United States' claims to the legitimacy of its international dominance was received not only by other states, but by their publics. This is clearly beyond the scope of the present study.[145]

We can state, however, that Max Weber's view of political and economic life in the domestic realm does carry over, despite popular reception, into the international realm. From this view, states that are able to successfully regenerate themselves through highly legitimated domestic relationships are more able to have influence within an international society of states, including an influence on its regulatory and normative structure.[146] This view is also in accordance with recent constructivist work that emphasizes how the contestation of legitimacy in domestic realms explains changes in norms that hold prominence in the international political economy.[147] The key to this work is to differentiate how states treated their societies within particular historical periods and within various domestic political and economic contexts. It is a similar aim that now guides us through the empirical chapters in seeking to understand the social sources of financial power.

145. However, see Ian Hurd, "Legitimacy and Authority in International Politics," *International Organization* 53, 2 (1999).

146. John M. Hobson and Leonard Seabrooke, "Reimagining Weber: Constructing International Society and the Social Balance of Power," *European Journal of International Relations* 7, 2 (2001); Max Weber, *Gesammelte Politische Schriften* (Tübingen: J. C. B. Mohr, 1988), 143, 175–77.

147. Mlada Bukovansky, *Legitimacy and Power Politics: The American and French Revolutions in International Political Culture* (Princeton: Princeton University Press, 2002), 8, 26; Reus-Smit, *Moral Purpose,* 167. See also Jens Steffek, "The Legitimation of International Governance: A Discourse Approach," *European Journal of International Relations* 9, 2 (2003).

3

The Financial Reform Nexus in England

Engineering was the principal Great Power in the international financial order in 1900. Such primacy was built on foundations established in the preceding century, particularly improvements in the City of London's ability to draw capital from rapid growth in provincial joint-stock banking in the mid-nineteenth century.[1] During this period, the English state actively attempted to ensure its autonomy from the political and economic power of City financiers. A key element of this strategy was to develop a broader and deeper source of financial wealth by using positive state intervention to develop a public and private savings bank system targeted at enabling lower-income groupings (LIGs) to better fulfill their social wants. The success of these systems allowed provincial financial assets to quickly double City of London assets. These systems, as long as positive state intervention persisted, also permitted increased access to credit and property during a period in which LIGs developed economic social norms that outlined what the economy should be like, and how the state should intervene against the wealthy, particularly rentiers, to improve their lot.

The problem here was that positive state intervention did not persist. The development of both increased financial power and new norms on what LIGs should expect from their political representatives scared political and economic elites about the transformation of the English state from a "narrow plutocracy to a bureaucratic liberal welfare capitalism."[2] As such, from 1890 the

1. I specify English norms rather than British norms. This distinction does produce some problems in gathering statistics, since many studies provide only data on the United Kingdom (UK) or "England and Wales." There are sound reasons for specifying English norms. English investors accounted for 80 percent of all equity in the British system and 90 percent of the value of domestic equity. Moreover, the average London investor placed his or her private capital in a domestic/foreign/empire ratio of 24:37:39. Lance E. Davis and Robert E. Gallman, *Evolving Financial Markets and International Capital Flows: Britain, the Americas, and Australia, 1865–1914* (Cambridge: Cambridge University Press, 2000).
2. Avner Offer, *Property and Politics, 1870–1914: Landownership, Law, Ideology, and Urban Development in England* (Cambridge: Cambridge University Press, 1981), 3.

54

once-splintered factions of City financiers and landed aristocracy combined their skills to produce a rentier shift that sought to draw capital from the provinces into the City, while also raising barriers to prevent increased credit and property access to LIGs, as well as minimizing their own tax burdens through trade protectionism. This rentier shift manifested in the construction of a "gentlemanly capitalism" that sought to control the English financial reform nexus.[3] I maintain that gentlemanly capitalism was constructed following a historically determined path to emphasize that rentier actions did not lead a return to "sound" or "natural" financial practices (as argued by City bankers). Rather, their behavior was a reaction to the social and political change of the period, particularly to protect themselves from LIGs' call for greater political representation, access to credit and property, and greater taxes on the wealthy. A conglomerate of bankers, landowners, and aristocrats aided the concentration of financial services in the City, a process that became particularly intense after 1900 (for which data are selected below) and supported overseas portfolio investment. The consequent early 1900s addiction to rents from investments in foreign debt securities (governments, railways) agitated LIGs and led them to publicly contest the lack of positive state intervention and point out the declining legitimacy of the English financial reform nexus. Thus while English volumetric influence in the international financial order peaked around 1910, the social sources of English international financial capacity were being undermined. The capacity to sustain international capital quantities came back to domestic social qualities.

If we look at the key financial institutions late in the period, we may be immediately overcome with English grayness. Nothing much, it would appear in Figure 3.1, happened. However, the process of bank concentration in the commercial bank category (which should be separated into private and joint-stock categories, but this is not differentiated in the available statistics) is critical to change in the English financial reform nexus. The number of commercial banks in England and Wales decreased from 168 in 1900 to 77 in 1914, while branch numbers increased from 4,315 in 1900 to 6,395 in 1914.[4] Aggressive bank concentration in England led to an increased alienation of LIGs' and provincial financing requirements.[5] If we look at insurance companies we notice some increase in assets. This increase was, in large measure, due to the capacity of insurance companies to directly appeal to LIGs, and to marry financial innovations to established economic social norms on "proper behavior" (like death insurance), as well as emerging economic conventions (like life insurance).

3. Geoffrey Ingham, *Capitalism Divided? The City and Industry in British Social Development* (Basingstoke: Macmillan, 1984).

4. Forrest H. Capie and Alan Weber, *A Monetary History of the United Kingdom, 1870–1982* (London: George Allen and Unwin, 1985), 576–77.

5. Contra Forrest H. Capie and Michael Collins, "Banks, Industry and Finance, 1880–1914," *Business History* 41, 1 (1999).

Figure 3.1 Key English financial institutions' assets as a percentage of total financial assets, 1900–1915.

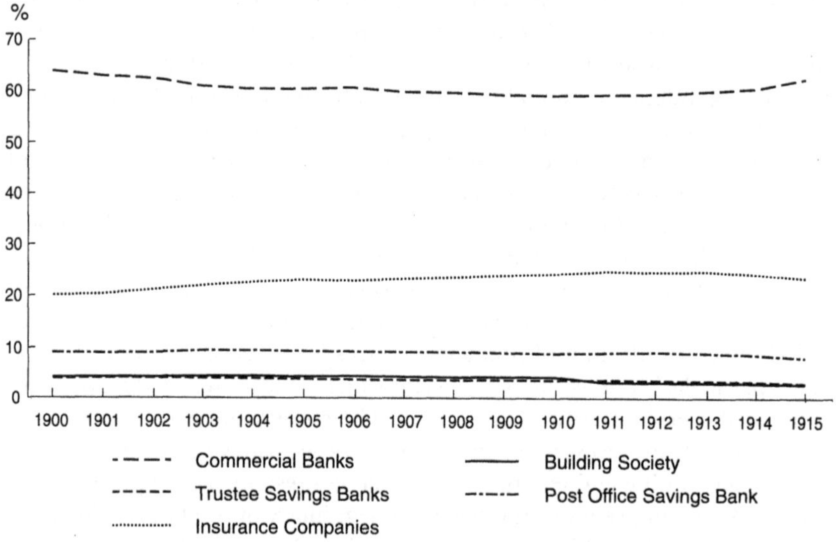

Source: David K. Sheppard, The Growth of UK Financial Institutions, 1880–1962 (London: Methuen, 1971), 184–85, Table (A) 3.4.

Still, insurance companies were not powerful enough, and not supported enough by the state to make up for the failings of post office savings banks and trustee savings banks. The former became closely associated with supplementing government revenue, following legislation passed by the Tories in 1904–05, and LIGs turned away from them.[6] In 1907 the post office savings bank had 15,000 branches compared to 6,000 for joint-stock banks and 400 for trustee savings banks. In 1902 Henry Warren suggested that the "small depositor . . . might remember that the post office savings bank allows 2 1/2 percent; and why he should prefer the banker's miserly 1 1/2 percent is a mystery."[7] However, given confidence problems within the institutions and their incapacity to allocate sufficient amounts of credit, LIGs instead spent more on immediate gratification.

While growth in the financial services sector nearly doubled between 1890 and 1918, credit allocations to LIGs actually diminished.[8] This was be-

6. Peter H. J. H. Gosden, "Savings Banks? The Savings Function and the Development of Savings Institutions from the 19th Century," in Franz Bobasch and Hans Pohl, eds., *Das Kreditwesen in der Neuzeit: Ein deutsch-britischer Vergleich* (Munich: K. G. Saur, 1997), 154.
7. Henry Warren, *A Bee among the Bankers* (London: R. A. Everett and Co, 1902), 35. This bears out from the data provided in David K. Sheppard, *Growth and Role of UK Financial Institutions, 1880–1962* (London: Methuen, 1971), 56.
8. Edgar Jaffé, "Die Konzentration des Bankwesens in England," *Bank-Archiv: Zeitschrift für Bank- und Bank Börsenwesen* 4, 7 (1905): 102–6.

cause as capital became increasingly concentrated, gentlemanly capitalist assessments of creditworthiness prevented LIGs and the provinces from receiving credit. Access to credit became evermore dependent upon social, political, and economic rank than before. Gentleman's clubs flourished to permit potential creditors and debtors the opportunity to meet each other face to face and assess one another's credentials. The English state did nothing to stop this tightening *redistributive* grip on who could access credit and, therefore, who could obtain property (and therefore the vote).

As a consequence groups such as Liverpool's Financial Reform Association produced a clear line on what should become the norm: more credit access for the poor, less indirect taxes, more free trade, and pro-housing reform to deal with overcrowding. All these changes reflected the basic conception that in Edwardian England "the poorer a person is, the greater the burden."[9] As such LIGs railed against the injustices of the investors' "unearned increment," that landlords incomes "rose while they slept," and the use of "the public purse for the purposes of private profit-making" as the state militarily protected rentiers' international investments while they refused to pay fair taxes.[10]

The post-1905 Liberal government, despite its rhetoric against rentier and electoral successes, did not positively intervene in the financial reform nexus on behalf of LIGs. The English state was not able to encourage private financial institutions to lend credit for property, nor was it able to reverse the Bank of England's (BoE) "locks-up" policy on credit generation in the provinces.[11] To quote George Dangerfield's classic summary of the period, the "Liberals had reached a point where they could no longer advance; before them stood a barrier of Capital which they dared not attack."[12] This inaction agitated LIGs, particularly as it was out of step with expectations about how the state and economy should work based on recent experience.

From the Alehouse to the Abacus

The period that many scholars cite as the height of English "hegemony" was also the period in which the English state positively intervened in its finan-

9. Financial Reform Association, *Almanack and Year Book 1905* (Liverpool: Financial Reform Association, 1905), 102.

10. Avner Offer, "Ricardo's Paradox and the Movement of Rents in England, c. 1870–1910," *Economic History Review* 3, 2 (1980): 237–8; also John A. Hobson, *Imperialism: A Study* (London: Archibald Constable, 1902), 60. Lloyd George quoted John Stuart Mill's phrase "The incomes of the landlords are rising while they are sleeping" in his 1909 People's Budget speech.

11. "Locks-up" was Ernest Edye's description of the Home Office's policy change after 1899 that put a halt to credit generation in the principal branches. Edye was the Bank of England's Principal of Branch Banking.

12. George Dangerfield, *The Strange Death of Liberal England* (New York: Capricorn Books, 1935), 8.

cial reform nexus. Between 1840 and 1890 the English state decreased indirect taxes that hurt the poor and increased income taxes on wealthy groups. It encouraged the development of joint-stock banks and the establishment of a post office bank system explicitly designed to attract LIGs' savings and reduce the government's dependence upon the City of London for debt financing. In short, between 1840 and 1890, positive state intervention heightened the legitimation of the English financial reform nexus, and assisted international financial capacity through the nationwide deepening and broadening of credit generation.

Of course, I am not the first to note the importance of positive state intervention in the development of English capitalism. Max Weber recognized that the source of English financial power was positive state intervention: that the expansion of empire required the BoE to introduce a widespread credit system for fiscal purposes.[13] Since its inception in the late seventeenth century the BoE's objective was to legitimate "promises to pay" from small savers as gold was converted to paper notes.[14] The BoE spread throughout Britain to create a credit network and, in turn, from the mid-nineteenth century its branch banking systems assisted capital provision to industries in the provinces.

One important social source of financial power for England during this period was the humble joint-stock bank. By 1810 there were 600 joint-stock banks in England, but they were considered financially unstable. Following a financial crisis in 1825, in which eight "country" banks failed, the English state legalized joint-stock banking with the view that broadening its investor base would create a more durable source of capital. As a consequence joint-stock banks "gained [capital] from all classes without exception," providing an important example of the broader social source of financial power, and heightened legitimacy of the English financial reform nexus, in the 1840–90 period.[15]

While it would be overstepping the mark to argue that the lower-middle classes greatly contributed to English finance (this phenomena was unique to the United States in the 1985–2000 period), the middle classes certainly did so (although their contribution to the English financial system lessened after 1900). Stanley Chapman's description of the Preston Bank's 101 shareholders in 1844, an institution he views as "typical," comprised nearly 70 percent middle class occupations (in order of representation: cotton spinners, retailers, corn merchants, linen merchants) with only 18 percent represented by "Gentlemen, spinsters and a parson" and 10 percent by profes-

13. Max Weber, *Staatssoziologie* (Berlin: Duncker und Humblot, 1956), 26.

14. Geoffrey Ingham, *The Nature of Money* (Cambridge: Polity, 2004), 125–30.

15. Adolf Weber, *Depositenbanken und Spekulationsbanken: Ein Vergleich deutschen und englischen Bankwesens* (Leipzig: Duncker & Humblot, 1902), 36–37. Here Weber quotes Joseph Mendelssohn's account of English provincial finance, which asserts that "in every city in Britain one finds bankers. They take money from and issue securities to any man."

sionals (lawyers and doctors).[16] During the mid-nineteenth century joint-stock banks constituted the largest part of the money supply and source of credit for the English financial system. It was their capital that was then placed through London's banks for investment in government securities, foreign loans and, particularly, credit for international trade. Bill discounting by joint-stock banks rivaled private City banks as well as the BoE's extensive operations during this period.[17]

Another indicator of the broader socially based financial system is access to mortgages. Using Raymond Goldsmith's figures, I estimate that mortgages as a percentage of financial assets in 1850 represented approximately 15 percent, which declined to 8 percent by 1913.[18] Mortgages as a percentage of total financial assets declined from 15.4 percent in 1880 to 7.6 percent in 1915 as rentier activity and dependence on foreign portfolio investment increased. Again, while lower income groups did not have access to mortgage credit (although they increasingly called for it, as discussed below), the role of joint-stock banks in responding to social wants is important. Certainly the middle classes had more access to mortgage credit in the 1840–90 period than after 1890 following the process of financial concentration into the City of London.[19]

Also important during a period of high legitimacy for the English financial system in the nineteenth century was the emergence of a national savings banks system that tapped LIGs' savings, and allowed them to "escape the debauchery of the alehouse" and encourage "saving and spending as complementary virtues."[20] The English state explicitly encouraged LIGs to shift from a dependence on a cash economy to the practice of saving their money in institutions. This legitimation was initiated by the Savings Bank Act of 1817, which established 80 trustee savings banks in its first year. By 1841 the trustee savings bank system had 841,000 depositors with £24.5 million in savings (it had grown 106–fold since 1817), with the 1874 Royal Commission on the role of savings banks referring to them as "self-help to the whole of the industrious classes."[21]

William Gladstone's efforts in 1861 (while Chancellor of the Exchequer) to create a post office savings bank system also intended to provide a means

16. Stanley Chapman, "Characteristics of English Joint-Stock Banking, 1826–1913," in Franz Bobasch and Hans Pohl, eds., *Das Kreditwesen in der Neuzeit: Ein deutsch-britischer Vergleich* (Munich: K. G. Saur, 1997), 57–67, quote at 59.

17. Rondo Cameron, *Banking in the Early Stages of Industrialization: A Study in Comparative Economic History* (New York: Oxford University Press, 1967), 49–51.

18. Raymond Goldsmith, *Comparative National Balance Sheets: A Study of Twenty Countries, 1688–1978* (Chicago: University of Chicago Press, 1985), 232, Table A7.

19. Calculated from Sheppard, *Growth and Role of UK Financial Institutions*, 184–85, Table (A) 3.4.

20. Timothy Alborn, "The Thrift Wars: Savings Banks and Life Assurance in Victorian Britain," paper presented at Session 61 of the Thirteenth Congress of the International Economic History Association at Buenos Aires, 23 July 2002, 1–2.

21. Gosden, "Savings Banks?" 150–51.

of attracting deposits from LIGs. This system would then coincide with state intervention to alter the "portfolio choices of the privately controlled institutions to finance its needs or other desired social objectives, e.g. housing."[22] Its continued growth would, according to Gladstone, address the existing "anti-social and immoral" mortgage policies of private financial institutions and ease the frustrations of LIGs.[23] Savings within the post office savings bank system would also allow the state to keep rentiers at bay and lessen the power of the City.

But this did not happen. The increased talk of state intervention from Gladstone and others spurred on the development of gentlemanly capitalism and a rentier shift. The first step was to move provincial capital to the City. While the ratio of provincial joint-stock bank assets to London joint-stock bank assets was 3.2:1 in 1844, it had grown to 1:1.06 by 1880.[24] This process involved rapid bank mergers, so that while there were approximately 2,000 joint-stock banks in 1844, by 1913 there were only 43 independent institutions. As commented by the German political economist Edgar Jaffé in 1905, this process was prominent only after 1890:

> Is it not amazing that *only in the 90s* was the survival of provincial banks threatened when capital city banks turned the tables and sought to get hold of an advantage through the extension into the Provinces. On the part of the London and Provincial banks this furthered their concentration and drove a wedge between the [merged banks and] others, leading to today's principle, that only big banks that are established both in London and the Provinces are competitive enough to fight their way through with a view of success.[25]

Joint-stock banks turned away from their provincial origins, as City bankers were able to control merged institutions following the incremental post-1890 rentier shift.

The BoE's "Locks-Up" on Its Provincial Branches

English primacy in the international financial order imbued it with characteristics that reflected the domestic legitimation of its financial reform nexus. Minimal state intervention and the "ideological fiction" that precious metals have intrinsic value were two dominant characteristics within the order.[26] The construction of gold as a "natural" asset to permit an interna-

22. Sheppard, *Growth and Role of UK Financial Institutions*, 4.
23. Offer, *Property and Politics*, 141.
24. Calculated from Michael Collins, "Long Term Growth of the English Banking Sector and the Money Stock," *Economic History Review* 36, 3 (1983): 376.
25. Jaffé, "Die Konzentration," 104, my emphasis.
26. Geoffrey Ingham, *The Nature of Money* (Cambridge: Policy, 2004), 80.

tional balance of payments system placed more ad hoc discretion in the hands of the BoE and the gentlemanly capitalist networks between the City, the BoE, and the Treasury.[27] This was especially the case after the Boer War (1899–1902), which permitted the BoE to propagate concern about holding sufficient liquid assets to facilitate ongoing trade in the world economy while impoverishing provincial finance.

One of the City's defenses for the Gold Standard was that it benefited free trade, and that free trade benefited all English peoples since it allowed cheaper access to staple foods and greater choice of goods. However, it did not take long for the City to change its mind on free trade once its maintenance came at a cost to the banker's personal income. In short, the ideological commitment of the City to free trade was not sufficient for it to be an explanation of the BoE's adherence to the Gold Standard as a reason for "crowding out" the English financial system.

During the 1890–1915 period the BoE had eleven branches, nine in the provinces and two in the City of London. The story of how the BoE moved away from the provision of bill discounting through its branches is commonly told as market competition forcing out antiquated quasi-government-supported bill discounting for industry.[28] But there is, of course, a great deal more politicking than tales of market competition convey. Daniel Verdier's recent study, for example, reveals that "governments in Britain . . . would press in vain their central bank to open branches in the countryside. . . . When it did, it would discriminate against them."[29] This latter point proves most interesting, since it implies a fracture between the interests of government and their rejection for other interests by the BoE. But why?

Dieter Ziegler's work comes closest to providing the answer. He suggests that the Boer War brought the BoE out of an "experimental phase" of providing adequate lending through its provincial branches and came to "concern itself exclusively with the success of the emergent services and rentier economy, to create conditions only for that."[30] The main story here is that during and after the Boer War the BoE virtually abandoned its provincial branches on the grounds that liquidity in London had to be maintained, requiring a withdrawal of capital from provincial branches, the same capital used in discounting. As a consequence the provincial branches had to rely on their own devices for liquidity and turned increasingly to the use of short-term investments. This led to further support for private banking concentration and to less availability of credit for local customers in the provinces.

27. John Maynard Keynes, *A Treatise on Money, Vol. 1: The Pure Theory of Money* (London: Macmillan, 1930), 17.

28. Davis and Gallman, *Evolving Financial Markets,* 806.

29. Daniel Verdier, *Moving Money: Banking and Finance in the Industrialized World* (Cambridge: Cambridge University Press, 2002), 109.

30. Dieter Ziegler, *Central Bank, Peripheral Industry: The Bank of England in the Provinces, 1826–1913* (London: Leicester University Press, 1990), 90–91.

While Ziegler's assessment is the most well researched account of these changes, he also asserts that "virtually nothing is known of the provincial branches of the Bank."[31] My archival research reveals a "smoking gun," so to speak. Reports and memos from the Principal of Branch Banking for the BoE in the early 1900s, Ernest Edye, consistently demonstrate that, in his words, the BoE pursued a redistributive policy of "Free Trade" for private banks while maintaining socially "non-progressive Protection" for the BoE branches.[32]

One of the key problems with the view that the English financial system naturally favored private banking to an increasingly antiquated BoE provincial branch banking system is that the provincial branches were very successful economically. Beginning in 1889–1900 the provincial branches showed consistent profits from their discounting activities. The Liverpool, Manchester, Birmingham, and Newcastle branches all made profits during the 1889–1900 period and the Leeds, Bristol, Hull, and Plymouth branches recorded profits going into the 1900s. At the same time, the London offices of the BoE lost earnings during the first half of the 1890s. The provincial banks were too competitive with London BoE branches and were actively competing with private savings banks despite not being allowed to pay interest on deposits.[33]

In February 1899 a Court of Directors meeting called for a halt to long-term lending from provincial branches on the basis that it used capital at a time of domestic financial uncertainty, and that this capital should be placed into the London Stock Exchange (LSE) to assist with demand for credit from investors interested in the booming South African mining industry. As a consequence, business in London increased by £1 million within a year and the provincial branches' lending operations were pegged back.[34] Of course credit support for "new customers in London" and investment in South African mining coincided with a fast approaching Boer War. Three months following the February 1899 decision all provincial branches were asked to stop lending due to low gold stock. Critically, this action demonstrates a policy plan put in place before the escalation of the Boer War, as opposed to conventional explanations about the tightening of domestic branches lending *during* the Boer War.

Perhaps such action could be excused in wartime. However, the use of the Boer War as a reason to impoverish the BoE's provincial branches was spurious, especially once the war had ended. For example, Sir John Clapham's study of the BoE's activities found that "war conditions put no real strain on the Bank."[35] Justifiably, Edye complained to the governor of the BoE (Au-

31. Ibid., 2.
32. E. Edye, "The Branch Question," 20 February 1906, Letter to A. J. Wallace.
33. Letter of May 1903, BoE Archive G/5/39 2486/1.
34. 18 January 1900, Orders of Court, Branch Bank Office, 1898–1911, 6, C7/16 692–2.
35. John H. Clapham, *The Bank of England: A History*, Vols. 1 and 2 (Cambridge: Cambridge University Press, 1944), 375.

gustus Prevost) in 1903 that the discontinuation of bill discounting (advances) had no real basis:

> The result of the policy of reductions in Advances is further evident—the reason being that stagnation in banking is not possible—you must either go with the times and meet the necessary demand of Customers, or keep to conservative methods and lose business. I am not saying that this latter is our case, but it was supposed at the commencement of the [Boer] War that our County Advances were more or less locks-up: my reply was that they were as liquid as any Advance of this magnitude could be.[36]

Edye traced the decline in advances to the provincial branches to be from £7 million to £4.588 million in 1902, and called for the "locks-up" on provincial advances to be released. Edye continued: "It must also be remembered that the Branches have been placed in Commercial and trade centres without Capital and the natural inference is that they should have reasonable means to carry on reasonable business."[37] Edye pointed to the fact that the "locks-up" on advances had no real economic rationale following the end of the Boer War, especially as the branches had consistently returned a profit to the Head Office and had never been as profitable before the "locks-up" (1897–1902 profits were £500,000 more than the total of 1877–97 profits). He commented further that the impoverishment of the provincial branches was leading to a different conception of the role of the BoE in the provinces, away from an interventionist role to a more discreet and inadequate private role:

> The raison d'être of a Bank is to meet the legitimate requirements of its Customers, and if this is not the business of the Bank of England Branches . . . the question resolves itself into "what can the object of Branches be, except as profit earning branch establishments"?[38]

In a 1904 report to the BoE, Edye commented to the governor (now Samuel Hope Morely) that the BoE was moving more and more toward a financial system not based on "banking" but based on "trust funds." He explicitly stated that it had become clear that the BoE's aim was not to generate finance within England but "to protect the Gold Reserve of the country."[39] Edye noted that the more enterprising private London banks were accessing the "accumulated funds of the residential districts," which should be the aim of BoE branch banks, and that private banks that "have confined themselves to London have lagged behind in the race, whilst those that have

36. Letter of May 1903, BoE Archive G/5/39 2486/1.
37. Ibid.
38. Ibid.
39. Principal of Branch Banking Report to the Governor, 1904, BoE Archive G/5/39 2486/1.

sought provincial outlets for their surplus funds are forging ahead."[40] For Edye, the BoE had changed in its aims, and its legitimacy was weakening as a consequence. At the same time it was clear that the Court of Directors was encouraging the concentration of banks and the expansion of London joint-stock banks in the provinces.[41]

It was argued by the BoE that concentration also aided liquidity through the provision of national networks that allowed access to ordinary deposits. But there is no clear relationship between bank mergers and the "productive economy." On the contrary, merger activity had no relationship to economic growth.[42]

Banking concentration allowed London private banks to expand their capital base and increase their prominence and position. The aspect of social position should not be ignored, for the banker in Edwardian England sought to augment his position among the upper classes and the aristocracy (from which the Treasury, the BoE, and the main City banks continued to draw their staff). Those from the upper-middle classes who participated in high finance mimicked aristocratic behavior to ingratiate themselves into the circles of power.[43] Thus, rather than the English financial system encouraging an economic social norm of enterprise, it increasingly propagated rentier elite norms which were increasingly out of step with broader social norms, as best represented in the election of the Liberals in 1906.

The Threat of "Unpractical and Revolutionary Souls"

In the late nineteenth century, one of the key changes was that the English state was no longer clearly determined by elite property-holders due to shifts in electoral reform (the 1884 Reform Act gave the vote to all men who owned property or paid annual rent of more than £10) in response to changing social demands and economic social norms on how the state and economy should work for LIGs.[44] As a consequence the propertied classes felt threatened in every part of the financial reform nexus. LIGs called for increases in taxation of wealthy individuals' personal income, and demanded access to property ownership to alleviate "overcrowding." This contestation required reform of the English financial system away from the perceived interests of gentlemanly capitalism and threatened social standing.

40. Ibid.
41. Governor of the BoE, Charles George Arbuthnot, in the 15 February 1906 Minutes of the Court of Directors, BoE Archive Ce 231 G4/128.
42. Forrest H. Capie and Ghila Rodrik-Bali, "Concentration in British Banking, 1870–1920," *Business History* 24, 3 (1982): 291.
43. Youssef Cassis, "Bankers in English Society in the Late Nineteenth Century," *Economic History Review* 38, 2 (1985).
44. Offer, *Property and Politics*, 152.

By the time of the Boer War, direct taxes had increased to 38 percent of government income from 19 percent in the 1870s and 33 percent in 1900.[45] On the grounds that increased indirect taxation excises would lead to electoral losses, the Chancellor of the Exchequer, Michael Hicks Beach, raised income tax to 1s 3d in the pound in 1903, leading to an outcry from Conservative supporters and a subsequent withdrawal of the policy and lowering of the tax rate in 1904 to 11d in the pound.[46] All the same, by the early 1900s the Conservative Party under Arthur Balfour was threatening its core constituency with increased taxes, leading its members to complain about the "creeping rate" of taxation and unfair burden placed upon them.

The 1903 revocation of the corn tariff placed even stronger emphasis on the need for income taxes on the well-off and led to a split in the Conservative Party, with Joseph Chamberlain, the Colonial Secretary, calling for tariff protectionism to provide tax relief to their key constituency. Chamberlain sought to legitimate tariff protectionism as a broader societal interest, arguing that tariffs on wheat and industrial products would permit the funding of social reform and protect English industry from unfair competition. He posited that should tariff protectionism be rejected, then social reform in the form of old-age pensions would not be possible. While increased income taxes may make up for the absence of tariffs, they would, it was argued, inhibit domestic economic consumption and lead to a stagnation of the economy.[47]

A problem with Chamberlain's selling of tariff protectionism was that the public contested it on the grounds that it would lead to the "dear loaf" and therefore punish LIGs despite gains to any potential "productive" industry (this problem also emerged in Germany, as discussed in the following chapter). *The Times*, among other popular publications, pointed out that Chamberlain's scheme would indeed hurt the pockets of the poor. LIGs had already shown disfavor toward the prospect of a consumption tax on wine, beer, or tobacco, and especially toward higher bread prices. The City, however, threw its weight behind the scheme, and by 1903–04 publications like the *Bankers' Magazine*, which had attributed the death of protectionism to the City's superior guidance, supported tariff protectionism as a sound fiscal strategy.[48]

The City's support for tariff protectionism reflected LIGs' contestations for increased state intervention and redistribution to access credit and prop-

45. John M. Hobson, *The Wealth of States: A Comparative Sociology of International Economic and Political Change* (Cambridge: Cambridge University Press, 1997), 125.
46. Hugh V. Emy, "The Impact of Financial Policy on the English Party Politics Before 1914," *Historical Journal* 15, 1 (1972): 113.
47. Hobson, *Wealth of States*, 129–32.
48. Youssef Cassis, "British Finance: Success and Controversy," in J. J. Van Helten and Youssef Cassis, eds., *Capitalism in a Mature Economy: Financial Institutions, Capital Exports and British Industry, 1870–1939* (Aldershot: Edward Elgar, 1990), 13.

erty, as well as minimize tax burdens. Gentlemanly capitalists wanted none of this. It threatened established social and political positions of the landed aristocracy and the aspirations of newly monied gentlemen. Both groups drew their political, economic, and social authority from their social position. The undermining of its economic base was due to its waning legitimacy as an acceptable economic social norm among LIGs, who then sought to attack rentiers and gentlemanly capitalists through the state. Early-twentieth-century changes in how LIGs viewed the economy and how it should work for them intensified their contestation of perceived rentier privileges through their complaints to the state. However, rather than accepting the normative changes in the broader population, rentiers and gentlemanly capitalists decried potential changes to the English financial reform nexus as the rise of "socialism." Within the Conservative Party the movement to tariff protectionism was presented as a way of providing partial social reforms to keep LIGs happy and "socialism" at bay. Prime Minister Balfour argued that socialism was spreading as an ideology through the working classes and that "what is going on is a faint echo of the same movement which has produced massacres in St. Petersburg, riots in Vienna and Socialist processions in Berlin."[49]

Socialism was spreading in England, but not to the extent imagined by Balfour. Rather, socialism in the English context was associated with a legitimation of political and economic relationships that would allow LIGs to develop "spiritual personality." The aim was therefore not one of economic class solidarity, but one of "social unity and growth toward organic wholeness."[50] All the same, "socialism" required a change to the financial reform nexus instigated by "unpractical and revolutionary souls" for the benefit of a broader societal interest.[51] For example, in the *Socialist Budget*, Philip Snowden argued for the doubling of income tax on the grounds that "the cost of bettering the condition of the people must be met by the taxation of the rich."[52] The idea that *excessive* incomes could be taxed as a social property became increasingly popular in the early 1900s, with scholars like John A. Hobson arguing for a redistribution of wealth on the grounds that LIGs should increase their consumption and thereby access to credit to fuel English economic growth.[53]

The 1906 landslide election win of the Liberal Party over the Conservatives represented a clear withdrawal of consent for the direction of the En-

49. Arthur Balfour in Alan Sykes, *Tariff Reform and British Politics, 1903–1913* (Oxford: Clarendon Press, 1979), 115.

50. M. J. Daunton, "Payment and Participation: Welfare and State-Formation in Britain 1900–1951," *Past & Present* 150 (February 1996): 208.

51. Criticism of Conservative perceptions of property taxation by Charles Trevelyan, the Liberal MP for Elland in Leeds, in 1901. Cited in Offer, *Property and Politics*, 246.

52. Cited in Peter Fraser, *Joseph Chamberlain* (London: Cassell, 1966), 287.

53. See Leonard Seabrooke, "The Economic Taproot of US Imperialism," *International Politics* 41, 3 (2004): 295–99.

glish financial system under Conservative leadership and a call for a legitimation across the financial reform nexus that benefited LIGs. For the City, one of the more frightening outcomes from the election was the idea that financial affairs within the City might be brought before parliamentary scrutiny. In 1906, for example, bankers campaigned to prevent a Royal Commission into the source of financial crises. This fear was not only confined to Conservative bankers. At the head of the campaign was Edward Holden, manager of the Midland Bank and Liberal member for Heywood in Lancashire from 1906 to 1910, who argued that the legislation should be blocked on the basis that "if any Banking measure goes into the House, none of us can tell how it will come out."[54]

Significantly, the changeover of Chancellor of the Exchequer from Herbert Henry Asquith to David Lloyd George marked a turning point in the relationship between the City and the English state. The appointment of Lloyd George brought with it a recognition by the English state that social change had provided the background for formal institutional change on taxation. The City, however, opposed Lloyd George's appointment on the grounds that it would lead to financial recklessness. The *Bankers' Magazine* argued that "Mr Asquith, as Premier, seems to have thrown off with his *rôle* of Chancellor all regard to principles of sound finance."[55] Sound financial principles were used to counter calls for increased death duties and, especially, changes to income tax.

The BoE's antagonistic relationship with Lloyd George also reflected the uneasy relations between a government being called upon to intervene by LIGs, and City-based gentlemanly capitalists who feared losing position. Lloyd George, for example, had little impact on BoE policy, which could hardly be typified as sound. As gentlemanly capitalism accelerated, personal perceptions of creditworthiness intensified and led to an increased emphasis on overseas investment to the detriment of the domestic economy. For example, the years 1906 and 1907 represent the highest domestic returns on industrial equity for the entire 1900–15 period, while actual investment stagnated in relative terms, and the LSE was a source of funds for only 10 percent of domestic industrial development.[56] The City's reaction to the threat of socialism was to further the *construction* of gentlemanly capitalism and steer London's focus away from the domestic economy and toward an international rentier economy. From this view, perceptions of how the English economy should work, and more importantly for whom it should work, thoroughly informed investment decisions regardless of how investors' utility-maximizing preferences may be objectively assessed *ex post facto*. As the

54. Youssef Cassis, *City Bankers, 1890–1914* (Cambridge: Cambridge University Press, 1994), 272.

55. *Bankers' Magazine* 81 (1908): 849, cited in ibid., 287.

56. A. J. Arnold, "Profitability and Capital Accumulation in British Industry During the Transwar Period, 1913–1924," *Economic History Review* 52, 1 (1999): 58, Table 3.

threat of "socialism" drew closer, rentiers discounted the future by investing overseas and ignoring the domestic economy. Such action violated LIGs' expectations on how the economy should work and fueled calls for the state to intervene against rentiers across the English financial reform nexus.

Positional Premiums and Shoddy Dwellings

With land comes position. Accordingly, property politics was crucial in changes to the financial reform nexus. The English upper classes, including all associated with gentlemanly capitalism, sought to defend their social, political, and economic "positional premium" of owning property by denying others access to it. Thus while property was in relative decline as a proportion of national wealth (from 53.3 percent in 1850 to 23.9 percent in 1900 and 18.6 percent in 1913) it was an "explicit expression of wealth . . . traded above its economic value."[57] Throughout the nineteenth century, agrarian property ownership "facilitated the control of tenants in local and parliamentary elections as well as the dominance and deference typical of patron-client relations."[58] The declining economic value of property would ideally have allowed greater ownership. However, gentlemanly capitalists defended their "positional premiums"—in both town and country—by blocking access through assessments on creditworthiness and by, instead, increasing their dependence on rents from LIG tenants. As such, property politics became a focal point for contestation between LIGs, the state, and the propertied classes. The English state's failure to intervene on this most important subject greatly diminished the legitimacy of the financial reform nexus and undermined an important potential social source of financial power.

There was LIG demand for mortgage credit in Edwardian England. Avner Offer asserts that "House-ownership was an aspiration of well-paid workers in regular employment."[59] Demand for mortgages was particularly intense among the poorer of wage earners who were exposed more to predatory, and less legitimate, rental practices than higher earners who had more uniform rents.[60] However, in 1914 only 10.6 percent of households in England were owner-occupied. Nearly all owner-occupied housing was in the north in places like Oldham. In comparison, in the south of England short leaseholds dominated. According to Offer, as "many as seven-eighths or more of

57. Quote from Tom Nicholas, "Businessmen and Land Ownership in the Late Nineteenth Century," *Economic History Review* 52, 1 (1999): 41–43. Figures from Charles H. Feinstein and Sydney Pollard, eds., *Studies in Capital Formation in the United Kingdom, 1750–1920* (Oxford: Clarendon Press, 1988), 469.
58. Reinhard Bendix, *Kings or People: Power and the Mandate to Rule* (Berkeley: University of California Press, 1978), 215.
59. Offer, *Property and Politics*, 119–20.
60. Elizabeth Roberts, "Working-Class Standards of Living in Barrow and Lancaster, 1890–1914," *Economic History Review* 30, 2 (1977): 318.

English households enjoyed no more than a working-class dwelling held at a week's notice" that, in short, was "shoddy and expensive" (a parallel can be found in the Japanese case in Chapter 6).[61] Rent as a proportion of expenditure for working-class people increased from 25 to 30 percent over the 1900–15 period despite downturns in property prices and upturns in wages more generally.[62] Indeed, while England experienced strong growth between 1900 and 1915, the construction of new dwellings declined dramatically (one of the only two periods during the twentieth·century, the other period being 1939–45).[63]

Much of the reluctance for mortgage credit came from the perception that LIGs could not be relied upon to repay their debts, and that land values were "a lottery ticket" taken as "collateral only with the gravest misgivings and placed it among the lowest grades of security."[64] As such banks and other financial institutions only provided 39 percent of the funding for all mortgages in 1900. Private wealthy individuals supplied 82 percent of credit used by individual mortgagors between 1904 and 1914. There was real growth of 100 percent, in a fifteen-year period, of "small fry" landlords who owned more than seven or eight properties, accounting for some 2.5 million properties in 1909.[65] While there was a general decline in mortgages, "small fry" landlords' actual returns on investment in LIGs' housing were excellent. A 1912 study of London found that the average mortgage rate was around 4 percent, but further examination reveals that higher interest rates (what would be referred to as "sub-prime lending" in the contemporary context) were charged to LIGs, at around 8 percent in Stepney in 1906, for example.[66] In addition, to acquire a mortgage LIGs were required to put forward a down payment of two-thirds of the value of the property, effectively disabling most from ever acquiring property (a scenario repeated for Japanese LIGs and in sharp contrast with U.S. LIGs, as discussed in Chapters 5 and 6). In short, "Investors were warned off working-class housing."[67]

The consequence was a lack of mortgage credit for LIGs and an increasing problem of "overcrowding." This led to calls for the state to address the "unearned increment" of the landlord and encourage investment in a housing policy to meet LIGs' economic social norms. The Liberal Party responded by moving against the "positional premium" by proposing a land values tax that would punish landlords and encourage them to use their land in productive ways, as well as opening up a credit market for home pur-

61. Offer, *Property and Politics*, 116, 120.
62. Offer, "Ricardo's Paradox," 239.
63. Alec K. Cairncross, *Home and Foreign Investment, 1870–1913: Studies in Capital Accumulation* (Cambridge: Cambridge University Press, 1953), 157.
64. Quotes from Offer, *Property and Politics*, 114.
65. Ibid., 119.
66. Offer, "Ricardo's Paradox," 244.
67. Offer, *Property and Politics*, 121, 144.

chases. This, in part, came from an incremental acceptance of reform ideas that framed land values as the consequence of a community's work rather than merely the possession of an individual.[68] The Liverpool-based Financial Reform Association, for example, argued in 1908 that the thievery of the "landed interest" should "force the middle and industrious classes to understand how they have been cheated, robbed, and bamboozled upon the subject of taxation."[69]

Housing policy was seen as a key aspect of social reform for Lloyd George and part of the electoral success for the Liberal Party in 1906. Reform to property politics required changes to the taxation system at the national level (increased income tax) plus reform of local taxation in the form of lower rates to encourage property development and access to mortgage credit. As a social reformer, Winston Churchill recognized the crucial need for the English state to legitimate the financial reform nexus with regard to property, taxation, and increased access to credit. His comments from a 1908 speech give a clear idea of how economic social norms were evolving:

> They [the Liberals] must go forward and repeat in the arena of local taxation the same sort of triumphs as were won sixty years ago in the arena of national taxation when the Corn Laws were repealed. . . . *Under the old system people had dear food, under the present system they had dear houses* . . . [what is required is] an equitable partition of corporate and individual increments from day to day and from year to year through the operation of just law regulating the acquisition of wealth.[70]

As recognized by Churchill, bolstering the legitimacy of the English financial reform nexus required the Liberal Party to provide LIGs with greater access to credit and defend their interests against groups guarding their "positional premiums." The problem with this scenario, however, was that while the Liberal Party did provide greater symbolic representation for LIGs, it did not provide greater access to credit to fulfill social wants through intervention and redistribution. In short, the Liberal Party was a *party of thrift* and not a party that extended state intervention for social reform (as is commonly assumed). While called-up government capital under the Conservative government of 1900–05 represented approximately 49 percent of total called-up private capital, under the Liberals it dropped to 26 percent during 1905–09 (they were elected in 1906, but provided a caretaker government in 1905) and 34 percent from 1910 to 1914 (which included war prepara-

---

68. Much of this argument was originated by Henry George and then advocated by others. See Michael Freeden, *The New Liberalism: An Ideology of Social Reform* (Oxford: Clarendon Press, 1978), 140–41.

69. Financial Reform Association, "How the Landlords Threw Their Burden on the People," *Financial Reformer* (1908): 6.

70. *The Times*, 22 April 1908, my emphasis.

tions).[71] Lloyd George as Chancellor was "extremely hesitant and cautious about committing public money to the direct relief of poverty" but at the same time spoke of the "still unconquered territory of social reform."[72] The gap between rhetoric and action weakened the legitimacy of the English financial reform nexus for LIGs as it intensified their frustrations.

The Paucity of the People's Budget

Much has been made of the "People's Budget" in studies of the Edwardian period.[73] Indeed, the budget handed down on 29 April 1909 provided a real shock to rentiers and threatened to transform the English financial reform nexus in favor of social reform for LIGs. On the grounds that "death is the most convenient time to tax rich people," Lloyd George increased death duties by one-third, increased a "super-tax" of 2d in the pound for incomes over £5,000, and a general increase in income tax from 12d to 14d in the pound.[74] Furthermore, the budget provided a tax-free allowance of £10 per annum for working children under sixteen, and "abatements" on taxes were increased for LIGs and decreased for higher income groups. The land clauses of the People's Budget included several duties on land and required an Inland Revenue assessment of all land to enable fair taxation. Also included was an "Increment Value Duty" of 20 percent, which was placed on all land changing ownership other than agricultural land used for agricultural purposes only.

The Times referred to the budget as "social ransom" and argued that "the fundamental *right of ownership* was at stake."[75] Simply put, the budget frightened the City and rentiers with the prospect of them losing political and economic standing. Lord Walter Rothschild, for example, formed a public meeting in June 1909, calling for government to represent the interests of the City and shift to tariff protectionism rather than income taxes for the good of the economy. The immediate response, most explicitly stated by Lord Lansdowne, was that the Rothschild meeting was "really a meeting of the rich men who won't pay for the dreadnoughts they were clamouring for."[76] This provided a particular sore point for rentier interests, and Lloyd George used

71. Calculated from the estimates provided by Lance E. Davis and Robert Huttenback, *Mammon and the Pursuit of Empire: The Political Economy of British Imperialism, 1860–1912* (Cambridge: Cambridge University Press, 1987), 40.

72. John Grigg, *Lloyd George: The People's Champion, 1902–1911* (London: Harper Collins, 1997), 158.

73. The best work in this area is Bruce Murray, *The People's Budget 1909–10: Lloyd George and Liberal Politics* (Oxford: Oxford University Press, 1980).

74. Cited in Niall Ferguson, *The Cash Nexus: Money and Power in the Modern World, 1700–2000* (London: Penguin, 2001), 69; Hobson, *Wealth of States*, 138.

75. *The Times*, 30 April 1909, my emphasis.

76. 25 June 1909, cited in Murray, *People's Budget*, 129.

the 1907 sending of naval forces to Peru to secure investments in the nitrate industry, to attack rentiers on the basis that while they wanted dreadnoughts to defend their investments in far-flung lands, they were unwilling to pay increased direct taxation, and allowed the burden for "their dreadnoughts" to fall on the common man.[77] The City's reaction was to assert that Lloyd George had lost the respect of "all fair-minded businessmen."[78]

Demonstrating their support for gentlemanly capitalism, the House of Lords rejected the 1909 Finance Bill and forced a constitutional crisis which then led to a general election and the passing of the bill into the Finance Act of 1909–10 with the landslide reelection of the Liberals in 1910. However, the main problem with the People's Budget was that the rhetoric of social reform was not met with increased government revenue and expenditure to push forward positive state intervention across the English financial reform nexus.

Within the budget the biggest tax increases were on "unearned income" (starting at a 13 percent increase for those on £500 per annum, rising to 77 percent increase for those on £50,000 per annum), which did reflect LIGs' contestation for action to be taken against rentier interests. However, the People's Budget was not for most of the people. The budget is often considered to have directly benefited the lower-middle classes, as it benefited only those earning less than £2,000 per annum.[79] The problem with this view, however, is that only 30,000 English people earned over £3,000 per annum (0.08 percent of the population), so £2,000 is an extraordinarily generous annual income to attribute to LIGs. In addition, only 1.13 million people in total paid income tax, which obviously lessened the impact of the budget.[80] In fact, there was only a marginal change for those at the bottom of the lower-middle class bracket (a 2 percent decrease for those on £150 per annum), with significant tax relief for those toward the top and the quite wealthy (a 14 percent reduction for those on £200 per annum and 11 or 12 percent for those earning from £500 to £2,000 per annum).

When calculated as a proportion of government expenditure, the People's Budget's revenue enhancement was only 0.2 percent of national income between the 1905–09 and 1910–13 periods, while government expenditure *dropped* 2.5 percent in comparison to the 1900–04 period.[81] The People's

77. Grigg, *Lloyd George,* 203.

78. *Bankers' Magazine* (1909), cited in Cassis, *City Bankers,* 287.

79. Hobson, *Wealth of States,* 138–39, Table 4.7.

80. Theo Balderston, "War Finance and Inflation in Britain and Germany, 1914–18," *Economic History Review* 42, 2 (1989): 236, Table 7. Population figures are for 1911 and from Brian R. Mitchell, *European Historical Statistics 1750–1970* (New York: Columbia University Press, 1975), 24, Table B1.

81. Undoubtedly the end of the Boer War was important in this decline, but realizing calls for positive state intervention would have required large increases in expenditure, as demonstrated in the immediate post–World War I experience. Hobson, *Wealth of States,* 124, 126–27, Tables 4.3–4.5.

Budget was therefore primarily of rhetorical importance rather than demonstrating belief-driven actions that could legitimate the English financial reform nexus for LIGs.

The Liberal Party's minimal state intervention on taxation was repeated on property. In response to calls from LIGs, the Housing and Town Planning Act of 1909 sought to "crack-down" on conservatism within local government to provide easier means for housing planning and encourage more owner-occupied housing.[82] But in reality the Liberal government was reluctant to penalize local governments because it was also a key constituency for the Liberal Party. For example, although the Finance Act of 1909–10 required the payment of estate duties to go to the Chancellor of the Exchequer, in practice they were paid into a Local Taxation Account to avoid ongoing conflict between the Liberal Party and local government.[83] As discussed in the previous section, property construction actually declined throughout this period.

Given the above we should not exaggerate the People's Budget as engendering an early example of twentieth-century social reform because, as argued by Michael Mann, "the Liberal Party was not the ideal instrument to advance reformism."[84] Thus while the Old Age Pensions Act of 1908 (for which English politicians traveled to Germany to learn how to emulate) and the National Health Insurance Act of 1911 were significant in recognizing changing social norms within England (and which were rejected by the City as "socialistic"), the financial system was not changed.

The lack of positive state intervention was also demonstrated in changing behavior in LIGs' participation with financial institutions. As outlined earlier, the post office savings banks system and the trustee savings banks system were allowed to rot on the vine following Conservative challenges to make them tools to supplement government revenue.

State inaction provided more autonomy for private financial institutions, although without the means to permit capital to flow through from LIGs into bigger financial institutions and, eventually, to influence the international financial order. Insurance companies, for example, noticed the trend toward obtaining "ordinary deposits" and changed strategies to create teams of employees who walked door-to-door offering policies (primarily burial insurance) to LIGs. Economically, the small cost of contributing pennies on a weekly basis for a burial policy was attractive to LIGs because it helped ensure a "proper funeral" and avoided the joint moral disgust of a pauper's funeral or engaging a moneylender at usurious rates to bury one's dead. Insurance companies, therefore, were able to attract capital in ways, and for

82. Offer, *Property and Politics*, 325.

83. Henry Higgs, *The Financial System of the United Kingdom* (London: Macmillan, 1914), 97–98.

84. Michael Mann, *The Sources of Social Power, Vol. 2: The Rise of Classes and Nation-States, 1760–1914* (Cambridge: Cambridge University Press, 1993), 619.

a purpose, held to be in step with changing economic social norms of the day. At the same time, government attempts to get into the life insurance business were rejected and eventually post office savings banks stopped offering insurance policies.[85]

Elephant Marriages and the BoE Bull-Headedness

During the Edwardian period the English financial system was changing dramatically as banks became increasingly concentrated within London while the provinces were impoverished of credit. Between 1901 and 1911, for example, London-originated banks decreased their share of the English bank deposit market from 19.3 to 6.9 percent, as did provincial-originated joint-stock banks from 27 to 19.3 percent, while merged London and provincial joint-stock banks increased their share from 55.7 to 71.9 percent. Furthermore, between 1901 and 1911, London banks' branches, as a percentage of total bank branches, decreased from 3.2 to 0.5 percent, as did provincial joint-stock bank branches from 35.2 to 24.1 percent, while merged London and provincial joint-stock banks increased their share of total branches from 47.4 to 73.6 percent.[86]

Ideally this process of bank concentration would permit both a broader and deeper domestic pool of capital, as well as provide incentives for institutions to mutually benefit from one another by linking investment up the chain from the local to the international. But such a scenario only occurs with positive state intervention to legitimate relationships between players in the chain. This did not occur in England and produced, instead, an increasingly top-heavy system of international investment supported by a weakening domestic base contested by LIGs. Commercial banks, for example, were happy to gain access to the deposits of ordinary savers but did not provide access to credit in return. The Liberal government did not address this issue or sufficiently compete for investment from LIGs. In addition, through all of this, the BoE supported banking concentration, although it weakened its own powers within the system.

One important change that undermined the generation of a social source of financial power in England was the assessment of creditworthiness. As concentration proceeded, the number of bank loans made from local bank managers to local industrialists, or for mortgage credit, declined.[87] Once again we can turn to Jaffé's study of the changing social dynamics within English finance:

85. Alborn, "Thrift Wars," 7–9, 13.
86. Philip L. Cottrell, "The Domestic Commercial Banks and the City of London, 1870–1939," in Youssef Cassis, ed., *Finance and Financiers in European History, 1880–1939* (Cambridge: Cambridge University Press, 1991), 46.
87. Sheppard, *Growth and Role of UK Financial Institutions,* 184–85, Table (A) 3.4.

The change [in bank concentration] is of great importance, for the English banking system and its prevailing forms of personal credit is critical to the national economy. . . . [However,] in the last decade the underlying commercial spirit of enterprise has begun to weaken. . . . The revolution being carried out in the character of the bank system is making it increasingly harder for "younger forces" to raise even small amounts of capital . . . a result of concentration in the classification of large enterprises [banks] with firmly ranked administrative hierarchies.[88]

The City's view was that cutting out the role of local branch managers was essential to having a more transparent financial system, even though the success of local knowledge had assisted the successful development of provincial joint-stock banks. The Midland Bank, for example, created a centralized managerial control of bank branches, putting in place supervisors of local bank managers that could view credit provision "dispassionately and from the point of view of business suitability alone."[89] This aim clashed directly with the assessment of creditworthiness within the City, where social positioning among gentlemen permitted "trust and confidence," and credit access became increasingly "heavily dependent upon personal relations between the lender and the borrower."[90]

Provincial banking had no means to resist these changes. Resistance from groups like the English Country Bankers' Association was "meaningless" during the concentration of finance between 1890 and 1915, because negotiations did not take place between organized public groups. Political power was, rather, exercised through "informal means" among the City, the BoE, and the Treasury. Without positive state intervention against them they could not be penetrated by outside pressure groups from the provinces.[91]

During this period the BoE asserted that it should play a minimal role but also still compete with large commercial banks despite having shut down its competitive-profit-making provincial branches in the early 1900s. Unsurprisingly, it soon became dwarfed in size by merging banks. For example, the 1909 "marriage of elephants" merged the London and County bank with the London and Westminster bank to form the London, County, and Westminster bank with £72 million of assets (compared with the Midland with £70 million and Lloyds with £76 million).[92] In comparison the BoE at the time held between £20 million to £37 million. The BoE Head Office re-

88. Jaffé, "Die Konzentration," 105.
89. From the *Bankers' Magazine*, cited in Lucy Newton, "English Banking Concentration and Internationalisation: Contemporary Debate, 1880–1920," in Sara Kinsey and Lucy Newton, eds., *International Banking in an Age of Transition: Globalisation, Automation, Banks, and Their Archives* (Aldershot: Ashgate, 1998), 66, 72.
90. Forrest H. Capie and Michael Collins, "Industrial Lending by English Commercial Banks: Why Did Banks Refuse Loans?" *Business History* 38, 1 (1996): 35.
91. Cassis, *City Bankers*, 276–77.
92. Cottrell, "Domestic Commercial Banks," 49.

sponded by dealing more and more as a profit-making bank discounting bills for the larger commercial banks. Clapham claims that the BoE became obsessed with profit-making from discounts and moved away from its core agenda.[93] To stop BoE branches from doing likewise, in 1911 the BoE Head Office required all provincial customers to register in London whereby the "registry would be used for grading credit."[94] The consequence was a dampening of provincial activity and a further concentration within the City where creditworthiness could be more closely assessed. (A similar use of registers to hinder the growth of financial activity and protect elites would appear in Berlin—see Chapter 4.)

To make matters worse, the BoE also encouraged the same process of concentration for provincial stock exchanges to bolster the position of the LSE. This also involved a tightening of regulations on the role of BoE provincial branches, which were intimately tied to the provincial exchanges. In 1908 the BoE declared, in conjunction with the LSE, that no members of English stock exchanges were to conduct business with non-members.[95] The former informal regulation had been that "in order to retain really valuable connections, we [provincial branch managers] undertook in special cases to lend on the London Stock Exchange the Surplus balance of certain customers."[96] This allowed a "subterfuge for giving interests on deposits" (which was not allowed) and a means to compete with joint-stock banks. The BoE's restrictions prevented the continuation of this practice.[97] The consequence was that BoE's provincial branches and provincial stock exchanges both stagnated.

This series of events was all the more serious because the LSE was a highly inadequate provider of capital to the English domestic market. In the years immediately preceding World War I, the LSE was increasingly used to raise capital for foreign investment while domestic investment waned. Gentlemanly capitalists had not only rejected calls from LIGs for change to the English financial reform nexus, but they encouraged increased international rentier investments while domestic finance stagnated. Accordingly, with the weakening domestic legitimation of the English financial reform nexus, international financial capacity would suffer as a consequence.

---

93. Clapham, *Bank of England*, 1: 226.

94. 25 January 1911, Orders of Court, Branch Bank Office, 1898–1911, 6, C7/16 692–92.

95. 30 January 1908 and 18 June 1908, Orders of Court, Branch Bank Office, 1898–1911, 6, C7/16 692–92. This enforced an earlier recommendation from 26 April 1900, Orders of Court, Branch Bank Office, 1898–1911, 6, C7/16 692–92.

96. Special Report #619B, "Loans to Markets—Sundry Correspondence," 1913, BoE Archive C65/10 3700/615, BBO Reports.

97. Ibid.

The Strange Dearth of Liberal England

While the Liberal Party was reelected in 1910 by a considerable margin, there was growing recognition that it was not going to push through its promised social reforms as LIGs increasingly voted for the Labour Party. For example, while the Liberal reelection was a consequence of an electoral pact with the Labour Party, the latter won forty-two of the fifty-six working-class seats.[98] Put simply, the Liberal Party had failed to provide positive state intervention into the English financial reform nexus for LIGs, a case of rhetoric without redistribution. In May 1914, Lloyd George proposed income tax increases and, most important, a tax on income specifically from foreign earnings. But the "Cave" revolt within the party led Lloyd George to relent.[99] The Liberal Party was unable to push any harder against the City and, as a consequence, LIGs continued to vent their frustration.[100]

Such frustration could be seen in how LIGs acted toward financial institutions, public and private. One of these ways was an increase in immediate consumption of high quality foodstuffs (wages increased 8 percent between 1907 and 1915) because of the lack of choices and confidence in financial institutions.[101] Because of the lack of intervention, LIGs' demand for mortgages remained a source of frustration and increased spending on bacon and eggs was a legitimate alternative. (A similar scenario would occur in the Japanese context of "wardrobe deposits"—see Chapter 6.)

If we look at Figure 3.2 and recall that only 0.08 percent of the English population earned over £3,000 per annum, then we can see the massive concentration of wealth among the super-rich in England. We can also see that the amount of mortgage credit going to those in the lower-middle classes is virtually negligible. Furthermore, once we recognize that mortgage credit was hard to come by, and the fact that house and business property represents such a large proportion of English LIGs' wealth, then we gain a further idea of how LIGs were disabled from accessing credit. Indeed, the level of investment in stocks, funds, and shares for English LIGs provides a remarkable contrast with the United States, where over one-third of mutual fund assets come from households on or below median income (discussed in Chapter 5).

98. David Brooks, *The Age of Upheaval: Edwardian Politics, 1899–1914* (Manchester: Manchester University Press, 1995), 134–37.

99. The "Cave" was an informed group of 30 to 60 pro-business liberal MPs. In June 1914 the "Cave" published a letter in *The Times* that criticized the Liberal Party's leadership of not being "constitutional and businesslike" on the matter of taxation. The "Cave" was led by Richard Holt. See Ian Packer, "The Liberal Cave and the 1914 Budget," *English Historical Review* 111, 442 (1996).

100. George L. Bernstein, *Liberalism and Liberal Politics in Edwardian England* (Boston: Allen and Unwin, 1986), chapter 7.

101. Ian Gazeley, "The Cost of Living for Urban Workers in late Victorian and Edwardian Britain," *Economic History Review* 42, 2 (1989): 214–17; Mitchell, *European Historical Statistics*, 185, Table C4; Roberts, "Working-Class Standards," 313–15.

Figure 3.2 The distribution of privately held assets by wealth class in England by percentage and net capital value of assets, 1913–14.

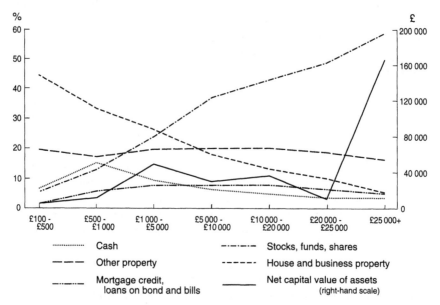

Cash ....

Other property — — —

Mortgage credit, loans on bond and bills —··—··—

Stocks, funds, shares —··—··—

House and business property — — — — —

Net capital value of assets (right-hand scale) ————

Note: Percentages according to income class on left-hand scale, net capital assets in thousands of pounds on the right-hand scale.
Source: Alan M. Hall, *The London Capital Market and Australia, 1870–1914* (Canberra: Australian National University, 1963), 40, Table 7.

Quite simply, English LIGs were not provided with very many alternatives. The post office savings banks and trustee savings banks were the only real vehicles available and neither provided them with any substantial credit. One indicator of the frustrations of English LIGs here was that there was a 16 percent reduction in the number of accounts held with the post office savings banks between 1908 and 1913 (from 11,018,30 down to 9,181,000) despite their competitive terms.[102] Trustee savings banks also dwindled. Despite calls for increased access to mortgage credit and the fact that the purchasing value of urban properties fell by over 14 percent during the 1898–1914 period, credit was not made available.[103]

The Liberal Party's solution to this ongoing problem was to provide income tax concessions to landlords to encourage the construction and maintenance of new rental dwellings.[104] But tax concessions to landlords were

102. In 1910, for example, deposits for the post office savings banks were £168.9 million, of which £21 million was kept in the Metropolitan Water Board, local government bonds and £146 million in national government and guaranteed bonds. Davis and Gallman, *Evolving Financial Markets*, 131–32.
103. Offer, *Property and Politics*, 106, 142.
104. Offer, "Ricardo's Paradox," 243.

criticized by LIGs as yet another form of "unearned increment." As a consequence, LIGs increasingly turned to the Labour Party, which was not yet sufficiently strong enough to counter the English rentier shift.

By 1914, 40 percent of both outstanding long-term debt and equity securities were raised through London.[105] The pace of the rentier shift quickened in the years preceding World War I and with it a paradox became more apparent with its intensification: rentiers relied on foreign portfolio investment that was protected by the British navy, while the capacity to sustain returns on these investments was dependent upon averting war. While rentiers feared their capital being lent to LIGs for property, they had no problem investing it in a foreign government or railway "to *avoid* the risks of *enterprise* and *management*" as long as the state could provide warships should there be a serious risk of default.[106]

Most surprising about the City's reaction to World War I was that "London did not believe in its coming."[107] This contradiction was further exposed when City banks quickly fell into crisis because they had long-term loans to what soon became enemy states. World War I therefore created the first major financial crisis for the City in half a century as non-performing loans quickly piled up. The reliance on foreign portfolio investment made English international financial capacity particularly sensitive because the domestic pool of capital to cope with a financial crisis had been so thoroughly drained and narrowed. Indeed, matters went from bad to worse. When the war began, LIGs demonstrated belief-driven economic actions and created a run on banks, a sure sign of the English financial reform nexus's waning legitimacy.

In August 1914 savings banks in Manchester, Leeds, Hull, and Liverpool all faced the prospect of collapse. The BoE's immediate response was to issue more notes.[108] Still, such action only inflamed the situation. The failure of the National Penny Bank in 1914 led "Angry Depositors" to demonstrate at Westminster on the grounds that the bank had "deceived many depositors into believing that they had national security," but that the state could, in fact, provide no such guarantee. Facing the crowd Lloyd George was required to intervene and promise depositors 5 shillings in the pound as well as the closure of the National Penny Bank.[109]

To finance the war, the government established a London Exchange Committee in 1915 (followed by a Government War Obligations Bill). With

---

105. Ranald Michie, *The London and New York Stock Exchanges, 1850–1914* (London: Allen & Unwin, 1987), 91.
106. Avner Offer, "The British Empire, 1870–1914: A Waste of Money?" *Economic History Review* 46, 2 (1993): 222, emphasis in original; Davis and Gallman, *Evolving Financial Markets*, 121.
107. Clapham, *Bank of England*, 1: 415.
108. Special Report #742: "The Great War—The Branches of the Bank of England 1914/1921," C65/17 3707, BBO Reports.
109. All detailed in ibid. and in "Angry Depositors," *The Times*, 24 August 1914.

much cajoling England's largest banks contributed nearly one-third of their deposits in loans to the government.[110] As a consequence, from 1913 to 1918 the amount of government debt as a percentage of banks' assets rose from seven to 29 percent. The rest had to be raised from foreign investors, primarily American.[111] As a consequence of closed channels of investment from the world conflict, rentier profits from finance capital declined as the war continued.[112] English influence upon what had become an international rentier economy declined accordingly.

Many studies have followed John A. Hobson's questioning of whether international or domestic investment was more profitable. Most conclude that domestic investment actually provided more stable and higher returns given the expense and failure rate of potentially lucrative international investments.[113] It is here that we can contribute to this debate by raising a counterfactual concerning the potential for the development of a broader and deeper domestic social source of financial power that may have placed England in a better position to handle the financial shock of World War I.

By 1914, mortgage credit as a percentage of net national income had declined from 11.5 percent in 1885 to 8 percent in 1913. In the United States, in 1985 mortgage credit represented 66.5 percent of net national income, rising to 76.9 percent of net national income in 1999.[114] The benefits of increased credit access for LIGs, which coincided with very low savings rates, was a consequence of positive state intervention and also led to increased investment in government debt. There is no sufficient argument to assert that this was not technically possible in England during the 1890–1915 period, since mortgage securitization (the repackaging of income flows to a mortgage into a security that provides the asset-support to permit the issue of new

110. See, in particular, Balderston, "War Finance and Inflation," 240.
111. Sheppard, *Growth and Role of UK Financial Institutions*, 32. One interesting development with branch banking once World War I started was that the BoE *branches* could unofficially provide interest on deposits over £50,000 from other banks. Special Report #619C, "Loans to Markets on Account of Customers and Deposits, 1900–1917," BoE Archive C65/10 3700/ 615, BBO Reports. The crisis of war spurred the need for credit generation in the provinces.
112. Arnold, "Profitability and Capital Accumulation," 65.
113. Michael Edelstein, *Overseas Investment in the Age of High Imperialism: The United Kingdom, 1850–1914* (New York: Columbia University Press, 1982); Davis and Huttenback, *Mammon;* William P. Kennedy, *Industrial Structure, Capital Markets and the Origins of British Economic Decline* (Cambridge: Cambridge University Press, 1987).
114. English calculations: Sheppard, *Growth and Role of UK Financial Institutions*, 184–85, Table (A) 3.4; Charles H. Feinstein, "Income and Investment in the United Kingdom, 1856–1914," *Economic Journal* 71, 282 (1961): 184, Table 4. U.S. calculations: Board of Governors of the Federal Reserve, *Flows of Funds of the United States, 1985–1994: Annual Flows and Outstandings* (Washington, D.C.: U.S. Federal Reserve, 2002), 85, L. 217; Board of Governors of the Federal Reserve, *Flows of Funds of the United States, 1995–2001: Annual Flows and Outstandings* (Washington, D.C.: U.S. Federal Reserve, 2002), 85, L. 217; International Monetary Fund, *International Financial Statistics, November 1990* (Washington, D.C.: International Monetary Fund 1990), 554, line 99c; International Monetary Fund, *International Financial Statistics, June 2000* (Washington, D.C.: International Monetary Fund, 2000), 808, line 99e.c.

debt) was experimented with in the United States during the mid-to-late nineteenth century (but failed due to a lack of positive state intervention).

My point here is simply that if the English state had intervened positively to redistribute credit to LIGs it would have been able to raise credit for war expenditure domestically by having a deeper and broader financial system. More generally, as a consequence of having firmer ground from which to sustain international financial capacity, England may have been able to sustain its primacy in the international financial order even through the financial shock of World War I. But to do so would have required, as argued by Hobson, an "intellectual and moral ability to accept and execute a positive progressive policy which involves a new conception of the functions of State."[115]

Conclusion: Moderate Legitimation of the Financial Reform Nexus

The English financial reform nexus reflected everyday economic struggles between rentier interests and propertied classes' defense of their "positional premiums," and LIGs' calls for representation and access to credit to fulfill social wants. The emergence of banking concentration, new political machinations over creditworthiness, and the BoE's "locks-up" policy after 1890 all represented a rentier shift that the Conservative and, especially, Liberal Parties were unable to counter despite increased calls for positive state intervention on credit, property, and tax from the increasingly politically powerful LIGs.

Institutional and social change within the English financial reform nexus was both rapid *and* incremental. Change was not engendered by crises and there was little "Knightian uncertainty" over what ideas should be pushed forward to transform the financial reform nexus.[116] Rather, the experience of financial growth between 1840 and 1890, alongside political changes in enfranchisement for LIGs, provided normative weapons with which to attempt to resist and fight the post-1890 rentier shift. As demonstrated by the failure of the Liberal Party to provide sufficient positive state intervention, actors such as Lloyd George were able to change the institutions within which they worked (developing the "super-tax") but were also constrained by interests who held their own ideas about how the economy should work (such as local landlords and Dangerfield's "barrier of Capital"). The everyday struggle did not resolve in policy coherence, and there was no new clear institutional or social equilibrium within the English financial reform nexus.

As such, neither rentiers nor LIGs behaved in an economically utility-maximizing manner during the period under study. Transaction costs among

---

115. John A. Hobson, *The Crisis of Liberalism: New Issues of Democracy* (London: P. S. King and Son, 1909), xi.

116. Mark Blyth, *Great Transformations: Economic Ideas and Institutional Change in the Twentieth Century* (Cambridge: Cambridge University Press, 2002).

the key institutions of the English financial reform nexus did not lower but increased as political and social barriers were erected by rentiers (through their "positional premium" on land and investments, for example) and by LIGs (through their rejection of state financial institutions who provided the most obvious option).[117] The state's capacity to intervene to lower transaction costs and generate a social source of financial power by linking local financial institutions to the international realm had weakened.

We could argue that the People's Budget reflected a new normative "logic of appropriateness" on tax redistribution. However, while the Liberal Party made significant symbolic changes to the taxation system, the government's *actions* did not live up to electoral *rhetoric*.[118] Appeals to public sentiment meant little without policy implementation. Indeed, in general the notion of a new norm-setting logic of appropriateness for financial relations is both too general and too structural to permit an understanding of the period. It is impossible to isolate a general social norm of appropriateness that was imposed from the top-down from the state onto LIGs. Instead, contestation over the legitimacy of changes to the English financial reform nexus demonstrated that there were a number of competing ideas and new social norms about how the economy should work for the state, for LIGs, and for rentiers.

LIGs' expectations about how the financial reform nexus should work for them evolved with increased political representation and with increased fervor against how rentiers were able to use state intervention for their particular purposes rather than for a broader social purpose. LIGs made claims not so much by appealing to revolution, as rentiers claimed and feared, but by cobbling together their rejection of changes to the financial reform nexus in everyday terms.[119] As Churchill commented, while LIGs had contested state policy on "dear bread" in the late Victorian period, in the Edwardian period they contested state policy to encourage state intervention into credit and property access. LIGs operated with everyday ideas about how the economy worked and should work for them. Economic social norms were at once strong but also liquid, as LIGs held a dynamic relationship with both the state and rentier interests. During World War I in 1915, for example, LIGs' protest about predatory landlord practices led to the imposition of rent controls that encouraged landlords to invest elsewhere. Importantly, this action raised LIGs' standards for the legitimation of the English financial reform nexus to strongly argue for state intervention to increase access to property ownership and the need for direct taxation of the wealthy.[120]

---

117. Douglass C. North, *Institutions, Institutional Change and Economic Performance* (Cambridge: Cambridge University Press, 1990).

118. James G. March and Johan P. Olsen, *Rediscovering Institutions: The Organizational Basis of Politics* (New York: Free Press, 1989).

119. John L. Campbell, *Institutional Change and Globalization* (Princeton: Princeton University Press, 2004).

120. Sven Steinmo, *Taxation and Democracy: Swedish, British, and American Approaches to Financing the Modern State* (New York: Yale University Press, 1993), 156.

But such groundwork was all far too late. The failure of the English state to sufficiently respond to LIGs, and the shutting out of LIGs by key financial institutions (especially the BoE), weakened England's social source of financial power and, eventually, undermined English international financial capacity. This may have provided Germany with an opportunity to wrestle primacy in the international financial order from England. But, as we shall see, Germany was fundamentally unable to challenge England because its financial reform nexus was even less legitimate.

4

The Financial Reform Nexus in Germany

In the late nineteenth and early twentieth centuries, Germany was an active participant in the international financial order, primarily through its Great Banks (*Großbanken*). These financial institutions were heralded as the means through which Germany could assert its primacy in the international financial order as English capacity crumbled from domestic social disaffections.[1] The *Großbanken* were championed as exemplars of how links between the state and private banks could boost domestic financial power. Moreover, state intervention had created local financial institutions that apparently provided efficient financial services to people in German lower-income groupings (LIGs). German state intervention, one may believe, was able to generate a domestic social source of financial power and, therefore, boost Germany's international financial capacity.

State intervention, as discussed earlier, should be disaggregated into positive and negative forms, and we should seek to specify if intervention transforms a financial reform nexus in favor of LIGs or against them. In *Kaiserreich* Germany, state intervention into its financial reform nexus was predominantly negative and its international financial capacity was at all times inferior to the English. Localized rentiers systematically extracted rents from LIGs, including the use of local financial institutions for personal gain, the erecting of barriers to credit access and property ownership, and increased tax burdens through indirect taxation. Such behavior could be seen across the financial reform nexus and reflected Germany's "polycratic but uncoordinated authoritarianism."[2] It was exemplified by the influence of large agrarian landholders' political hold on financial and fiscal institu-

---

1. Jacob Riesser, *The German Great Banks and Their Concentration in Connection with the Economic Development of Germany,* National Monetary Commission, Senate Document No. 593, 61st Congress, Second Session (Washington, D.C.: Government Printing Office, 1911); Otto Jiedels, *Das Verhältnis der deutschen Großbanken zur Industrie* (Leipzig: Duncker & Humblot, 1905).
2. Hans-Ulrich Wehler, *The German Empire, 1871–1918* (Leamington Spa: Berg, 1985), 62.

tions, and by local rentiers' abuse of the largest public savings banks (*Sparkassen*) due to a fiscal battle between the Reich and the federal states (*Länder*). Despite Germany's intention of increasing its international financial capacity to rival England, it was not able to deepen and broaden the domestic pool of capital through positive state intervention. In stark contrast, negative state intervention provided persistent obstacles to the establishment of channels of capital and credit from the local to the international.[3] In Germany the rentier shift intensified after 1900 and altered financial institutions (see selected data below).

If we look at the key financial institutions in Germany for the period after 1900, we may be surprised by the prominence of institutions other than the *Großbanken,* especially the *Hypotheken* (mortgage banks) and *Sparkassen* (Figure 4.1).[4] Regional banks also held a significant amount of assets, but their political treatment compared to other institutions is unproblematic and they do not play much of a part in the story here. The most common argument concerning *Großbanken* is that they formed cartels and "interlocking directorates" that underwrote German industry.[5] Alexander Gerschenkron famously argued that *Großbanken* were invaluable for rapid industrialization as they could coordinate industrial firms' development "from the cradle to the grave."[6] Such a view was indeed pronounced by *Großbanken* leaders, who saw themselves as the most "powerful and capital-rich . . . the first and most resounding [*klangvollsten*] name in the financial world."[7] This view of *Großbanken* dominance also fits with a cultural explanation of path dependence, whereby institutional change conforms to a "German propensity for bigness."[8] As with all explanations we should seek to look for the politics and not depend upon the path.

Großbanken did invest heavily in industry: overwhelmingly in heavy industries like mining and metallurgy to the discrimination of others. There is lit-

3. Daniel Verdier, *Moving Money: Banking and Finance in the Industrialized World* (Cambridge: Cambridge University Press, 2002), 96.

4. The number of *Großbanken* did not change in the period, although they were able to swallow up smaller regional banks. However, this is not to suggest that the number of provincial joint-stock banks decreased, as their numbers rose from 109 to 140 over the period. Deutsche Bundesbank, *Deutsches Geld- und Bankwesen in Zahlen, 1876–1975* (Frankfurt: Fritz Knapp, 1976), Table 1.01. See also Paul Wallich, *Die Konzentration im deutschen Bankwesen—Ein Beitrag zur Geschichte der Gegenwärtigen Wirtschaftsorganisation* (Berlin: J. G. Cotta'sche Buchhandlung Nachfolger, 1905), 163, 170–73.

5. Hugh M. Neuberger and Houston H. Stokes, "German Banks and German Growth, 1883–1913: An Empirical View," *Journal of Economic History* 34, 3 (1974): 713. Rainer Fremdling and Richard Tilly dispute this evidence in "German Banks, German Growth, and Econometric History," *Journal of Economic History* 36, 2 (1976).

6. Alexander Gerschenkron, *Economic Backwardness in Historical Perspective: A Book of Essays* (Cambridge, Mass.: Harvard University Press, 1962), 13–14.

7. As declared at the first General Meeting of German Bankers in 1902. *Tagesblatt der Ersten Allgemein deutschen Bankiertages,* 18 September 1902, 1.

8. Charles P. Kindleberger, *A Financial History of Western Europe* (London: Allen and Unwin, 1984), 128.

Figure 4.1 Key German financial institutions' assets as a percentage of total financial assets, 1900–1915.

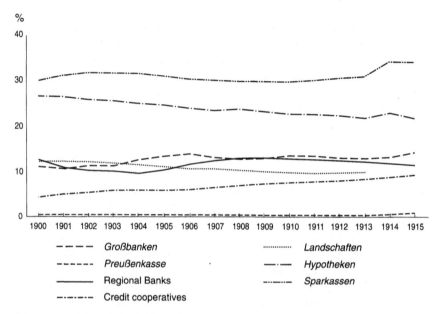

Source: Deutsche Bundesbank, *Deutsches Geld- und Bankwesen in Zahlen, 1876–1975* (Frankfurt: Fritz Knapp, 1976), Tables 1.03–1.08.

tle support for the light industries from commentators of the period, particularly as internally generated funds still represented more than 80 percent of industrial investment.[9] There is also strong evidence to suggest that most German "interlocking directorates" represented not the concentration of financial power, but coordination to provide a short leash to the industrial firms *Großbanken* did support.[10] In short, we should downgrade our view of the role of *Großbanken*. They were not the only, or even the most important, players in town.

The development of the *Sparkassen* provides a key insight into changes within the German financial reform nexus, since it was the *Sparkassen* that had the greatest contact with LIGs. The role of the *Sparkassen* is remarkably unrecognized in English works on the German financial system.[11] *Sparkassen*

9. Werner Baumgarten, "Der Bankkredit der 'leichten' Industrie," Ph.D. diss., Albert-Ludwigs-Universität zu Freiburg im Breisgau, Freiburg, 1914, 27–29, 33. Figures from Wilfried Feldenkirchen, *Die Eisen- und Stahlindustrie des Ruhrgebiets, 1879–104: Wachstum, Finanzierung und Struktur ihre Grossunternehmen* (Wiesbaden: Steiner Verlag, 1982), 287.

10. Caroline Fohlin, "Universal Banking in Pre-World War I Germany: Model or Myth?" *Explorations in Economic History* 36, 4 (1999): 326.

11. Volker Berghahn refers to them as financially "insignificant" while Richard Tilly asserts that "the savings banks seem to have been of minor importance." Volker Berghahn, *Imperial Germany, 1871–1914: Economy, Society, Culture, and Politics* (Oxford: Berghahn Books, 1994),

were first formed at the end of the eighteenth century as an alternative savings institution to moneylenders and pawnshops.[12] The rhetoric behind the formation of *Sparkassen* was to serve "penniless persons," although in reality they played a key fiscal role for the *Länder* and local governments they served.[13] As such they became particularly important for *Länder* sovereignty, as will be clarified below.

As can also be seen in Figure 4.1, one of the largest types of financial institutions was the poorly named private mortgage banks *Hypotheken* (poorly named because the bulk of their business was in exchange trading). The *Hypotheken* were decried as the "Banks of Palaces" and associated with the urban rich financiers and commerce people. During the *Kaiserreich* these institutions came under sustained re-regulation from conservative politicians, who used *Hypotheken* as a diversion away from their unscrupulous use of mortgage credit from their own favored financial institutions.[14] Chief among these favored institutions were the cluster of public land credit institutes (*Öffentlich-rechtliche Bodenkreditinstitute*), of which the lion's share of assets were held by the highly regressive, mainly Prussian, *Landschaften*.[15] With state support nobles and agrarian large landholders used *Landschaften* to gain access to mortgage credit and to minimize their tax burdens, which effectively increased the tax burden for LIGs. Instead of discussing the *Bodenkreditinstitute* in general, in this chapter I concentrate on the extreme case provided by the *Landschaften* (and accordingly identified in Figure 4.1).

By contrast, LIGs had a difficult time getting credit given the limited choices. Their isolation from all the institutions mentioned already (including, increasingly, the *Sparkassen*) led LIGs to Schulze-Delitzsch and Raiffeisen credit cooperatives, which grew rapidly during the *Kaiserreich*.[16] However, despite the accolades often given to German credit cooperatives

---

26; Richard Tilly in Rondo Cameron, *Banking in the Early Stages of Industrialization: A Study in Comparative Economic History* (New York: Oxford, 1967), 165.

12. On the mutual development of pawnshops and *Sparkassen* see Josef Wysocki, "Die Wirtschaftliche Entwicklung von Sparkassen und Leihhäusern," in Hans Pohl and Wilhelm True, eds., *Zeitschrift für Unternehmensgeschichte* (Stuttgart: Franz Steiner, 1987), 168–75.

13. Gabriele Jachmich, "Grundzüge der Entwicklung der deutschen *Sparkassen*," in Franz Bobasch and Hans Pohl, eds., *Das Kreditwesen in der Neuzeit/Banking System in Modern History: Ein deutsch-britischer Vergleich* (Munich: K. G. Saur, 1997), 134–35.

14. J. Budde, "Die Entwicklung der deutschen Hypothekenbanken seit Erlass des Reichs Hypothekenbankgesetzes," *Bank-Archiv: Zeitschrift für Bank- und Bank Börsenwesen* 11, 6 (1911): 82.

15. While the common usage of *Landschaften* in German is "landscapes," as it was in the nineteenth century, this term was also used to denote institutions that provided credit for agrarian large landholders through mortgage bonds placed on the stock exchange or traded freely. As discussed later, they provide an extreme example of access to credit for property in the German context. The institutions within *Öffentlich-rechtliche Bodenkreditinstitute* are the *Landschaften* (in and outside of Prussia), the *Stadtschaften* (their much smaller city equivalents), and the provincial property credit institutes, the *Landeskreditkassen* and *Landesbanken*.

16. Membership of the credit cooperatives grew from 1.26 million participants in 1901 to just under 2.6 million in 1915. The number of cooperatives grew from 12,779 to 19,761. Deutsche Bundesbank, *Deutsches Geld*, 65, Table 1.06.

as precursors of microcredit institutions (most famously the Grameen bank),[17] these institutions reflected feudal-like social norms that sought to "preserve a more conservative and decentralized society" and contributed to the lack of legitimacy within the German financial reform nexus for LIGs.[18]

In general, problems within the financial system reflected problems within the political system, particularly Prussia's effective veto power within the *Bundesrat* and the conservative influence of the Prussian politicians upon the *Reichstag*.[19] Prussia's three-tier voting system (assessed by taxes paid) did not help because 3 percent of the population had one-third of the vote and 10 percent of the population held two-thirds of the vote. Generally, Germany's mixed electoral laws (from three-tier systems to universal male suffrage) gave elites a great deal of power.[20]

The political landscape, however, should not be simply seen as politicians marching Germany along its own "special path" (*Sonderweg*) to assert *Weltpolitik* and suppress the rise of liberalism and socialism. Such a view ossifies social norms and blinds us to LIGs' contestation for greater political representation and access to credit. The German state's rejection of these calls should not dissuade us from acknowledging them. Indeed, Germany's weak international financial capacity was a consequence of state intervention for rentiers and against LIGs that prevented it from developing a social source of financial power. Such incapacity also left Germany more exposed to the drive toward war and, once it arrived, more vulnerable to its financial costs.

Fighting the Anonymous Powers of Financial Speculation

While in England the formation of the BoE provided a national network upon which the joint-stock banks could flourish in the 1840s, the Prussian Bank was founded in 1846 to protect the credit available to the landed elite and dampen the power of the financial bourgeoisie.[21] In the previous chapter I illustrated the City's artificial support for the free movement of capital and goods and use of the "ideological fiction" of the Gold Standard to

17. Abhijit V. Banerjee, Timothy Besley, and Timothy W. Guinnane, "Thy Neighbor's Keeper: The Design of a Credit Cooperative with Theory and a Test," *Quarterly Journal of Economics* 109, 2 (1994).

18. Richard Deeg, "On the Development of Universal Banking in Germany," paper presented at Conference on the Origins of Universal Banking, Fiesole, Italy, 2–4 March 2000, 11.

19. John M. Hobson, *The Wealth of States: A Comparative Sociology of International Economic and Political Change* (Cambridge: Cambridge University Press, 1997), 39–40.

20. James Retallack, "Liberals, Conservatives, and the Modernizing State: The *Kaiserreich* in Regional Perspective," in Geoff Eley, ed., *Society, Culture, and the States in Germany, 1870–1930* (Ann Arbor: University of Michigan Press, 1996), 225.

21. Ulrich Ramm, "Die deutschen Aktienbanken seit der Mitte der 19. Jahrhunderts," in Bobasch and Pohl, eds., *Das Kreditwesen in der Neuzeit*, 70–71.

"crowd out" credit provision within the English domestic financial system. In Germany, agrarian interests agitated in the late nineteenth century against any possible increase in the generation of claims against gold in the domestic economy.[22] This led Prussian agrarian interests to oppose financial speculation.[23] Furthermore, Prussian agrarian interests argued that speculation on grain prices was being generated by cheap grain from the east, which sought to justify Chancellor Otto von Bismarck's raising of agricultural tariffs through his famous 1879 "marriage of iron and rye."[24] As a consequence, bread prices in Berlin doubled and raised widespread discontent among LIGs. In their defense, Prussian and then Reich politicians propagated norms against "finance capital" as a threat to the German standard of living from the "anonymous powers" behind "international capitalism and Judaism."[25]

The subsequent 1890s restrictions on the Berlin stock exchange trading are important for our understanding of the establishment of regulatory restrictions to actively fragment the financial system and prevent the generation of credit between different levels and types of financial institutions. The most important move against "speculation" came from June 1896 legislation that banned futures trading on mining and industrial shares, as well as on grain and wheat, established a "gambling register" of traders, and prevented any company worth less than one million marks from listing, including the added pain of having to wait twelve months before listing for those with sufficient capital.[26]

As a consequence all securities which were not of "considerable public interest" were restricted from trading. The legislation also led to the appointment of a Commisar in each *Länder*, so that once a security had been rejected by one stock exchange it was not allowed onto any other. This process allowed the *Großbanken* to specialize rather than expand their role in providing capital, while smaller financial institutions were unwilling to take the risks and costs of trading by themselves.

Max Weber's assessment was that the 1896 stock exchange law was "intrinsically one of the worst and most unsatisfactory products of agrarian leg-

22. In part because bimetallism was preferred. Verdier, *Moving Money*, 82.
23. "Junkers" were a wealthy agrarian landholding elite. It would be simpler to speak of the Junkers rather than the "Prussian agrarian interests" but this would distort the picture. While politically powerful, the Junkers were economically subordinate to the large agrarian landowners in Prussia who did not self-identify as Junkers. It was a coalition of interests between the Junkers and these landowners that assisted the movement against "speculation."
24. This decision reflected Prussian agrarian interests' desire for tax relief at the *Länder* level (particularly on land tax) by decreasing the Reich's fiscal dependence upon the *Länder*, a relationship discussed in the following section. For details see Hobson, *Wealth of States*, chapter 2.
25. Hans-Jürgen Puhle, *Agrarische Interessenpolitik und preußischer Konservatismus im wilhelmischen Reich (1893–1914)* (Hannover: Verlag für Literatur und Zeitgeschehen, 1966), 234.
26. Henry C. Emery, "Ten Years Regulation of the Stock Exchange in Germany," *Yale Review* 17 (1908): 8.

islative methods," which would lead to a "decline of Germany's economic position and power."[27] The legislation introduced a great deal of legal uncertainty over the status of contracts traded on the stock exchange, increased the number of bankruptcies, and *reduced* the revenue from taxes on stock exchange transactions (from RM20 million in 1895–96, or 2.5 percent of government revenue, to RM13 million in 1902–03 or 1.4 percent of government revenue).[28] There was no economic sense to the changes and all rewards from the changes were political.[29]

The effect of the legislation was to protect agrarian interests, disempower the use of the stock exchange by medium and small enterprises, and increase the role of the *Großbanken* in isolation from broader society. All of this, however, was relatively oblivious to the Prussian agrarian establishment, since their credit interests were served by the agrarian credit banks which effectively funneled state revenues from taxation to the large landowners. These same interests sought to minimize the fiscal power of the Reich and assert the power of *Länder* governments, a process repeated throughout much of Germany during the *Kaiserreich*.

Franckenstein Goes to the Bank

In Germany, the tax burden placed upon LIGs was clearly worse than in England. German LIGs, like their English counterparts, complained about the "dear loaf," but while the corn tariff was eliminated in England, Leo von Caprivi, Bismarck's replacement, raised the corn tariff and fueled widespread discontent and increased support for the Social Democratic Party (*Sozialdemokratische Partei Deutschlands,* SPD) in the 1903 election. The decision to increase indirect taxes through trade tariffs was a consequence of the revenue arrangements between the Reich and *Länder* governments, where the latter sought to insulate themselves from Prussia's dominance within the Reich and its "centralizing ambitions."[30] This deal, the 1879 "Franckenstein Clause," named after its Bavarian author Georg Arbogast von und zu Franckenstein, dramatically altered the German financial reform nexus. The basic content of the clause was that if the Reich's revenue from tariffs and excises (such as tobacco, brandy, sugar, salt) was over RM130 million, then the ex-

27. Cited from Wolfgang J. Mommsen, *Max Weber and German Politics 1890–1920,* trans. Michael S. Steinberg (Chicago: University of Chicago Press, 1984), 75; Max Weber, "Commerce on the Stock and Commodity Exchanges [Die Börsenverkehr]," trans. Steven Lestition, *Theory and Society* 29, 3 (2000): 366–67.
28. Calculated from Emery, "Ten Years Regulation," 17; and Brian R. Mitchell, *European Historical Statistics 1750–1970* (New York: Columbia University Press, 1975), 711, 719.
29. Karl Mommsen, "Zur Börsengesetzreform," *Bank-Archiv: Zeitschrift für Bank- und Bank Börsenwesen* 4, 9 (1905): 129–30.
30. Sheri E. Berman, "Modernization in Historical Perspective: The Case of Imperial Germany," *World Politics* 53, 3 (2001), 437.

cess would go to the *Länder* governments. But if Reich expenditures were higher than its revenue, then the *Länder* were required to provide "matricular contributions" to the Reich. This deal, according to the "Miquel Clause" that accompanied Franckenstein's design, only lasted as "long as federal [direct] taxes have not been introduced."[31] As such it provided an ongoing source of frustration for both LIGs and the Reich by giving local political and economic elites an effective veto over reforms to fiscal and financial institutions.

The distinction between direct and indirect taxes is important here. The *Länder* depended upon direct taxes on property and income (especially in more progressive cities like Frankfurt)[32] while the Reich became increasingly dependent upon indirect taxes (customs and excise).[33] During the 1870s the Reich was dependent for up to 20 percent of its income from the *Länder*. This pattern would require increased taxation at the *Länder* level, which would require the *Länder* governments to go against the interests of local rentiers by raising both income and property taxes. For Germany as a whole, matricular contributions from the *Länder* to the Reich increased from RM15.2 million in 1901 to around RM24 million per annum during 1902–06 and then RM31.6 million in 1907, RM48.5 million in 1909, and RM51.9 million in 1912–13.[34]

As a consequence of the fiscal struggle, LIGs were effectively hit from both sides: by paying higher food prices for Reich revenue, and being denied credit access and property ownership as local rentiers increasingly used public *Sparkassen* for profit-making activities to defend their political, economic, and social position.[35] Like Mary Shelley's famous character, Franckenstein's well-intentioned creature bred animosity and public outcry once local rentiers abused it for their own gain.

Sparkassen activities became increasingly blurred between the private and public sectors, particularly as they were part of a "triangular interdependence between prosperous local sectors, well-entrenched local banks, and politically powerful local governments."[36] Despite the fact that *Sparkassen* were meant to provide a progressive savings institution for LIGs, personal

31. This latter *clausula Miquel* was put in place by Finance Minister Johannes von Miquel. Jürgen von Kruedener, "The Franckenstein Paradox in the Intergovernmental Fiscal Relations of Imperial Germany," in Peter-Christian Witt, ed., *Wealth and Taxation in Central Europe: The History and Sociology of Public Finance* (Leamington Spa: Berg, 1987), 114.

32. Jan Palmolski, *Urban Liberalism in Imperial Germany: Frankfurt am Main, 1866–1914* (Oxford: Oxford University Press, 1999), 299–306.

33. Contra E. R. A. Seligman, "Progressive Taxation in Theory and Practice," *American Economic Association Quarterly* 9, 4 (1908): 53.

34. John M. Hobson, "The Tax-Seeking State: Protectionism, Taxation and State Structures in Germany, Russia, Britain and America, 1870–1914," Ph.D. diss., London School of Economics and Political Science, 1991, 101; von Kruedener, "The Franckenstein Paradox," 123.

35. Nearly all *Sparkassen* paid no taxes.

36. Daniel Verdier, "Financial Capital Mobility and the Origins of Stock Markets," mimeo, European University Institute, Florence, October 1999, 18.

credit was not permitted until 1908 and the legitimacy of their intended institutional purpose was increasingly challenged before World War I.[37] As with the English case, German rentiers sought to capture financial institutions to build up their own position to defend themselves against an emergent "socialism." In Germany, however, the rentier shift was more localized.

Regional differences in the treatment of *Sparkassen* were therefore important. In Bavaria, where financial relations were more dynamic and where access to private property was greater, restrictions were placed on *Sparkassens'* ability to attract securities investment to only those of sufficient creditworthiness. In Prussia, however, *Sparkassen* were allowed to take any securities that would help build a "surplus" to be used for a "public purpose."[38] Following a 1905 Minister of the Interior decree, "surplus" came to mean any interest from 10 percent of reserve funds greater than a savings bank's liabilities. This ruling inevitably drove the *Sparkassen* to increasingly become a profit-oriented institution, leading Robert Schachner to comment in 1906 that "in savings bank affairs the antisocial tendency . . . has become more pronounced."[39]

One consequence of the squabble between the *Länder* and the Reich over the fiscal and financial composition of the German political economy was a mutual attack on the *Hypotheken*. As the *Hypotheken* were seen as "gatherers and administrators of fortunes" in urban areas, an attack upon them represented a movement against the *potential* financial strength of the urban upper classes. A common argument of the time was that the *Hypotheken* were a "capital vacuum" which crowded out investment in Reich debt and caused the low international standing of German public debt, all for the benefit of a tiny urban financial and commercial elite.[40] The *Großbanken* also attacked the *Hypotheken* as a source of speculation within the financial system.[41]

A concerted attack against the *Hypotheken* (including an 1899 law restricting their expansion and a 1909 law imposing a lending ceiling) led to their decline as well as a 44 percent drop in urban land values. Access to mortgages also declined.[42] The same opposition toward mortgages for private property did not apply to agrarian regions.

37. For example, W. Hoffman, "Der Zweck der Sparkassen," *Bank-Archiv: Zeitschrift für Bank- und Bank Börsenwesen* 14, 21 (1915): 366–67.

38. Jachmich, "Grundzüge der Entwicklung," 135.

39. Schachner called for Germany to adopt an English-style Post Office Savings Bank system that would better serve the needs of LIGs than provide for the particularistic interests of the *Sparkassen*. The Reich had attempted to introduce a postal office savings system in 1878, but this was blocked by *Sparkassen* interests. Robert Schachner in National Monetary Commission, *Miscellaneous Articles on German Banking,* Senate Document No. 508, 61st Congress, 2nd Session (Washington, D.C.: Government Printing Office, 1910), 417–18, 426.

40. Karl Kimmich, *Die Ursachen des Niedrigen Kursstandes deutscher Staatsanliehen—Eine Untersuchung über englischen, französischen und deutschen Staatskredit* (Berlin: J. G. Cotta'sche Buchhandlung Nachfolger, 1906), 34–46, 53–55.

41. Centralverband des Deutschenbank—und Bankiergewerbes, *Reichbanks-Direktorium,* n. 5263, DB Archiv 50072, 6 May 1907.

42. Walter Immerwahr, "Der Einfluß der Grundsteuerreformen auf den Hypothearkredit," *Bank-Archiv: Zeitschrift für Bank- und Bank Börsenwesen* 5, 20 (1906): 233–34.

Land Hunger and the *Landschaften*

While many of the cities in the western and southern areas of Germany were hotbeds of both liberalism and socialism during the *Kaiserreich,* the LIGs in agrarian areas of northern Germany, particularly Prussia, lived under legal and social conditions of the mid-eighteenth century in which "the Lord of the Estate owned the police force and patrimonial jurisdiction in which credit relations took place."[43] As such, the Prussian financial reform nexus was particularly important for the rest of the nation given the influence of large agrarian landowners on the *Landtag* (the Prussian upper house) and, by proxy, the *Reichstag* (federal upper house). Within the Prussian order, LIGs' request for access to credit for land was declined, and tax burdens disproportionately fell upon them (including the continued denigration of the Poles). The financial system of the region reflected these power dynamics and hindered the development of a cohesive German financial system. Tax, property, and credit intertwined in Prussia to serve the interests of the landed elite and actively worked against enabling LIGs' access to property despite their "land hunger."

In the early 1900s farmers on small estates complained that they were persecuted. They paid high bread prices, land taxes, and, importantly, a surtax on outstanding mortgage debt. Such fiscal impositions restricted the transfer of property and led to its concentration among the politically favored Junkers and large agrarian landowners. During a period in which rentiers feared the rise of "socialism," changes to taxation made the system more regressive. For example, in 1904 the Prussian *Landtag* passed legislation which permitted the deduction of local government taxes from amounts payable in Prussian state taxes. This clearly benefited large Prussian agrarian landowners because while in theory they paid local government taxes, in reality they paid very little, if any, tax: some 0.94 percent of their annual income in Prussia in general and even less in "deep" Prussia.[44] In addition, Prussian agrarian landowners were allowed to deduct approximately half the amount they should pay when assessed at the *Länder* level. Worse still, because the three-tier electoral system was divided based on taxes paid, Prussian agrarian landowners' votes were weighted on the taxes they should have paid rather than the taxes they did.[45] The inequities of this system worsen once we account for the role of the *Landschaften* in supporting Prussian large agrarian landowners.[46]

43. Sven Möller, "Entwicklung der Kreditwesens im ehemaligen Herzogtum Schleswig unter besonderer Berücksichtigung des Agrarkredits seit dem ausgehenden Mittelalter bis ins 20. Jahrhundert (1931)," Ph.D. diss., Universität Hamburg, 2001, 42.
44. The numbers are 0.71 percent in Königsberg, 0.58 percent in Danzig, and 0.55 percent in Gumbinnen. See Mark Hallerberg, "The Political Economy of Taxation in Prussia, 1871–1914," *Jahrbuch für Wirtschaftsgeschichte* 2 (2002).
45. Ibid. Contra R. C. Brooks, "The New Unearned Increment Taxes in Germany," *Yale Review* 8 (1907): 237.
46. A key, albeit rare, text here is Morduch Tcherkinsky, *The Landschaften and Their Mortgage Credit Operations in Germany, 1770–1920* (Rome: Institut International d'Agriculture, 1922).

In addition to tax manipulation, large Prussian agrarian landowners manipulated the value of real estate to gain easy credit from *Landschaften,* in turn making the financial institutions "state institutes for money-hungry nobility to organize debts, both actual and potential."[47] Max Weber commented that *Landschaften's* function was to increase mortgage credit to large landholders and to enhance the creditworthiness of land by grossly overvaluing it.[48] One of the key privileges of the *Landschaften* was to "levy executions on mortgaged real estate without legal process."[49] Thus when land was sold it was, on average, 1.5 times higher than the assessed price used in acquiring a mortgage, and well out of the reach of all but the elite. And as *Landschaften* assessed creditworthiness according to taxes paid on the land, Prussian large agrarian landowners successfully grossly overvalued their properties based on land tax they did not pay. Moreover, *Landschaften's* cheap mortgages were funded from taxes that larger agrarian landholders did not pay but did claim! In Weber's view the use of *Landschaften* for such purposes had intensified and sought to entrench a "repressive political position" that could keep both liberalism and socialism at bay among the general population.[50]

I calculate that mortgages provided by the *Bodenkreditinstitute* within Germany as a whole represented 40.2 percent of total mortgages in 1900, reducing slightly to 34.5 percent of total mortgages in 1913.[51] As *Landschaften* represented 60 percent of all *Bodenkreditinstitute* in 1900 and 48 percent in 1913, the unfair practices used by *Landschaften* to support large agrarian landholders had a significant impact on the general provision of credit for property.[52] It is not difficult to then view this behavior as a key element in the weakening legitimacy of the German financial reform nexus for LIGs.

Prussian large agrarian landowners defended their access to state-sponsored mortgage credit on economic and security grounds. The Reich also propagated this idea. They argued that any increase in property taxes, particularly the concept of a Reich tax not administered by local particularistic interests, would place the *Landschaften* in serious financial difficulties in the event of war, depress land prices, and place external forces in control of Ger-

My thanks to Oliver Grant for alerting me to it. A comparison of Landschaften in Westfalen can be found in Maria Blömer, "Probleme des institutionalisierten Agrarkredits in Westfalen im Zuge der Agrarreformen des 19. Jahrhunderts," *Westfälischen Forschungen* 40 (1990): 416–35. My thanks to Carmen Huckel for this one.

47. Max Weber, "Die Kredit- und Agrarpolitik der preussischen Landschaften," *Bank-Archiv: Zeitschrift für Bank- und Bank Börsenwesen* 8, 6 (1908): 87. I believe this piece is something of a find considering that it does not appear in Richard Swedberg's extensive bibliographic survey "Max Weber's Economic Sociology: A Bibliography," Work-Organization-Economy Working Paper No. 61 (Stockholm: Department of Sociology, Stockholm University, 1998).

48. Weber, "Kredit- und Agrarpolitik," 88.

49. Andreas Hermes in National Monetary Commission, *Miscellaneous Articles,* 293–301.

50. Weber, "Kredit- und Agrarpolitik," 87.

51. Calculated from Deutsche Bundesbank, *Deutsches Geld,* Tables 1.01–1.04.

52. Ibid., Table 1.03.

man lands.[53] Indeed, such scaremongering about the potential greater Polish influence in Prussia intensified throughout the period and gained active political support, including Reich Chancellor Bernhard von Bülow's 1908 laws permitting the expropriation of *large* Polish landholdings and the ban placed on the use of Polish language within public assemblies.[54] Prussian large agrarian landowners argued that *Landschaften* should assist the "inner colonization" of lands in Prussia by pushing out Poles and moving German "settlers" (actually tenants) onto large estates in the area to cope with the supposed Polish menace.[55]

Weber argued that the rationale for "inner colonization" was weak and that the struggle really reflected a clash of political and economic groups, the nobles and large agrarian landowners versus the small farming communities (*Bauerntum*), as well as small merchants. The way to deal with the injustice of the large Prussian landholders was to introduce a national property tax, which would lead to a collapse in land prices and be "naturally politically very agreeable for the interests of people of small means, the 'widows and orphans.' "[56] But a comprehensive property tax did not occur and land prices did remain artificially high. This spread social discontent, as gaining access to property was an aim of LIGs. Carl Heiligenstadt, president of the Prussian Cooperative Central Bank (simply known as the *Preußenkasse*), argued:

> If you consider what is it that the small customer most often thinks of in connection with the money that he saves, you will find that he is very frequently saving in order that he may some day be able to purchase a little piece of ground. The land hunger of the little people is proverbial; in my opinion it is entirely logical for the savings bank to turn to that kind of investment which the little people would themselves choose if they had command of sufficiently large sums of money.[57]

But, as discussed, LIGs had difficulty obtaining credit from any financial institution. Of course this draws a parallel with the English case. However, the crucial difference here is that due to the tax and voting systems, LIGs actively paid for *Landschaften* to sponsor large agrarian landholders—a clear case of rent extraction for rentiers (a similar scenario recurs in the Japanese case, as discussed in Chapter 6). This generated frustration within Germany

53. Weber, "Kredit- und Agrarpolitik," 89.
54. Weber rejected these laws as "morally and politically impossible and nonsensical." See Max Weber, *Gesammelte Politische Schriften* (Tübingen: J. C. B. Mohr [Paul Siebeck], 1988), 123; Max Weber, *Briefe 1906–1908* (Tübingen: J. C. B. Mohr [Paul Siebeck], 1990), 548.
55. Möller, "Entwicklung der Kreditwesens," 34.
56. Weber, "Kredit- und Agrarpolitik," 90.
57. Cited from National Monetary Commission, *German Banking Inquiry of 1908–9: Point VI*, Senate Document No. 407.2, 61st Congress, 2nd Session (Washington, D.C.: Government Printing Office, 1910), 169.

because, despite some of the "socialist" rhetoric accompanying social reform, LIGs sought private property. Even the SPD, which in some areas called for the abolition of private property, recognized this and had electoral success in the universal male suffrage system in Bavaria by offering mortgage protection to peasants. In 1903, the anti-Semitic Christian Social Party, also in Bavaria, was voted in on the basis of limiting mortgage generation from *Landschaften*.[58] The legitimacy of the financial reform nexus was very much a concern for LIGs and they intensified their calls for change to an entrenched and obstinate German state.

Peasant Nosiness and Parish Boundaries

Due to the relative absence of private property that could be used as collateral to secure a loan, LIGs' access to credit within the German financial reform nexus became dependent on direct power relationships. The most important element was the existence of a "co-signing" system. This system represented the continuation of feudal-like social relations in Germany as it allowed local political and economic elites to control LIGs' access to credit. As explained by Timothy Guinnane, banks' loans had to be agreed upon the co-signing of a contract. This meant that a non-wealthy person could acquire a loan as long as the co-signer was a person of means:

> Banks' reliance on wealthy co-signers meant that to obtain credit the borrower would have to approach someone of his social and economic superior. Accounts mention that co-signers extracted some surplus from the relationship, insisting that borrowers make up their lost time with free labor and sometimes using the threat of non-renewal notes to gain other advantages.[59]

Co-signing existed at the cooperative level and for savings banks. As with other aspects of the German financial system, the southern regions had a stronger use of private property, and in Bavaria and Baden 40 percent of loans were secured by such collateral. The overall figure for Germany was 23 percent, suggesting a system in which community self-monitoring and playing up to patrimonial ties were important.[60] Despite the generally rosy assessment normally given to credit cooperatives, they reflected the German state's incapacity to transform the financial reform nexus in favor of LIGs because the state did not intervene to provide institutions who could re-

---

58. Michael Mann, *The Sources of Social Power, Vol. 2: The Rise of Classes and Nation-States, 1760–1914* (Cambridge: Cambridge University Press, 1993), 707–9.
59. Timothy W. Guinnane, "Cooperatives as Information Machines: The Lending Practices of German Agricultural Credit Cooperatives, 1883–1914," Economic Growth Center Discussion Paper 699 (New Haven: Economic Growth Center, Yale University, 1993), 16.
60. Ibid., 29, Table 5.

distribute credit, property, and taxation to mitigate economic information asymmetries.

This problem was evident in how credit cooperatives were regulated to be intensely localized. Credit cooperatives retained their tax-free status only as long as they lent exclusively to local customers within the boundaries of the local parish (*Kirchspiel*). This severely limited their credit-generating powers since—at least with the Raiffeisen type of credit cooperative—80 percent of cooperatives in 1913 had less than 3,000 members.[61] "Peasant nosiness" therefore became the primary means of assessing creditworthiness within the parish boundary, a situation made worse by the fact that because cooperatives had unlimited liability the responsibility of all members was to ensure that no other member would default.[62] This regulatory scenario also permitted local elites to dominate credit allocation, a complaint that was especially prominent in Prussia.[63] One indicator of such abuses was that while there were no other alternative institutions, in Sachsen the percentage of small farmers as members declined from 50 to 30 percent between 1900 and 1915.

One inadequate institutional solution to overcome a reliance on "peasant nosiness" was the foundation of "Centrals." In 1899 the Cooperative Law placed Prussian cooperatives under the supervision of the *Preußenkasse*, which was capitalized by the Prussian government. The *Preußenkasse*, however, soon reflected the inequities present in the *Landschaften* system.[64] Once more, LIGs were left without a state to intervene on their behalf to redistribute access to credit and property, or to provide tax relief. The legitimacy of the German financial reform nexus was therefore weak and becoming worse due to intensifying squabbles between the Reich and the *Länder*. Indeed, by 1907 it appeared that these squabbles had grown worse and were leading to a potential constitutional crisis.

Electoral Politics and *Länder* Obstinacy in the Reich's Fiscal Reform

By the early 1900s the inequities present in the German financial reform nexus were frustrating the population and leading them to turn to more "socialist" policies that might represent their interests, provide them with real political representation, and empower their access to credit. Accordingly, in 1905 there were open demonstrations for electoral reform in Dresden,

61. Ibid., 8.
62. Michael Prinz, "German Rural Credit Cooperatives, Friedrich-Wilhelm Raiffeisen and the Organisation of Trust, 1860–1914," paper delivered to the Thirteenth International Economic History Association Conference, Buenos Aires, July 2002, 12.
63. Willi Wygodzinski, *Das Genossenschaftswesen in Deutschland* (Berlin: Teubner, 1911), 60.
64. Arnd Kuge, "Andere Kreditinstitute," in Hans Pohl, ed., *Das Bankwesen in Deutschland und Spanien, 1860–1960* (Frankfurt: Fritz Knapp Verlag, 1997), 153. Over the last century the *Preußenkasse* has transformed into the *Deutsche Genossenschaftsbank*, more commonly known as DG.

Leipzig, Chemnitz, and Plauen. Bülow's reaction to the demonstrations in Saxony was to inform the local minister that the Kaiser supported the use of troops to shoot down the protestors.[65]

The presence of a three-tier voting system in some regions meant that for much of the German population approximately 13 percent of their peers held the top two tiers of the votes. As a consequence there were some extreme cases in which the tax brackets for the first-tier system were so unjust that in the cities of Essen and Elbing one person held 33 percent of the vote. The system actively discriminated against LIGs, as even Conservative interests began to recognize the potential for crisis as contestation from LIGs increased. In Saxony, for example, Conservative leaders called for electoral reform on the grounds that 80 percent of voters were effectively unrepresented and beginning to align themselves with "socialist" elements. A 1909 reform of the electoral system led to a widening of the tax brackets in order to bring in the middle classes, but still by 1913, 20 percent of voters elected two-thirds of the delegates.[66]

One of the problems with reforming electoral and fiscal systems was that they relied on the Franckenstein clause's prevention of direct taxation without the collapse of matricular contributions. From 1907 there were public calls for an end to the matricular contribution system and introduction of federal direct taxes on income and property that could provide relief to LIGs by dropping tariffs on staple food items. In 1909 Gustav Cohn asked: "How is it possible that a Reichstag based on a universal suffrage displays a spreading resistance against a tax-bill [on personal income and property] that affects merely a minority of the Reich's people [the upper classes]?"[67] The Reich failed to push through reform due to the obstructions put in place by the *Länder* governments (particularly the Prussian *Landtag* which did represent the Prussian large agrarian landholders). Indeed, both the Kaiser and Bülow favored the implementation of direct taxes in the face of growing public contestation. But, crucially, this required the cooperation of the *Länder* to cede some of their autonomy.

As a political compromise Bülow dropped the property tax and pushed for an inheritance tax that would raise only a modest amount (RM310 million). Still, the reaction from rentiers was fierce. In Prussia the proposal was attacked as a "national act for the middle classes" and rejected by Conservatives on the grounds that "with a democratically elected Reichstag . . . the move would be a slippery slope threatening all private property."[68] Fur-

---

65. Retallack, "Liberals, Conservatives," 242–44.

66. Ibid., 235, 255.

67. Gustav Cohn, "Die Stand der Reichsfinanzreform," *Bank-Archiv: Zeitschrift für Bank- und Bank Börsenwesen* 8, 17 (1909): 265.

68. Income tax was rejected unanimously by the "propertied class indebted to the Reich." Johann Plenge, "Zur Diagnose der Reichsfinanzreform," *Zeitschrift für die gesamte Staatswissenschaft* 65, 2 (1909): 294.

thermore, it was warned that, should it be implemented, "the private land-owners . . . [would be forced to] brazenly prepare themselves with the right tools to fight against a communal agrarian economy."[69] Without *Länder* support Bülow could not push through the reform, and he soon resigned as chancellor and was replaced by Theobald von Bethmann-Hollweg.

The failure of Bülow's financial reform was greeted by the bankers and industrialists with anger. However, this anger was not directed at the Prussian establishment, but against LIGs. Significantly, the business community, including bankers, rallied *against* progressive electoral or fiscal reform (dismissing the idea that the urban bourgeoisie was inherently progressive). The 1911 formation of industrialists, merchants, and bankers under a *Hansabund* argued that they wished to "cease being the stepchildren of German law-making" and saw that the way to do so was to align themselves with conservative interests against LIGs' calls for reform.[70] Thus the failure of Bülow's reforms resulted not only in assuring the weak legitimacy of the German financial reform nexus among LIGs—which continued to be unrepresented and overtaxed—but encouraged a movement against them.

Effortless Profits from Peoples' Pockets

In the previous chapter I detailed how the BoE supported the process of banking and stock exchange concentration, which subsequently led to the impoverishment of the provinces and the suspect introduction of new means to assess creditworthiness. These processes weakened the legitimacy of the English financial system. Banking concentration also occurred in Germany, and in 1908 the restrictions put in place on stock exchanges in 1896 were removed. The effects of bank concentration in Germany were different from England because the *Großbanken* were already far removed from LIGs. Indeed, the significance of banking concentration for LIGs was the flow-on effects to *Sparkassen*.

Attempts at stock exchange reform were made by Liberals in 1901, 1904, and 1906, all of which failed due to a lack of support from Conservatives and from the Center Party. However, in 1907, and despite a renewed attack from large Prussian agrarian landowners on the stock exchange for encouraging "effortless profits," the Reich conceded that the "prohibition of trading for the account in mining and industrial shares has proved injurious to the public, without accompanying its original purpose."[71] Other than

69. Otto Wöhler, "Das Interesse des Bankgewerbes an der privaten Bodenwirtschaft," *Bank-Archiv: Zeitschrift für Bank- und Bank Börsenwesen* 9, 15 (1910): 239.
70. See W. Daniel Garst, "From Factor Endowments to Class Struggle: Pre-World War I Germany and Rogowski's Theory of Trade and Political Cleavages," *Comparative Political Studies* 31, 1 (1998): 28.
71. Cited in Emery, "Ten Years Regulation," 18–20.

simple policy failure, there were also other reasons for reforming the exchange. For example, Paul Damme suggests that a trade-off from stock exchange reform was that *Großbanken* would be prepared to purchase some of the bad mortgage debts plaguing large agrarian landowners by this stage.[72] A 1909 reform of the German Bank Act to permit the sale of bonds of "quasipublic agricultural credit institutions" to the *Reichsbank* followed up on this problem (and provides an interesting comparison with the Japanese state's bailout of *jūsen* housing loan companies in the mid-1990s discussed in Chapter 6).[73] The reform to the stock exchange was also informed by foreign perceptions of Germany's weak stock exchanges as a sign of default risk, making the "economic reconstruction of the German stock exchanges . . . of national significance."[74]

Beyond stock exchange reform, the most important aspect of banking concentration among the *Großbanken* is that it was not really that important. In Germany, concentration meant swallowing smaller regional banks, not each other.[75] Nor did *Großbanken* create large regional networks, despite their mergers with regional banks, as by 1911 the six biggest *Großbanken* had no more than 98 branches throughout Germany.[76]

In contrast, between 1900 and 1915 the number of *Sparkassen* in the Reich expanded from 2,685 to 3,137 (55 percent of which were in Prussia).[77] Their reform in the post-1908 period demonstrates the extent of negative state intervention in Germany. In the English case the BoE drew money out of its provincial branches in order to concentrate financial power in London and thereby impoverish the provinces. It also actively downgraded its own assets while those of commercial banks grew. In the German case the power of the *Sparkassen* led local governments and the *Länder* to use their financial resources to begin competing with commercial banks and further neglect their depositors, many of whom were small-saving LIGs. Thus while in the English case savings banks stagnated, they still provided some—if inadequate—resources to LIGs. In the German case the only vehicle for most Germans became a quasi-private enterprise that had never substantively addressed their social wants and increasingly ignored them.

72. Paul Damme, "Die Landwirtschaft und ihr Interesse an der Reform der Effeketenbörse," *Bank-Archiv: Zeitschrift für Bank- und Bank Börsenwesen* 6, 5 (1906): 51.

73. R. Koch, *German Imperial Banking Laws,* National Monetary Commission, Senate Document No. 574, 61st Congress, 2nd Session (Washington, D.C.: Government Printing Office, 1910), 131.

74. As argued by Max Warburg in Deutsche Bank, *Verhandlungen des III. Allgemeinen deutschen Bankiertages zu Hamburg am 5. und 6. September 1907* (Berlin: Verlag von. J. Guttentag, 1907), 33–34.

75. The largest of the *Großbanken* were the "Four D's": Deutsche Bank, Diskonto Gesellschaft, Dresdner Bank, and Darmstädter Bank. See Deutsche Bundesbank, *Deutsches Geld,* 56–58, Table 1.01.

76. Adolf Weber, *Depositenbanken und Spekulationsbanken: Ein Vergleich deutschen und englischen Bankwesens* (Leipzig: Duncker & Humblot, 1902), 67.

77. Deutsche Bundesbank, *Deutsches Geld,* 63–64, Table 1.04.

In a 1908 inquiry into the financial system it was debated whether *Sparkassen* should be considered public or quasi-public or whether they should become private institutions. Certainly the legislation following the inquiry encouraged *Sparkassen* to act for private profit under the guise of tax-free public institutions. To fulfill this aim the key reform in 1908 was the passage of a Reich law allowing *Sparkassen* to accept checks as deposits. This law coincided with the end of the "atomization" of *Sparkassen,* whereby each institution could place 10 percent of total assets into trading for profit.[78] The legislation was a consequence of the *Länder* governments' lobbying the *Reichstag* for fiscal relief considering the increasing difference between the Reich's revenues to the *Länder* and their matricular contributions to the Reich.

As a consequence of this change, the *Sparkassen* "by no means performed the function of an almshouse for those proletarians who are in need of such an institution."[79] *Großbanken* began to place large temporary deposits in the *Sparkassen* to take advantage of the higher rates of interest. The basic relationship entailed the *Großbanken* depositing funds in the *Sparkassen,* which, after 1908, invested the extra deposits commercially to increase revenue. The *Sparkassen* then demonstrated "a mistrust of state credit, and a misuse of the savings institutions" by increasing the costs of capital to their *captive* market, small and medium enterprises, while still drawing from, but not providing credit to, their smaller savers.[80] This active redistribution against LIGs was profitable for *Sparkassen,* whose profits increased more than threefold between 1908 and 1909.[81]

Sparkassen had become commercial enterprises run by local rentiers who now wished to use the tax-free status of the *Sparkassen* to compete with the *Großbanken.*[82] The transformation of the *Sparkassen* represented a significant rentier shift. Schachner's 1910 study of the 1908 reforms to *Sparkassen* argued that "all of the [*Sparkassen*'s] social and political characteristics were embattled." Thus while Schachner estimated that 50 percent of *Sparkassens'* savers were from working classes, *Sparkassen* had an "absolute ignorance of the budgets of the small people" by continuing to deny them credit.[83] In response, LIGs turned to the moneylenders and pawnbrokers that *Sparkassen*

78. Fritz Wilhelmi, "Sparkassen, Stadt- und Kreisbanken," *Bank-Archiv: Zeitschrift für Bank- und Bank Börsenwesen* 20, 11 (1921): 235; Jürgen Mura, "Die Sparkassen," in Pohl, ed., *Das Bankwesen in Deutschland und Spanien,* 136.
79. Robert Schachner, "Die grossen Einlagen bei den Sparkassen," *Bank-Archiv: Zeitschrift für Bank- und Bank Börsenwesen* 11, 1 (1911): 7–9.
80. Ibid.
81. Deutsche Bundesbank, *Deutsches Geld,* 63, Table 1.04.
82. W. Kühne, "Wollen die Sparkassen Banken werden?—Der Giroverband der Sparkassen und das Postcheckkonto," *Bank-Archiv: Zeitschrift für Bank- und Bank Börsenwesen* 11, 21 (1912): 341; Robert Schachner, "Scheck- und Kontokorrentverkehr bei den öffentlichen *Sparkassen,*" *Bank-Archiv: Zeitschrift für Bank- und Bank Börsenwesen* 9, 14 (1910): 213.
83. Schachner, "Die grossen Einlagen," 7.

were meant to replace.[84] These activities further weakened the legitimacy of the German financial system. It was no surprise, then, when considering LIGs' other troubles, that *Sparkassens'* activities helped fuel the widespread social dissent that led to the election of the SPD in 1912.

The Dear Loaf

By 1912 the German financial reform nexus was clearly out of step with German LIGs' economic social norms. Again this disjuncture can be traced back to fiscal and electoral relations that impacted upon the German financial reform nexus. As discussed, the fiscal relationship established under the Franckenstein clause encouraged the Reich to increase its indebtedness and to use tariffs as sources of revenue. By 1910 the Reich's debt had increased to RM4,844 million and led to further tariff increases, including increased tariffs on imported cereals (which added RM100 million from increases in the corn tariff alone).[85]

German political economists of the period noted that the German state was violating economic social norms by taxing "indispensable needs" for LIGs and thereby increasing political instability.[86] In the years preceding World War I, Berlin bread prices were approximately 26 percent higher than world bread prices.[87] In addition, the "dear loaf" was *not* offset by the provision of the often-lauded social insurance, which, in reality constituted only 5 percent of Reich social expenditure, and was extremely hard to attain, and whose funds were under the administration of *Länder* governments.[88] As a consequence LIGs were not hoodwinked by "social reform" and voted for the SPD in droves at the 1912 election.

The electoral success of the SPD can be attributed to its calls (dating back to 1905) for electoral reform, federal income and property tax, and its policy on increasing access to mortgage credit. The SPD reflected changes in the German polity, with increased migration to the cities in search of opportunity, and accompanying social norms as Germans faced massive housing overcrowding in some cities (notably Berlin) as well as the "dear loaf." The SPD also propagated the idea (like the Liberal Party in England) that LIGs were paying for the construction of warships that served only the elite.[89] Again this was popular in the cities. The party won over 50 percent

84. As asserted by W. Lexis to the National Monetary Commission, *German Banking Inquiry*, 52.
85. Hobson, *Wealth of States*, 58.
86. For example, Plenge, "Zur Diagnose," 314, 320.
87. Hobson, *Wealth of States*, 66.
88. To obtain an old-age pension one had to be seventy years old and able to demonstrate that one had worked over three hundred days a year for forty-eight years.
89. Gustav Cohn, "Die finanziellen Beziehungen des Reichs zu den Einzelstaaten, II," *Bank-Archiv: Zeitschrift für Bank- und Bank Börsenwesen* 8, 2 (1908): 18.

of votes in areas of over 100,000 people compared to the Conservative Party's 2.2 percent. Most votes came from the urban Protestant working class since the SPD was too "godless" for Catholics in the south and too focused on "Marxist productivism" for those in agrarian areas.[90] The outcome of the 1912 election was that the SPD had twice as many votes as the nearest party, but had no political influence over the government.

In some regions the electoral results were clearly manipulated. For example, in one Berlin district 83 percent of third-tier votes and 66 percent of second-tier votes went to the SPD, but the seat went to a Left Liberal. In the 1913 Prussian state elections the SPD doubled the votes of the nearest party but received only a handful of seats. Indeed, Mark Hallerberg's study demonstrates the overwhelmingly favorable treatment given to the Conservative Party, that while their vote declined from 25 percent in 1898 to 15 percent in 1913, they consistently held 33 percent of seats throughout the period.[91]

Increased contestation from LIGs led to violence and a further weakening of legitimacy. The Reich's response to the "unstoppable avalanche of what they called the 'masses' rolling towards them" was to clamp down even harder on the potential for "socialist" activities.[92] The most dramatic of these was the December 1913 detention of protesting civilians by the German army in the town of Zabern, leading to the passing of a no-confidence motion against the government.[93] Clearly Germany was becoming more, not less, authoritarian, and by 1910 the financial community was clearly complicit. Bankers' main concern was smoothing over their relationship with the Reich in order to allow greater capital mobility and opportunities for profit.

Imperial Strategy and Financing the War

In 1909, when attempting to push through his financial reforms, Bülow argued that it was critical "to convince the German people that morally and materially the reform is a matter of life and death."[94] Bülow recognized that Germany's domestic pool of capital was deep in some pockets, but certainly not broad. Moreover, Germany's international financial capacity was in serious trouble due to perceptions within the international financial community that the domestic retardation of financial reform made Germany an unsafe bet. In 1909 and 1910 attempts to float Reich debt on international

90. Berman, "Modernization," 452.
91. Hallerberg, "Political Economy of Taxation."
92. Norbert Elias, *The Germans: Power Struggles and the Development of Habitus in the Nineteenth and Twentieth Centuries,* ed. Michael Schröter (New York: Columbia University Press, 1996), 85–86.
93. Berman, "Modernization," 453.
94. Cited from Volker R. Berghahn, *Germany and the Approach of War in 1914* (New York: St. Martin's Press, 1973), 83.

debt markets led to the conclusion from foreign observers that Germany's "financial armament" did not match its "military armament."[95] Germany's failure to implement progressive domestic financial reform effectively led to the placement of an interest premium on German government loans within the international financial order (providing another parallel with Japan in the mid-1990s, as discussed in Chapter 6).

The Reich sought to overcome this problem by forging a closer, but short-lived, relationship with *Großbanken* in the years immediately preceding World War I; a relationship entered into willingly by financiers seeking to gain stable rents from the international financial order.[96] While we should be careful in asserting a clear union between domestically based rentiers like large agrarian landholders and those more internationally inclined rentiers like "monopoly" financiers,[97] after 1909 there was active cooperation between the Reich and *Großbanken* toward foreign policy objectives.[98]

It is of interest that the German strategy in foreign financial relations was to adapt to local conditions (at least in name and placement) rather than impose a coercive imperialism. The Deutsche Asiatische Bank provides a good example. The formation of the Deutsche Asiatische Bank in 1899 by the "four Ds" was guaranteed by the German government, as it explicitly encouraged the development of German colonies in China. By 1910 the Deutsche Asiatische Bank had branches in Hankow, Tsingtao, Peking, Tsinan, Canton, Hong Kong, Kobe, Yokohama, Singapore, and Calcutta. Its head office was in Shanghai and its trade was in Shanghai tael, a silver currency used in East Asia. Overall, however, the bank was a financial failure.[99]

While there was a cooperative international approach to encourage the spread of German banks, intervention into the domestic financial system undermined these efforts. The Reich's intervention in the placement of foreign stocks and raising of loans for foreign governments became more frequent in the years immediately preceding the war. Loans to Persia, Turkey, and Hungary were given on explicitly political grounds, the listing of American railway bonds was rejected on the grounds that the "cup is too full" for foreign capital in Germany, and there were numerous attempts to block Russia's loan-raising efforts in London and Paris. In 1911 the conflict over the status of Morocco led the French to withdraw their capital from the re-

95. Niall Ferguson, "Public Finance and National Security: The Domestic Origins of the First World War Revisited," *Past and Present* 142 (1994): 153–54.
96. Morten Reitmayer, "'Bürgerlichkeit' als Habitus: Zur Lebensweise deutscher Groß-bankiers im Kaiserreich," *Geschichte und Gesellschaft* 25, 1 (1999): 83–84; Horst Hanke, "Monopolkapitalismus, Bourgeoisie und imperialistische Außenpolitik, 1897 bis 1917," *Jahrbuch für Wirtschaftsgeschichte* 2 (1982): 231–37.
97. Willibald Gutsche, "Zum Funktionmechanismus zwischen Staat und Monopolkapital in Deutschland in den Ersten Monaten des Ersten Weltkrieg," *Jahrbuch für Wirtschaftsgeschichte* 1 (1973): 84.
98. As suggested by Max Warburg in E. Rosenbaum and A. J. Sherman, *M. M. Warburg & Co., 1798–1938: Merchant Bankers of Hamburg* (London: C. Hurst & Company, 1979), 105.
99. F. Barrett Whale, *Joint-Stock Banking in Germany: A Study of the German Credit Banks Before and After the War* (New York: A. M. Kelley, 1968), 71–79.

formed German stock exchanges.[100] These actions had political consequences for war financing. For example, in 1914 Charles Grant Robertson wrote that Germany "cannot float a loan . . . in the neutral money markets. Only one of the great money markets . . . remains . . . and a loan in New York is neither a political nor a financial possibility."[101]

In the year preceding World War I, the fiscal and financial difficulties plagued the Reich as Germany mounted for war. In comparison to England, where the onset of the war was met with a run on banks from LIGs, the primary problem for Germany was financing war expenses. In 1913 the *Länder* actively continued to resist the imposition of direct taxes from the Reich and even Bethmann-Hollweg's attempt to raise direct taxes under a "patriotic contribution" in 1913 was quashed by Conservatives but passed through with the support of the SPD.[102] Furthermore, the post-1909 alliance between the Reich and the *Großbanken* proved ineffective when it came to the war. While the large English commercial banks contributed one-third of their deposits to the war, *Großbanken* did not follow suit. Certainly loans to the Reich emerged on the balance sheets of commercial banks after 1912 in Germany, but the numbers involved are really quite insignificant (2.3 percent of *Großbanken* assets in 1912, 2.9 percent in 1915, 1 percent in 1917).[103] Interestingly, this suggests that the *Großbanken* were either more removed from the Reich than the City was from the English state, or that the Reich was incapable of commanding funds from the *Großbanken*. Both options force us to readdress common assumptions about the relationship between *Großbanken* and the German state.

As such, in August 1914 the Reich gained the cooperation of the *Länder* in gaining control of all deposits held by *Sparkassen* and credit cooperatives to finance the war effort directly.[104] The balance of *Sparkassen* savings had increased from RM140 million in 1900 to RM204 million in 1914 (after a high of RM647 million in 1909) but suffered a net loss of RM866 million in 1915.[105] This furthered the movement of *Sparkassen* away from their supposed social role. For example, in 1915 a *Sparkassen* newspaper advertisement read: "We seek large savings deposits, not under 5,000 marks."[106] By 1915 the *Sparkassen* were courting funds from the *Großbanken* and other fi-

100. As asserted in Rosenbaum and Sherman, *M. M. Warburg & Co.*, 95, 106; Herbert Feis, *Europe the World's Banker, 1870–1914: An Account of European Foreign Investment and the Connection of World Finance with Diplomacy Before the War* (New Haven: Yale University Press, 1930), 175.

101. Charles Grant Robertson, "Germany: The Economic Problem," *Oxford Pamphlets* 8, 34 (1914): 15.

102. Robert Axel Rüdorffer, "Reichsbank und Darlehnkassen in der Kriegsfinanzierung, 1914–18," Ph.D. diss., Universität zu Köln, 1967, 31.

103. Calculated from Deutsche Bundesbank, *Deutsches Geld*, 58, Table 1.01.

104. Jachmich, "Grundzüge der Entwicklung," 138.

105. Deutsche Bundesbank, *Deutsches Geld*, 63, Table 1.04. See also P. Crüger, "Zur Befriedung des Kreditbedürfnis des deutschen Mittelstandes während des Krieges," *Bank-Archiv: Zeitschrift für Bank- und Bank Börsenwesen* 14, 4 (1914): 57–60.

106. Cited from Hoffman, "Der Zweck der Sparkassen," 366.

nancial institutions within Germany to raise funds for war expenditure due to the incapacity of the Reich to raise sufficient funds in the international financial order or through direct taxation at home. Had Germany had a more legitimate financial system, its capacity to raise revenues internally and externally would have been greater.

Conclusion: Low Legitimation of the Financial Reform Nexus

Germany's fragmented political and financial systems failed to legitimate the financial reform nexus for LIGs and inhibited the development of a deep and broad pool of capital that could be used to boost international financial capacity. The German financial reform nexus weakened in legitimacy throughout the period as local rentiers, in the towns, cities, and in rural regions, sought to defend their particularistic interests and distorted the function and purpose of both private and public financial institutions. The constant conflict between the *Länder* and the Reich over the correct form of taxation encouraged these political manipulations by permitting room for localized rentiers, as well as providing Conservative interests with additional incentives to hoard financial and fiscal resources and prevent LIGs from accessing credit and property. More than this, rentiers within Germany systematically extracted rents from LIGs to defend their own political, economic, and social position to the detriment of German international financial capacity. As such Germany was unable to legitimate the financial reform nexus for LIGs due to the high level of political interference and rejection of changing social norms among LIGs during the period, especially after 1900. The everyday struggle for LIGs was not necessarily increasing their access to credit and property but, instead, seeking to minimize their increasing tax burden, both official and unofficial.

Institutional change in Germany was gradual and systematic as a rentier shift was applied locally and nationally. This rentier shift included the *construction of economic uncertainty* in the form of financial speculation by Conservative politicians influenced by Prussian agrarian interests.[107] This uncertainty led to the retardation of high finance within Germany for nearly a decade and was reformed when it became too expensive for the state. One further consequence of this change was the further removal of *Großbanken* from broader society, whose importance for German finance we can downgrade more generally. The most important lesson from the *Großbanken* is that state intervention should be disaggregated into positive and negative forms. While *Großbanken* could have provided a conduit for a deeper and broader

---

107. For a case of constructing monetary uncertainty in the postwar period see Wesley W. Widmaier, "Constructing Monetary Crises: Monetary Understandings and State Interests in Cooperation," *Review of International Studies* 29, 1 (2003).

pool of domestic capital to be used internationally, the state did not assist this potential.

Rather, Prussian large landholders and local business elites certainly had an idea of how the state and the economy should work for them, and this conception was very much a zero-sum game. As discussed above, this could be seen in the use of public institutions for private gain throughout the *Kaiserreich*. While changes to the *Landschaften* reflected the ongoing abuse of the system to support the Prussian large agrarian landowners, changes to the *Sparkassen* to become profit-driven institutions under the control of local rentiers actively frustrated German LIGs. The same is true for the much-lauded credit cooperatives, whose co-signing system replicated feudal power relationships.

We could ascribe institutional change under rentier and elite influence to a punctuated equilibrium or path dependence model (recall the *Sonder-weg* "special path"), but this would simply read back through history to find moments in which they won out. Indeed, German LIGs had a marginal chance of accessing credit, property, and tax relief from any part of the financial reform nexus. But a chance was still possible and LIGs did try to transform their own political, economic, and social environment rather than conform to a "logic of appropriateness" dictated by static social norms.[108] A more interesting question, therefore, is how institutional change was contested, and how these contests were ignored. Financial and fiscal institutions increasingly represented rentier interests, and their claims to legitimate changes (landed elites and anti-capitalist rhetoric and "inner colonization," or *Sparkassen* and the need for more flexible finance through a check system) did not gain consent from LIGs. Rather, LIGs protested about the widening gulf between them and the institutions supposedly constructed to serve them. They complained about regressive taxation and the crippling lack of access to either credit or property. LIGs' belief-driven actions, such as taking to the streets and coming under fire, reflected the severe lack of legitimacy within the German financial reform nexus.

The German state's negative intervention clearly violated social norms on legitimate governance, and highly unequal power relationships were replicated across the financial reform nexus, including taxation, property, and access to credit. The state's failure to positively intervene and address the creeping rentier shift inhibited the development of the German social source of financial power. The ultimate consequence was policy incoherence that left Germany financially vulnerable on the eve of World War I and facing regime collapse in its aftermath.

108. James G. March and Johan P. Olsen, *Rediscovering Institutions: The Organizational Basis of Politics* (New York: Free Press, 1989).

5

The Financial Reform Nexus
in the United States

In 1985 the United States was principal in the international financial order and also its largest debtor. The U.S.'s postwar development of the "international creditor economy" was premised on state support for international financial liberalization while maintaining stringent domestic financial regulations. Following the collapse of the Bretton Woods regime in the early 1970s, the massive expansion of private credit in the international financial order provided greater room for rentiers within the U.S. domestic economy. This power was demonstrated during a rentier shift in Ronald Reagan's first administration. This rentier shift, however, was blocked after 1985, through positive state intervention into the financial reform nexus for lower-income groupings (LIGs). Bill Clinton's first administration, in particular, intervened on behalf of LIGs and was able to increase U.S. international financial capacity: the capacity to draw credit from and increase the generation of credit to the international financial order, as well as influence the order's regulatory and normative structure.

The key proposition in this book is that if a state intervenes positively in its financial reform nexus for LIGs, it can broaden and deepen its domestic pool of capital that then enhances international financial capacity. In the introductory chapter I posed an ideal type scenario whereby, through state support for a "cumulative process" of credit generation, capital could flow up through various institutions from every person's pocketbook to the global financial marketplace. The U.S. case provides the closest empirical case to this ideal type, and this is a consequence of the high degree of legitimacy conferred upon U.S. financial reforms. Legitimacy, in turn, was a product of contestation that ensured that financial reforms *should* represent a broader social interest. This does not mean that legitimacy alleviated income inequality in the United States, but that financial reforms proceeded according to U.S. economic social norms.

In the period from 1985 to 2000, U.S. LIGs achieved greater access to credit and property, and faced lower tax burdens. LIGs' social wants were aided by both domestic and international forces. Domestically, the providers of credit for LIGs were mainly private financial institutions with regulatory and economic support from agencies tied to the U.S. government. These agencies, particularly what I refer to as Federal Mortgage Agencies (FMAs), enhanced U.S. international financial capacity by providing a source of capital for U.S. financial institutions and corporations with global interests, as well as increasing their own capacity to attract foreign investors to their debt—which in turn assisted credit access for LIGs. This ability was assisted by financial innovations, particularly securitization (the greater use of securitized assets by banks),[1] and bank concentration that coincided with increased community-driven regulatory initiatives to ensure credit provision to LIGs. The pressure upon U.S. regulators to ensure that financial reform could demonstrate a broader social interest could also be seen in the management of financial crises within the United States, including the savings and loans associations (S&Ls) and commercial bank crises of the 1980s.

Despite valid perceptions of the strength of the banking lobby in the United States, the state often acted against the interests of the financial community for a broader social concern and, in doing so, provided much greater capital to the American financial system. The contestation of the legitimacy of financial reform from community activists, banking lobby groups, between regulatory agencies, and political representatives resulted in the increased process of redistribution from the U.S.'s main depository financial institutions—commercial banks—to allow credit access to LIGs. This process blocked the 1980–84 rentier shift and assisted the propagation of economic social norms concerned with improving the fairness of creditworthiness assessments for property ownership.

Needless to say, these findings sit uncomfortably with the bulk of political economy literature on the United States. Within much of the literature the United States is seen as a state and society with very weak legitimacy due to its high income inequality, which increased dramatically in the last quarter of the twentieth century. Some scholars suggest that only the top 5 percent of U.S. income earners provide any assistance to U.S. international financial capacity and that LIGs are actively reduced to a state of "legitimalaise."[2] My task here is not to demonstrate that the United States was "good" or "just," but that from the case studies under investigation it was able to achieve the highest degree of legitimacy for LIGs and permitted unprecedented levels

1. A securitized asset is a regulated flow of capital that has been "packaged" or "pooled" and then sold by a financial intermediary (bank, finance company, etc.) to a third party, who then uses the income stream for an asset-backed security that is sold to investors—overwhelmingly corporate investors. In doing so, the original intermediary removes the asset from their balance sheet. The securitized asset includes the total amount outstanding (on a mortgage obligation, for instance) and all payable income that has been securitized in present and previous months (fixed payments).

2. Richard M. Merelman, "On Legitimalaise in the United States: A Weberian Analysis," *Sociological Quarterly* 39, 3 (1998).

of state-empowered credit in pursuit of their life-chances.[3] Crucially, unlike other cases under study, in the U.S. case I find no significant or systematic extraction of rents from LIGs to support rentier interests. Rather, LIGs' access to credit and property increased during the 1985–2000 period, while tax burdens dropped. This access was a greater legitimating factor than the expanding income gap. Indeed, I find that U.S. economic social norms do not lead to rallying against income disparity but do call for redistributive interventions for increased access to credit for LIGs.[4] I believe that this can be explained by an economic social norm that encourages creditworthiness assessments for property ownership, which is combined with U.S. entrepreneurial norms that allow "economically weak" actors and institutions to fall behind.

Such an entrepreneurial spirit can be seen in Figure 5.1, where change in the key financial institutions is rapid. The key institutions during the period are commercial banks, savings and loan associations, pension funds, mutual funds, and, importantly, government-sponsored enterprises (GSEs) and their federal mortgage pools. I refer to the latter as FMAs to highlight their role and purpose since with "relatively small exceptions, the bulk of capital supplied through these entities fund residential mortgages."[5]

Among all the institutions under investigation, private pension funds provide the most consistency. In contrast, mutual funds demonstrated tremendous growth in the last quarter of the twentieth century, in part due to changes to commercial banking activity and their attractiveness to LIGs (households earning under $35,000 per annum represented 37 percent of the mutual funds' market participants in 2000).[6]

We notice in Figure 5.1 that commercial banks faced a steep decline from 26 percent of assets in 1985 to 17 percent in 2000. The number of commercial banks throughout 1985 to 2000 nearly halved from approximately

3. One key criticism of my argument would be that as most U.S. peoples identify as "middle class," associating "LIGs" with those on or below median income ($52,148 for a family in 2000) is absurd, and that "LIGs" should be represented by groups who are effectively alienated from the financial system, if for the simple reason that many do not hold a bank account. Any study which sought to argue that such groups significantly added to financial power would obviously be doomed to failure. In 2000, U.S. families earning between $15,000 and $49,999 made up 38.6 percent of the population (of which 15.8 percent earn $35,000 to $49,999), with 9.4 percent below $14,999 and 52 percent over $50,000. I am focusing on those below median income rather than the wealthy. It should also be noted that during the period under study the African-American population below the poverty line decreased from 31.3 percent to 22.5 percent, while for all Americans there was a drop from 14 percent to 11.7 percent. Median income and poverty statistics are from U.S. Census Bureau, *Statistical Abstract of the United States: 2003* (Washington, D.C.: U.S. Census Bureau, 2003), 458, Table 686, 465, Table 700.

4. Mérove Gijsberts, "The Legitimation of Income Inequality in State-Socialist and Market Societies," *Acta Sociologica* 45, 4 (2002).

5. See Jane D'Arista, "Is a Mortgage Bubble Filling the Treasury Debt Vacuum?" *Flow of Funds: Review and Analysis* Third Quarter (1999): 1.

6. Eric M. Engen and Andreas Lehnert, "Mutual Funds and the U.S. Equity Market," *Federal Reserve Bulletin* 86, 12 (2000): 801.

Figure 5.1 Key U.S. financial institutions' assets as a percentage of total financial assets, 1985–2000.

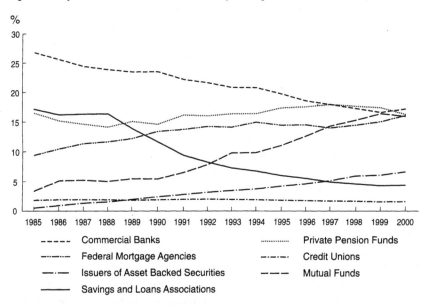

Source: Board of Governors of the Federal Reserve, *Flow of Funds of the United States, 1985–1994* (Washington, D.C.: U.S. Federal Reserve, 2002), L. 109–L.128, 61–72; Board of Governors of the Federal Reserve, *Flow of Funds of the United States, 1995–2000* (Washington, D.C.: U.S. Federal Reserve, 2002), L. 109–L.128, 61–72.

14,500 in the mid-1980s to 8,500 by 2000. Much has been made of this decline by political economy scholars. Philip Cerny, for example, cites the decline in banks' numbers as a key indicator that the U.S. system is trapped in a "gridlock" between different regulatory bodies.[7] But the decline in commercial banks' numbers or assets did not reflect a decline in their power. From the mid-1980s onward these institutions actively sought to remove assets from their balance sheets in order to avoid regulations that required them to keep capital aside in safe reserves (capital adequacy ratio regulations). Thus while their number and on-book assets declined by the mid-1990s, U.S. commercial banks were at their most powerful and profitable since the 1950s.[8] There was also regulatory change during the 1990s, both informal and formal. By 1999 the Glass-Steagall Act of 1933, which separated commercial and investment banking during a time when one in five banks failed, and the 1927 McFadden Act, which banned interstate bank-

7. Philip G. Cerny, "Gridlock and Decline: Financial Internationalization, Banking Politics, and the American Political Process," in Richard Stubbs and Geoffrey R. D. Underhill, eds., *Political Economy and the Changing Global Order* (London: Macmillan, 1994).
8. William B. English and Brian K. Reid, "Profits and Balance Sheet Developments at U.S. Commercial Banks in 1993," *Federal Reserve Bulletin* 80, 6 (1994): 483; Anatoli Kuprianov, "Tax Disincentives to Commercial Bank Lending," *Economic Quarterly* 83, 2 (1997): 68.

ing, were both repealed under the Gramm-Leach-Bliley Act of 1999 (GLBA), also known as the Financial Services Modernization Act. The decade-long passage of these reforms was due to the need to pass financial reforms that could be legitimated to LIGs. Banking concentration reforms were always "piggybacked" with socially minded financial reforms and under the scrutiny of groups like the National Community Reinvestment Coalition (NCRC), National People's Action (NPA), the National Fair Housing Alliance (NFHA) and a multitude of locally based Community Development Corporations (CDCs).

The real institutional decline was the managed collapse of S&Ls from 17 percent of total financial assets in 1985 to 4 percent of assets in 2000. The S&L scandal emerged as a direct response to the pro-rentier reforms of the first Reagan administration (1981–84), but were successfully cleaned up during the late 1980s and early 1990s. Furthermore, their role as mortgage providers was more than adequately picked up by institutions linked to the FMAs.

I especially wish to highlight the prodigious growth of FMAs, as this sector of the U.S. financial system has previously been ignored in political economy literature and demonstrates positive state intervention in the U.S. financial system on a massive scale (during the 1985–2000 period they moved from fifth position to third position in terms of their assets, and even then were only 1 percent behind the leader, commercial banks). The increased prominence of FMAs demonstrates that financial relations can be regulated to fulfill broad social goals and empower LIGs. An examination of changes in U.S. household portfolios shows an increase in financial assets as a percentage of all household assets from 29.4 percent in 1983 to 40 percent in 1998. Much of this growth can be attributed to the role of FMAs, as owner-occupied mortgage indebtedness increased by over 10 percent (43.1 percent of all households in 1998), even though there was a reduction in indebtedness for landlord investment.[9] There is a clear connection between increased mortgage indebtedness for LIGs and the role of FMAs. In 1994 and 1999, funding by these agencies to enhance mortgage credit for Americans equaled over 60 percent of outstanding U.S. Treasury debt. Moreover, while the capital going into this system is primarily domestic, 28 percent of the capital in this system came from foreign investors in 1999, who were primarily Japanese (this provides a particular irony when considering the Japanese equivalent of FMAs, discussed in the following chapter).[10] In short, the United States used positive state intervention to provide a sustainable social source of financial power, as well as drawing in international resources to augment the legitimation of the domestic financial reform nexus.

9. Carol Bertraut and Martha Starr-McCluer, "Household Portfolios in the United States," paper presented at the Conference on Household Portfolios, European University Institute, Florence, 17–18 December 1999, 26, 28, Tables 2–3.
10. D'Arista, "Is a Mortgage Bubble," 1.

This chapter demonstrates that in understanding institutional and social change it is vital to disaggregate state intervention into positive and negative forms rather than view state intervention as solely determined by the structure of the political system. For example, within the "varieties of capitalism" and "state capacity" literature, the United States is often viewed as a weak state due to its lack of regulatory centralization.[11] More generally, regulatory fragmentation and the U.S. system of "checks and balances" are seen to slow policy making and hinder national economic competitiveness.[12] However, as commented by Sven Steinmo, the U.S. political system's institutions were designed to be overlapping and fragmented to keep both the state and elites in check.[13]

Reagan's Rentier Push

In the English case we found that there was a rentier shift after the 1890s that intensified after 1900 under the guise of monetary responsibility and fiscal constraint. In the U.S. case there was a massive increase in the amount of private capital in the international political economy after 1970, and by 1980 a conservative bloc within the Republican Party was elected on arguments for monetary responsibility and fiscal constraint (including massive tax cuts).[14] The Reagan administration in its first term pushed forward an agenda that directly supported rentiers' interests across the financial reform nexus. It was this push in the very early 1980s that exacerbated the S&L crisis, which greatly increased the power of landlords within the U.S. domestic economy, and which allowed banks to behave more recklessly internationally and less socially responsible at home.

The first Reagan administration promoted rentiers' interests across the financial reform nexus, enabled by the Carter administration's Depository Institutions Deregulation and Monetary Control Act (DIDMCA) of 1980, then Reagan's Tax Reform Act of 1981 (TRA '81), and the Garn-St. Germain Act of 1982 (G.St.GA). The International Lending Supervisory Act (ILSA) of 1983 provided a corrective for international recklessness.

The DIDMCA of 1980 removed interest rate ceilings (Regulation Q), which had impeded commercial banks' and S&Ls' capacity to attract deposits at a time when non-bank financial intermediaries (NBFIs) were offering cash

11. An early example of this view is provided in John Zysman, *Governments, Markets, and Growth: Financial Systems and the Politics of Industrial Change* (Oxford: Martin Robertson, 1983), 267.
12. Robert Gilpin, "Economic Evolution of National Systems," *International Studies Quarterly* 40, 3 (1996): 417.
13. Sven Steinmo, *Taxation and Democracy: Swedish, British, and American Approaches to Financing the Modern State* (New Haven: Yale University Press, 1993), 8.
14. Mark Blyth, *Great Transformations: Economic Ideas and Institutional Change in the Twentieth Century* (Cambridge: Cambridge University Press, 2002), 166–74.

management accounts that provided higher returns. The DIDMCA also eliminated ceilings for usury during a time of high inflation, a change that affected LIGs negatively since they were the biggest clients of usurious or "sub-prime" lenders (this change also provides a contrast with community activism after the mid-1990s under the Clinton administration).

Compounding this change was the fact that the first Reagan administration clearly supported a move away from the government provision of housing for LIGs and used the savings from such programs to pay for tax cuts.[15] TRA '81 provided a 23 percent income tax cut but, importantly, permitted the deduction of payments on non-owner-occupied residential and commercial mortgage interest payments from income tax assessment.[16] This built upon 1980 changes to the Internal Revenue Code, which encouraged investment in new tax-exempt mortgage revenue bonds for the construction of rental housing for LIGs (there is a parallel here with changes within Japan discussed in the following chapter). By 1982 there were $5 billion of these bonds and by 1985 there were $20 billion, leading to the construction of an estimated 200,000 homes, or about one-quarter of all rental constructions during the period.[17] Furthermore, Reagan encouraged the growth of consumer credit to increase consumption and allowed interest payments on consumer credit to be deducted from tax-assessable income. The debts of the domestic non-financial sector nearly doubled as the better-off took advantage of Reagan's 1981 tax changes.[18]

The rhetoric at the time was that the United States would benefit from a more open financial system within which the state played a smaller role. The G.St.GA followed up on this aim in permitting commercial banks and S&Ls to use money market deposit accounts to compete with NBFIs. In addition to these changes the Federal Reserve Bank (Fed) allowed banks' capital adequacy ratios (capital kept aside in reserves in case of default, relative to all capital) to fall, from over 5 percent to 3 percent in some cases, to improve bank competitiveness, despite warnings during the late 1970s about the unsustainable character of U.S. banks' lending to states in Latin America. Of course this change heightened the risk of commercial bank collapse should banks' borrowers have trouble repaying their loans.

The debt crisis of the early 1980s demonstrated that U.S. commercial

15. See James M. Poterba, "Public Policy and Housing in the United States," in Yukio Noguchi and James M. Poterba, eds., *Housing Markets in the United States and Japan* (Chicago: University of Chicago Press, 1994), 252.
16. Gerard Epstein, "The Triple Debt Crisis," *World Policy Journal* 2, 4 (1985): 633; Blyth, *Great Transformations*, 175–76.
17. Stuart A. Gabriel, "Housing and Mortgage Markets: The Post-1982 Expansion," *Federal Reserve Bulletin* 73, 12 (1987): 896.
18. John F. Wilson, Elizabeth M. Fogler, James L. Freund, and Guido E. van der Ven, "Major Borrowing and Lending Trends in the U.S. Economy, 1981–85," *Federal Reserve Bulletin*, 72, 8 (1986): 511–12. The U.S. federal deficit also grew at a massive pace from $9 billion in 1981 to $207 billion by 1983.

banks were massively overexposed when it was revealed that the largest nine U.S. banks had lent 140 percent of their capital to Latin American states. The threat to the U.S. public that tax monies might be used to bail out U.S. banks' loans to sovereign entities animated contestation against the U.S. rentier shift.[19]

Despite the fact that U.S. commercial banks argued that the government had asked them to lend heavily to Latin American states as "a matter of public interest," there was widespread public dissent against the prospect of a taxpayer bailout of U.S. commercial banks. Accordingly, the ILSA forced banks to set aside special reserves for bad debts, increased capital adequacy ratio standards and implemented public disclosure on banks' concentration in overseas lending.[20] Furthermore, the ILSA led to the imposition of a domestic premium on commercial banks with bad debts to foreign sovereign entities.[21] The consequence was a clear shift by banks to engage in securitization and to stop Third World lending. The rentier shift of the first Reagan administration was clearly weakening the legitimacy of the U.S. financial system and, following the ILSA, there was a political shift to legitimate the U.S. financial system by encouraging banks to use securitization to positive social effect. But before discussing the post-1985 turn, it is necessary to discuss how the G.St.GA directly led to the S&L and commercial bank crises of the mid-to-late 1980s.

The Managed Decline of Cowboy Financiers

In U.S. financial history, the collapse of 1,295 S&Ls at a cost of $127 billion, and 1,617 commercial banks at a cost of $37 billion in the mid-to-late 1980s, occupies a special place.[22] Following regulatory changes in the early 1980s discussed above, the takeover of many "Mom and Pop" S&Ls to engage in commercial real estate speculation and junk bond trading makes for sensational reading and a demonstration of the gross inadequacies and inequities of the U.S. financial system.[23] However, the management of the crisis led to institutional and regulatory reforms that had payoffs for LIGs in the 1990s.

19. Wolfgang H. Reinicke, *Banking, Politics, and Global Finance: American Commercial Banks and Regulatory Change, 1980–1990* (Aldershot: Edward Elgar, 1995), 142.
20. Benjamin J. Cohen, *In Whose Interest? International Banking and American Foreign Policy* (New Haven: Yale University Press, 1986), 40.
21. Louis W. Pauly, "Institutionalizing a Stalemate: National Financial Policies and the International Debt Crisis," *Journal of Public Policy* 10, 1 (1990): 29.
22. Federal Deposit Insurance Corporation (FDIC), *Managing the Crisis: The FDIC and RTC Experience, 1980–1994* (Washington, D.C.: FDIC, 1998), 794–95.
23. As reflected in the titles of some of the key texts in this area. For example, Kitty Calavita, Henry N. Pontell, and Robert H. Tillman, *Big Money Crime: Fraud and Politics in the Savings and Loans Crisis* (Berkeley: University of California Press, 1997); Martin Lowy, *High Rollers: Inside the Savings and Loans Debacle* (New York: Praeger, 1991).

The managed collapse of the S&Ls and commercial banks during a crisis of unprecedented scale demonstrates the important place of society in institutional change, as contestation from socially minded advocacy groups led to an increased legitimation of the U.S. financial reform nexus for LIGs.

During the high housing growth period of the 1950s until the 1970s, S&Ls, under the supervision of the Federal Home Loan Bank Board (FHLBB), and with insurance provided by the Federal Savings and Loan Insurance Corporation (FSLIC), funded two-thirds of residential mortgages due to their preferential tax treatment in gaining access to cheaper credit than commercial banks.[24] But cheap access to credit from Regulation Q restrictions also led to severe constraints on their profitability in the late 1970s as inflation increased. As S&Ls provided only fixed interest rate mortgages for periods of twenty-five to thirty years, when interest rates climbed to 15 percent, a loan of 6 percent led to massive losses. While in 1979 3 percent of S&Ls were losing money, by 1981, 80 percent of S&Ls were in the red.

In response to the prospect of the sector collapsing, the first Reagan administration—on the advice of Alan Greenspan—allowed S&Ls and commercial banks to invest their way out of their problems through the provisions of the G.St.GA.[25] The act, which Reagan referred to as the "Emancipation Proclamation for America's Savings Institutions," provided S&Ls with greater lending powers to acquire commercial real estate and allowed commercial banks to buy up insolvent S&Ls.[26] Crucially, the act removed the rule that S&Ls must have at least 400 individual stockholders, instead allowing one individual to own them. As a consequence real estate developers became interested in S&Ls and abused them, most especially "cowboy financiers" in California and the U.S.'s own Prussia, Texas. Commercial banks followed the trend into real estate speculation with regulatory support, as over 200 new banks were chartered in Texas during 1983 and 1984, nearly half the U.S. total. Federal Deposit Insurance Corporation (FDIC) data suggest that banks that were formed in this period to engage in speculative commercial real estate lending were the same banks that failed in the late 1980s (of which there were 599 Texan failures or 37 percent of all U.S. bank failures in the 1980–94 period).[27]

Stories surrounding the abuse of S&Ls are well known. For example, in 1984 the Silverado S&L of Denver lost $500 million on investments in high risk speculative real estate bonds, with clear links to organized crime. At the

24. Patric H. Hendershott, "Housing Finance in the United States," in Noguchi and Poterba, eds., *Housing Markets*, 65, 68–69.
25. Interview with staff from Office of Thrift Supervision, Washington, D.C., November 2001.
26. FDIC, *History of the Eighties: Lessons for the Future* (Washington, D.C.: FDIC, 1998), 26.
27. Calculated from FDIC, *Managing the Crisis*, 832–35, Chart C. 40 and Chart C. 41. This calculation includes both state and federally chartered S&Ls. FDIC, *History of the Eighties*, 108, 160–61, 168, 14–15, Table 1.1.

same time the Columbia S&L invested 35 percent of its total assets in "junk bonds" (high yielding bonds with low investment ratings) and incurred losses of nearly $2.5 billion.[28] The collapse of commercial banks is also well known, particularly the 1984 failure of the Continental Illinois. But more important than the scandals is the much more mundane fact that only 10 percent of S&Ls' and commercial banks' losses were from fraudulent activities. Certainly for the S&Ls, the real beneficiaries of the collapse were not the real estate entrepreneurs but Americans who received cheap mortgage credit in the 1960s and 1970s.

While standard explanations of the S&L and commercial bank crises argue that the process of reform was slow and served only the interests of those involved with the collapsing institutions, U.S. federal regulators responded with speed and great efficacy. The statistics on commercial banks and S&L failures reveal that the overwhelming majority of costly failures were dealt with before 1989.[29] Even in the dramatic case of the Continental Illinois, the Office of the Comptroller of the Currency (OCC) took over its operations over a series of months, winding down the institution, while the FDIC paid its depositors (one glimpse of sunshine from the G.St.GA was the raising of the FDIC's deposit insurance guarantee from $40,000 to $100,000). Furthermore, to cement U.S. capacity in financial reform, a series of legislative changes established a new regulatory framework: the Competitive Equality Banking Act of 1987, which recapitalized the FDIC to deal with the crisis; the Financial Institutions Reform, Recovery, and Enforcement Act (FIRREA) of 1989, which established new institutions; and the FDIC Improvement Act (FDICIA), which provided $70 billion to pay depositors who had lost monies from collapsed banks and increased the FDIC's borrowing powers from the Treasury from $5 billion to $30 billion to provide more substantive deposit insurance.

During a period when the Democrats held the majority in the House and Senate, the FIRREA represented the capacity of the U.S. government to implement major socially progressive financial reform. The FHLBB, under the terms of the FIRREA, was dismantled and supervision was replaced by the Office of Thrift Supervision (OTS). The FIRREA provided $50 billion immediately for the S&Ls, removed their tax concessions, and immediately closed 12.5 percent (320) of all S&Ls nationwide.[30] A Resolution Trust Corporation (RTC) was established to deal with remaining S&L loans along with a Resolution Funding Corporation (REFCorp) to engage in bond trading to fund the RTC rather than rely on taxes. The RTC identified insolvent

28. David Silfen Glasberg and Dan Skidmore, *Corporate Welfare Policy and the Welfare State: Bank Deregulation and the Savings and Loan Bailout* (New York: Aldine De Gruyter, 1997), 45, 50–57.
29. FDIC, *Managing the Crisis*, 861, Table C. 14, 863, Table C. 16.
30. Interview with staff from Office of Thrift Supervision, Washington, D.C., November 2001.

S&Ls and required them to amortize all assets within seven years. Between 1989 and 1994, the RTC sold over $100 billion in failed S&L assets (35 to 40 percent of which were sold to commercial banks with FDIC support).[31] From 1991, FIRREA regulations stipulated that the S&Ls must hold at least 70 percent of their assets as residential mortgages and from 1993 S&Ls held only 2 percent of their assets in commercial loans.[32] In short, the FIRREA provided the regulatory arsenal sufficient to clean up the S&L and commercial bank collapses, especially the massive losses in Texas.

In addition to these changes, community agitation for public compensation from the S&L crisis led the Democrats to attach an important Affordable Housing Program (AHP) to the FIRREA. This institution came directly from LIG contestation. Citing their motives as "an insatiable desire to become a part, an integral part of this great American life," during the mid-1980s the Association of Community Organizations for Reform Now (ACORN) forcibly occupied housing that had failed from S&L collapses, and tied red ribbons around commercial banks, demonstrating a withdrawal of consent for Reagan's rentier shift.[33]

A range of localized Community Development Corporations (CDCs) also petitioned the Federal Reserve Board to draw attention to how financial institutions were treating credit for LIGs through extended public comment periods focused on the negative spillovers from bank mergers.[34] Furthermore, there was contestation of how FMAs were behaving. To take one example, the Northwestern Bronx Community and Clergy Coalition successfully campaigned against FMAs for supporting "infamous slumlords" and to support more generous terms to institutions that provided LIGs with credit to obtain property.[35]

The accumulated actions of LIGs and their advocacy groups had a large public profile and affect on the Democrats. Through their majority in the House and Senate, the Democrats amended the FIRREA to include at least $100 million per annum or 10 percent of Federal Home Loan Bank (FHLB) system earnings, whichever was higher, to fund an AHP for low-income groups.[36] The AHP led to the sale of 109,141 houses to buyers who earned,

31. *Economic Report of the President* (Washington, D.C.: United States Government Printing Office, 1991), 173; FDIC, *Managing the Crisis*, 803, Chart C. 10.

32. Mathias Dewatripont and Jean Tirole, *The Prudential Regulation of Banks* (Cambridge: MIT Press, 1994), 61.

33. Seth Borgos, "Low-Income Homeownership and the ACORN Squatters Campaign," in Rachel G. Bratt, Chester Hartman, and Ann Meyerson, eds., *Critical Perspectives on Housing* (Philadelphia: Temple University Press, 1986), 428–29.

34. Ibid., 445; Mara S. Sidney, *Unfair Housing: How National Policy Shapes Community Action* (Lawrence: University Press of Kansas, 2003), 84, 116.

35. Margaret Groarke, "Using Community Power Against Targets Beyond the Neighborhood," *New Political Science* 26, 2 (2004).

36. Discussed in U.S. Congress, Senate Committee on Banking, Housing, and Urban Affairs, "Discrimination in Home Mortgage Lending," Senate Hearing 101–0479, 101st Congress (Washington, D.C.: U.S. Government Printing Office, 1989), 774.

on average, less than 60 percent of U.S. median income.[37] It, like the reform of the U.S. financial system under the FIRREA, represented a clear qualitative shift to legitimate the U.S. financial reform nexus to LIGs through providing access to credit for property. And, while important, by 1989 change was already underway with a surprisingly socially progressive tax system. Importantly, this period of financial reforms included the 1989 bolstering of the Home Mortgage Disclosure Act (HMDA) of 1975, which requires financial institutions to disclose information on the race, age, gender, and other details of applicants for mortgages. The key reform here was more stringent requirements on the collection and presentation of HMDA data to regulatory authorities. Furthermore, in 1992 the Department of Housing and Urban Development's (HUD) Fair Housing Initiative Program was made permanent and HUD was also enabled to provide funding to nonprofit fair housing organizations on an ongoing basis. These organizations, including NPA, NCRC, NFHA, and various CDCs then used the HMDA information to contest the legitimation of the financial reform nexus.

"Super Keynesianism" and the Basle Accord

One reason why Reagan turned away from the rentier shift of his first administration is that, as demonstrated by the S&L and banking crisis, it was leading to public dissent and calls for the U.S. financial system to respond to LIGs' economic social norms. It is important to recognize within this context that while Reagan's victory over Walter Mondale (Reagan won 525 electoral college votes to Mondale's 13) in the 1984 election was crushing, the Democrats consistently had the majority in the House and took control of the Senate after 1986.

Given these changes, the extent and character of state intervention transformed after 1985. As has been recognized with regard to trade policy and international monetary cooperation, following the depreciation of the dollar through the Plaza Accord (the dollar had appreciated by more than 70 percent between 1981 and 1985), the second Reagan administration took an "activist turn" with regard to the domestic financial system and the international financial order.[38] Furthermore, it may be noted with some irony that despite the neoliberalism of the Reagan presidency, his administration was more "super Keynesian" in its public spending.[39] Indeed, there is a clear difference here in the growing level of state intervention at home, particularly in the provision of employment through defense-related industries, and the 1980s "neoliberal" ideal purported internationally. What was

37. FDIC, *Managing the Crisis*, 373–75.
38. James Shoch, "Party Politics and International Economic Activism: The Reagan-Bush Years," *Political Science Quarterly* 113, 1 (1998): 118.
39. My thanks to Richard Leaver for this point.

possible according to domestic economic social norms was informed by LIGs, which helps explain the absence of a national consumption tax in the United States while Value Added Taxes became increasingly implemented throughout the rest of the world. Moreover, the U.S. state was increasingly looking at ways to redistribute income from private financial institutions to the state, including not only domestic institutions but those abroad through the Basle Accord.

While the Tax Reform Act of 1986 (TRA '86) and the Basle Accord coordinated by the Bank for International Settlements (BIS) may seem strange bedfellows, both provided government revenue to assist the legitimation of the U.S. financial reform nexus. TRA '86 represented a major domestic political change, and the Basle Accord provided a form of redistribution to encourage foreign investment in U.S. government debt. Both therefore sought to maximize government revenue from higher-income groups and institutions, as well as increase the prominence of securitization in the U.S. financial system. These changes also led to greater private and public funds flowing into mortgage credit (discussed in the following section; one might also notice the rise of Issuers of Asset-Backed Securities post-1985 in Figure 5.1).

Of course the Reagan administration is not normally associated with a socially progressive tax regime.[40] However, TRA '86 provided a remarkable *volte-face* from the regressive TRA '81 in its scope and intended effects. The irony here is that although Reagan's electoral victory was in part a consequence of promised tax cuts—and Mondale's defeat a consequence of promised tax increases—with Democrat assistance his administration increased the tax burden on wealthy groups, actively discouraged landlord tax-benefits that helped fuel real estate speculation in 1981, increased the tax benefits of owner-occupier mortgage indebtedness and, once one scratches the surface, increased the effective tax burden on U.S. financial intermediaries operating at home and abroad.

The TRA '86 "attacked virtually every tax break on the books."[41] It removed the capacity to deduct interest repayment on commercial property, non-owner-occupier residential property, and consumer credit from one's income tax.[42] In its place, the "pro-family, pro-fairness, and pro-growth" act permitted the deduction of interest repayments on owner-occupier residential mortgages, scaled to benefit those with incomes of $25,000 and

40. The transformation of U.S. welfare was therefore less dramatic than many commentators have suggested. See Paul Pierson, *Dismantling the Welfare State?* (Cambridge: Cambridge University Press, 1994); John L. Campbell, *Institutional Change and Globalization* (Princeton: Princeton University Press, 2004), 152–61.

41. Charles E. McLure Jr, "The Political Economy of Tax Reforms and Their Implications and Interdependence," in Takatoshi Ito and Anne O. Krueger, eds., *The Political Economy of Tax Reform* (Chicago: University of Chicago Press, 1992), 103.

42. Poterba, "Public Policy," 244–45, 247–48.

greatly reduced deductibility for those with incomes of $250,000 and over. The following financial year, nearly half of all U.S. taxpayers claimed mortgage deductions from their tax.[43] Furthermore, TRA '86 created a Housing Tax Credit program (rather than reductions on personal income) for non-owner-occupied real estate that was targeted specifically to the construction or "acquisition with substantial rehabilitation" of low-income rental housing.[44]

These changes effectively increased the upper income group's tax burden. A congressional study of Internal Revenue Service data reveals that in 1988 the top 10 percent of taxpayers paid 57.2 percent of all income tax compared with 48 percent in 1981, those in the 50th to 90th percentile paid 48.7 percent in 1988 compared with 57.5 percent in 1981, and those in the bottom 49 percent of taxpayers paid 5.7 percent in 1988 compared with 7.5 percent in 1981.[45]

U.S. commercial banks were not immune to the effects of TRA '86 either, as their capacity to deduct interest payments on non-performing loan reserves from pre-tax profits was removed. This produced a strong incentive to go for "safe bets" within the domestic economy and reduce riskier international lending, further encouraging a process of securitization of assets. Furthermore, although TRA '86 officially reduced corporate tax from 46 percent to 34 percent, the *effective* tax rate increased as a consequence of the reform's base-broadening (including the outlawing of many "investment tax-related shields," as the amount of tax paid by U.S. commercial banks between 1985 and 1988 increased by 78 percent).[46] As commented by John Campbell, the 1986 tax reforms, which raised an additional $120 billion in corporate taxes between 1986 and 1991, were "not consistent with the intent of the neoliberal program."[47] The TRA '86 also closed a 1962 loophole that allowed U.S. financial institutions to defer payment of taxes on overseas income and then deduct the deferred tax payment against payable U.S. taxes.[48] The fixing of the loophole clearly demonstrated the will of the Rea-

43. Interview with staff from U.S. Federal Reserve, Washington, D.C., November 2001. Quote from Campbell, *Institutional Change*, 155.

44. See, for example, Ann Meyerson, "Housing Abandonment: The Role of Institutional Mortgage Lenders," in Bratt, Hartman, and Meyerson, eds., *Critical Perspectives*, 190–94.

45. U.S. Congress Joint Economic Committee, "The Reagan Tax Cuts: Lessons for Tax Reform," April 1996, ⟨www.house.gov/jec/fiscal/tx-grwth/reagtxct/reagtxct.htm⟩, 1; Eugene Steuerle, "Tax Policy From 1990 to 2001," paper presented at Conference on American Economic Policy in the 1990s, Center for Business and Government, John F. Kennedy School of Government, Harvard University, Cambridge, Mass., 27–30 June 2001, 6–7.

46. Calculated from English and Reid, "Profits and Balance Sheet," 497, Table A.1.

47. Campbell, *Institutional Change*, 161.

48. I estimate the windfall from changes to the tax law, from the largest 7,500 taxable entities alone, to be at least $4 billion in 1988 (or 5 percent of total corporate tax revenue). This loophole is Subpart F of the 1986 tax legislation. Rosanne Altshuler and R. Glenn Hubbard argue that as a consequence a U.S. financial subsidiary incorporated abroad has a tax burden which is 24.1 percent higher than French, German, British, or Dutch financial sub-

gan administration to extract rents from parties normally associated with their particularistic interests. And it is here that the Basle Accord is relevant.

While the Basle Accord has been hailed as an exemplar of international cooperation led by the Bank for International Settlements, its origins lie predominantly in U.S. domestic interests. It is here where explanations of the Basle Accord fall into the awkward position of arguing for the standard "gridlock" case outlined above, while also claiming that, when it mattered, the "U.S. policy network took relatively coordinated and decisive steps to reduce the challenge posed by the worldwide decline in banks' capital ratios."[49] I put forward a more consistent position in arguing that the Basle Accord reflected the U.S.'s capacity to increase revenue from public and private sources domestically and internationally, to secure funds to assist with the legitimation of the domestic financial reform nexus.

As mentioned above, the first Reagan administration allowed banks to drop their capital adequacy ratios in order to increase their competitiveness. During the debt crisis the Reagan administration rejected the notion that there should be a new international standard on capital adequacy rules, but soon changed its mind during discussions for the ILSA. Furthermore, at the same time as the ILSA, an application by Fuji Bank to establish a foreign subsidiary in New York brought Japanese banks' low capital adequacy ratios to attention.[50] Faced with the prodigious growth of Japanese international banking during the mid-1980s the Fed, in coordination with the BoE, began work on a new capital adequacy regime in 1986 which it then presented to the BIS in 1987. Following a series of negotiations on appropriate capital requirements, by 1988 the terms for the new regime stipulated that commercial banks should hold 8 percent of capital in reserves, split into "core capital" (of equity and disclosed reserves) and "supplementary capital" that could be represented by different forms of debt, including government securities.

Supplementary capital was risk-weighted, with OECD government securities receiving a zero risk rating, and with cash and commercial loans receiving a 100 percent risk weighting. As U.S. Treasury debt had the world's most active secondary market it became the most popular means for banks to make up their capital adequacy ratios to meet the terms of the Basle Accord. Critically, Japanese banks were the worse off in terms of the assets re-

---

sidiaries. They also point out that the change in corporate tax did not make the United States a low tax state, although other states followed the U.S. lead by lowering their corporate rates without closing similar loopholes. Rosanne Altshuler and R. Glenn Hubbard, "The Effect of the Tax Reform Act of 1986 on the Location of Assets in Financial Services Firms," paper presented at NBER Trans-Atlantic Public Economics Seminar, Gerzenzee, Switzerland, 22–24 May 2000, 4, 8.

49. Reinicke, *Banking, Politics*, 181.

50. This was also pointed out by the American Bankers' Association, who argued that the Japanese low capital adequacy ratios placed their banks at an advantage. See John D. Wagster, "Impact of the 1988 Basle Accord on International Banks," *Journal of Finance* 51, 4 (1996): 1322.

quired to meet the accord, because they had 2 to 4 percent capital adequacy ratios and had to meet the 8 percent set by the Basle Accord by 1992. Between 1988 and 1992 Japanese banks purchased $21 billion in U.S. Treasury debt. The Basle Accord therefore clearly enhanced the revenue for the second Reagan and Bush administrations' "super Keynesianism" at the expense of the world's commercial banks.[51]

Interestingly, the domestic implementation of the Basle Accord gave mortgage securities from FMAs only a 20 percent risk-weighting (non-FMA mortgages were given 50 percent), clearly encouraging their use by U.S. commercial banks and in line with the post-1985 legitimation of the U.S. financial reform nexus through positive state intervention.[52]

Freddie, Fannie, and Ginnie

If we look back at Figure 5.1, we can see the growth of FMAs, which securitize mortgages from institutions and provide, in return, more capital for new mortgages. By the mid-1990s, FMAs' assets were in excess of $1 trillion and represented, on occasion, 60 percent of U.S. Treasury debt. FMA assets increased more than sixfold during 1985 to 2000, making it the third-fastest-growing institution behind mutual funds and issuers of asset-backed securities (although FMAs have slightly more assets than mutual funds and 2.5 times more assets than issuers of asset-backed securities).[53]

As can be seen in Figure 5.2, the importance of FMAs' role as mortgage enhancers grew enormously during the 1985–2000 period as the role of S&Ls wound down. Figure 5.2 also demonstrates the increase in mortgage assets held by banks, although this is slightly deceptive since commercial banks keep one third to one half of their mortgages in securitization schemes, which allowed them to remove the asset from their balance sheet and from this graph. My calculations from U.S. *Flow of Funds* levels data indicate that, as a percentage of U.S. commercial banks' assets, mortgages increased from 21 percent in 1985 to 34 percent in 2000.[54] This massive

---

51. As also recognized by Thomas Oatley and Robert Nabors, "Redistributive Cooperation: Market Failures, Wealth Transfers and the Basle Accord," *International Organization* 52, 1 (1998): 45.

52. Mark D. Flood, "Basel Buckets and Loan Losses: Absolute and Relative Loan Underperformance at Banks and Thrifts," mimeo, Office of Thrift Supervision, Washington, D.C., 9 March 2001, 5.

53. Calculated from Board of Governors of the Federal Reserve, *Flow of Funds of the United States, 1985–1994: Annual Flows and Outstandings* (Washington, D.C.: U.S. Federal Reserve, 16 September 2002), 86, L.218; Board of Governors of the Federal Reserve, *Flow of Funds of the United States, 1995–2001: Annual Flows and Outstandings* (Washington, D.C.: U.S. Federal Reserve, 16 September 2002), 86, L.218.

54. Board of Governors of the Federal Reserve, *Flow of Funds of the United States, 1985–1994,* 61–72, L. 109–L.128; Board of Governors of the Federal Reserve, *Flow of Funds of the United States, 1995–2001,* 61–72, L. 109–L.128.

Figure 5.2 Key U.S. financial institutions' mortgage assets as a percentage of total home mortgage assets, 1985–2000.

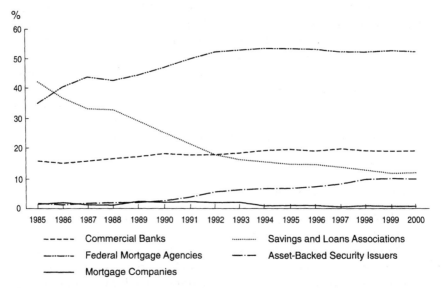

%

Source: Board of Governors of the Federal Reserve, *Flow of Funds of the United States, 1985–1994* (Washington, D.C.: U.S. Federal Reserve, 2002), 86, L.218; Board of Governors of the Federal Reserve, *Flow of Funds of the United States, 1995–2000* (Washington, D.C.: U.S. Federal Reserve, 2002), 86, L.218.

increase was a consequence of state-led incentives to increase their involvement with the owner-occupied residential mortgage market, an incentive permissible only with positive state intervention, as low-income lending became "no more and no-less profitable than non-low-income lending" for financial institutions.[55]

Positive state intervention was crucial to the growth of mortgage securitization in the 1985–2000 period, particularly through the emboldened role of the three siblings: Federal National Mortgage Association (Fannie Mae), the Government National Mortgage Association (Ginnie Mae) and the Federal Home Loan Mortgage Corporation (Freddie Mac).[56] The legitimation

55. David Malmquist, Fred Philips-Patrick, and Clifford Rossi, "The Economics of Low-Income Mortgage Lending," *Journal of Financial Services Research* 11, 1 (1997), 182.

56. The status of these agencies is referred to as public or quasi-public. Ginnie Mae is owned by the U.S. government, while Freddie Mac and Fannie Mae are sponsored by the U.S. government, although publicly traded companies owned by shareholders. Ginnie Mae's official mandate is to enhance the secondary mortgage market for mortgages guaranteed by the Federal Housing Administration (FHA) and the Veterans Administration (VA). Fannie Mae and Freddie Mac both operate in secondary markets for FHA, VA, and *conventional* mortgages. While Ginnie holds an official state guarantee to access Treasury funds in the case of default, Fannie and Freddie have an implicit guarantee. All of them are regulated by arms of the Department of Housing and Urban Development (HUD). "Wholesale" banks in the Federal Home Loan Bank system are also GSEs, but I focus here on the key institutions in the broader category of FMAs.

of these agencies to provide a social source of financial power differentiates the U.S. case from all others, including the United States in earlier periods.

The United States had attempted mortgage securitization during the late nineteenth century, with each attempt ending in disaster (including a loss of funds to English investors who invested heavily in mortgage schemes in the 1880s). These problems were repeated in the 1920s as real estate bond schemes failed, greatly contributing to the collapse of New York bond houses due to endemic problems in assessing the creditworthiness of borrowers without state intervention to improve monitoring.[57]

An attempt at positive state intervention for mortgage debt was made during the Great Depression under the Hoover administration, as it established the Federal Loan Bank system in 1932 and then the Homeowners' Loan Corporation (HOLC) in 1933, through which homeowners could borrow up to 80 percent of the house price. Within the first year of operation it received 40 percent of all mortgagor applications, and by 1936 (when the HOLC came to its demise) had one in ten residences encumbered to it, although the HOLC had to foreclose on 20 percent of its borrowers (compared to 2.6 percent in the private market) who were not government guaranteed. The National Housing Act of 1934 created residential mortgages with FHA insurance and, importantly, under Franklin D. Roosevelt, the National Mortgage Association of Washington was created in 1938 and soon renamed Federal National Mortgage Association (and known as Fannie Mae).

In addition to these institutional creations, the Fair Housing Act of 1968 provided a new legitimating context for credit and property politics, particularly its empowerment of the Department of Housing and Urban Development to investigate cases of racial, religious, sexual, and disability discrimination. This act was created in response to rioting following the assassination of Martin Luther King, Jr., and is actually Title VIII of the Civil Rights Act of 1968. This legislation was explicitly tied to the creation of Ginnie Mae (partitioned, like Adam's rib, from Fannie Mae) under the Housing Act of 1968 to expand credit for property access for LIGs.

In addition to these institutional changes that increased the legitimacy of the U.S. financial reform nexus in accordance with LIGs' economic social norms, the purpose of Fannie Mae was to provide a secondary market for FHA mortgages, and led to a sustainable system.[58] From 1970, Freddie Mac was chartered to provide a secondary market for mortgages, and permitted the packaging of mortgage-backed securities into a "pool" that was then sold to investors. Thus, from the early 1970s there was a means to transform mortgage debt into a source of capital to be used by U.S. financial interme-

57. Kenneth A. Snowden, "Mortgage Securitization in the United States: Twentieth Century Developments in Historical Perspective," in Michael D. Bordo and Richard Sylla, eds., *Anglo-American Financial Systems: Institutions and Markets in the Twentieth Century* (New York: New York University Salomon Center, 1995), 276–88.

58. Ibid., 291–93.

diaries and corporate America. The real importance of this change, however, did not occur until the 1980s with the blocking of the rentier shift.

In 1984 the passing of the Secondary Mortgage Market Enhancement Act
brought in a more active secondary market for mortgage-backed securities
with the intention of coupling increased homeownership with a means of
recycling capital through the U.S. financial system. The process was quite
simple for mortgage securitization, and its use by Ginnie Mae provides an
example. A bank provided a mortgage to several homeowners. The bank
then took this pool of capital income to Ginnie Mae for securitization, after
which the bank was free to lend the same amount of capital in new mortgages. Ginnie Mae accepted home loans (in 1998) with a value less than
$230,000 to be placed in a securitized pool and then placed the mortgages
in a trust against which mortgage-backed securities (MBS) can be drawn.
Mortgages were gathered together from different banks to increase the
pool's size and attractiveness to the corporate market.[59] As Ginnie Mae is
government guaranteed, corporate investors readily take up capital in the
form of an MBS. Freddie and Fannie operate in a similar "pass through"
manner but also buy mortgages from lenders and have an implicit guarantee that the U.S. government will intervene if default is possible. The important element here is the *perception* of state guarantee.

In 1981 the amount of securitized mortgages represented 4 percent of
mortgages in the United States. In the year following the Secondary Mortgage Market Enhancement Act the FMA siblings securitized one-quarter of
all mortgages in the United States, increasing to 69 percent of all mortgages
in 1989. As observed by Patric Hendershott: "In less than a decade, the agencies and their pass-throughs have gone from being a negligible factor to being the driving force in the market."[60] As clearly demonstrated in Figure 5.2,
this trend continued through the 1990s.

With regard to mortgage availability, the experience of the early 1980s led
the government from the mid-1980s onward to create an "efficient and eq-
uitable financial structure . . . making some attempt to legitimize itself in the
eyes of the public."[61] There was a shift in the provision of mortgages in the
early 1990s which continued through the decade as mortgages became
more accessible to LIGs.[62] In 1988 the required down payment for first-time
homeowners came down to 15 percent of the property value, and by the
mid-1990s LIGs required only 3 percent of the property value with HUD approval. This provided a dramatic contrast with Japan, where the average

---

59. FDIC, *Managing the Crisis*, 414.
60. Hendershott, "Housing Finance," 70.
61. Ann Meyerson, "The Changing Structure of Housing Finance in the United States," in
Sarah Rosenberry and Chester Hartman, eds., *Housing Issues of the 1990s* (New York: Praeger,
1989), 164–65.
62. Irina Barakova, Raphael Bostic, Paul Calem, and Susan Wachter, "Does Credit Quality
Matter for Homeownership?" *Journal of Housing Economics* 12, 4 (2003).

down payment during the 1985–2000 period was 40 percent (as discussed in the next chapter).[63]

Importantly, in 1991 the passing of the Federal Housing Enterprises Financial Safety and Soundness Act (FHEFSSA) obligated Freddie Mac and Fannie Mae to cater more to institutions lending to LIGs, particularly those at the lower end of the wage scale. In the same year the outstanding mortgage-backed securities were $1 trillion (total U.S. corporate debt was $1.4 trillion), with Ginnie Mae, Fannie Mae, and Freddie Mac issuing 90 percent of all new mortgage-backed securities.[64] In the early 1980s the bulk of mortgages within the U.S. financial system went to those in the middle- and upper-income groups, while in the 1990s it went to those in the lower- and middle-income groups. From 1991 to 1993 there was a turnaround of nearly 50 percent in mortgage originations for low-income groups. Furthermore, if we isolate lending by racial categories, there is a 60 percent increase from 1991 to 1993 for African Americans seeking mortgages.[65] By 1993, commercial banks were placing nearly 40 percent of their mortgages through the FMA siblings, reflecting their confidence in the system and increasingly becoming providers of mortgages for LIGs.[66]

Cautious Committees and the Informal Fed

We noted earlier that the key inhibitor to financial reform in the United States is often thought to be the fragmented political system. As suggested above, the response to the S&L and commercial bank crises was actually quite rapid as the main casualties were dealt with by 1988. Some other reforms were slow but at the same time socially progressive. As is well known, Clinton's electoral victory over George H. W. Bush was based on the regeneration of the U.S. domestic economy, contrasting Bush's short-lived war games with Iraq with "It's the Economy, Stupid." During the Clinton era, Democratic control of the presidency and Congress in the first two years led to reforms that increased the legitimacy of the U.S. financial reform nexus for LIGs according to their economic social norms. While there was slow reform of the Glass-Steagall Act, innovations that emerged from the banking community and the extent of mortgage securitization provided a real benefit to U.S. financial intermediaries operating in the international financial order. It was only once lobby groups could be satisfied, and a strong com-

63. Poterba, "Public Policy," 242.
64. Snowden, "Mortgage Securitization," 267.
65. Douglas D. Evanoff and Lewis M. Segal, "CRA and Fair Lending Regulations: Resulting Trends in Mortgage Lending," *Economic Perspectives* 20, 6 (1996): 33–37.
66. See also Allan D. Brunner and William B. English, "Profits and Balance Sheet Developments at U.S. Commercial Banks in 1992," *Federal Reserve Bulletin* 79, 7 (1993): 655; English and Reid, "Profits and Balance Sheet," 487.

munity element placed into legislation, that reform was permitted. I begin with the informal regulation of the Fed.

And what better place to start than with the promises of Alan Greenspan. As Chairman of the Fed, Greenspan promised that the repeal of Glass-Steagall was "one of the Board's highest priorities."[67] Repeatedly throughout the 1980s and early 1990s, congressional committees in both chambers discussed, without success, the reform of Glass-Steagall (which was permitted in 1999 with the Financial Services Modernization Act). The literature on this subject points to the lobbying of the American Bankers' Association (ABA) for reform and the Securities Industry Association against reform.[68] Moreover, the McFadden Act of 1927 that prevented interstate banking was not reformed until 1994, despite persistent attempts since the early 1980s. The frustrated reforms occurred during a time when U.S. banks were disappearing from Top 20 lists of the World's Biggest Banks (in the late 1980s, Japanese banks represented all of the Top 20). For many commentators, the U.S. banking system was suffocated by regulatory "gridlock." Despite such fears of extinction, banks were actually growing in power due to informal regulation by the Fed and the growth of asset-backed securitization use by U.S. banks. Indeed, by 1990 the "functional frontiers" of Glass-Steagall were relatively meaningless.[69]

Despite the Glass-Steagall restrictions that prevented commercial banks from engaging in investment activities, in 1987 the Fed permitted Citicorp, Bankers Trust, and J. P. Morgan to underwrite and deal commercial paper on the grounds that this form of activity could not exceed 10 percent of its trading capital. Furthermore, on the grounds that permitting some banks to enter investment banking would allow more Americans access to financial markets through lower brokerage costs, the Fed permitted J. P. Morgan in 1991 to underwrite an initial public offering (IPO) on the stock market, the first bank to do so since the Great Depression. The growth of securitization which—I emphasize here—provides the capacity to provide capital to enhance U.S. international financial capacity, while removing it from a commercial banks' balance sheet, led J. P. Morgan furiously to engage in securities trading. As a result, by November 1991 it had become the seventh largest underwriter in the U.S. market, while four of the top five global underwriters of securities were U.S.-based.[70] Following J. P. Morgan's success the Fed, in conjunction with the FDIC, allowed more commercial banks to enter securities markets, but, importantly, only those that could meet a 10

67. Alan Greenspan, "Innovation and Regulation of Banks in the 1990s," *Federal Reserve Bulletin* 74, 12 (1988): 786.
68. The lobbying activities of various groups are detailed in William D. Coleman, *Financial Services, Globalization, and Domestic Policy Change* (Houndsmill: Macmillan, 1996), 166.
69. As also argued by Michael Moran, *The Politics of the Financial Services Revolution: The U.S.A, UK and Japan* (London: Macmillan, 1991), 139.
70. Reinicke, *Banking, Politics*, 118.

percent capital adequacy standard that led to greater investment in U.S. Treasury debt and FMA mortgage-backed securities.

In addition, in the early 1990s the Fed permitted U.S. financial intermediaries of any description to borrow against the Fed as long as they used U.S. Treasury debt as collateral, providing a source of revenue for the U.S. Treasury. As corporate America turned increasingly to invest in securities such as FMA mortgage-backed securities and needed commercial banks less, commercial banks not only entered the securities industry with the Fed's permission but increased their stock of residential securitized mortgages (as mentioned above).[71] Following the success in these markets, the Fed allowed commercial banks in 1996 to increase their securities trading to total one-quarter of their activities. Rather than gridlocked, the U.S. financial system was undergoing a process of institutional innovation that also supported LIGs' wants. Such change was also profitable, as by the mid-1990s U.S. commercial banks were recording their best profits since the 1950s.[72]

One reform pushed through in 1994 was the Riegle-Neal Interstate Banking Efficiency Act (RNIBEA), which revised the McFadden Act of 1927 and permitted interstate banking as long as one organization could not control more than 10 percent of the national bank deposits.[73] The emphasis on the RNIBEA has been the efficiency component of the Riegle-Neal Act. It is less frequently noted that the act had a twin that was needed to push either both or neither of them through. And this twin was socially progressive. The Riegle Community Development and Regulatory Improvement Act of 1994 (RCDRIA) provided Community Development Financial Institutions and the Home Owner Equity Protection Act (HOEPA), which required regulators to impose premiums on any financial intermediaries offering sub-prime mortgage rates, and obliged all financial institutions to disclose full information on mortgage availability and conditions.[74] The RCDRIA followed up on the Clinton administration's aim to intervene positively to permit LIGs access to cheap credit for low-income housing ($382 million was provided for this purpose in the same year as RCDRIA).

The coupling of these acts is important in understanding U.S. financial reform, which was officially slow but in accordance with economic social

71. Gary A. Dymski, "How to Rebuild the U.S. Financial Structure: Level the Playing Field and Renew the Social Contract," in Gary A. Dymski, Gerard Epstein, and Robert Pollin, eds., *Transforming the U.S. Financial System: Equity and Efficiency for the 21st Century* (Armonk: M. E. Sharpe, 1993), 114.

72. Compare English and Reid, "Profits and Balance Sheet," 483, with William R. Nelson and Brian K. Reid, "Profits and Balance Sheet Developments at U.S. Commercial Banks in 1995," *Federal Reserve Bulletin* 82, 6 (1996): 484.

73. U.S. Congress, "The Riegle-Neal Interstate Banking and Branching Efficiency Act of 1994," H. R. 3841, 103rd Congress, Second Session, 1994.

74. Any interest rate which was 10 percent above the Treasury rate was classified as subprime. See U.S. Congress, "The Riegle Community Development and Regulatory Improvement Act of 1994," H. R. 3474, 103rd Congress, Second Session, 1994.

norms. I attribute this to the committee process when the Democratic Party held the House and Senate. During the 1985–2000 period, financial reforms that made it through had community-led concerns consistently "piggybacked" onto legislation to ensure its passage due to contestation from groups such as the NCRC, NPA, and the NFHA.[75] And regardless of what a cynic might argue about self-interests involved in "piggy-backing" social concerns onto financial reforms, the crucial point here is that this element led to increased credit access and political representation for LIGs, and with greater legitimacy for the U.S. financial reform nexus. In short, while the committee process undeniably slowed the process of financial reform in the United States, it was to the benefit of the legitimation of the U.S. financial reform nexus. The system reflected contestation that aided policy changes that emphasized redistribution and the propagation of economic social norms on access to credit and property and the use of financial innovations as everyday conventions.

Redlined Communities and Bank Concentration

Banks tend to ignore LIGs due to problems in assessing their creditworthiness, or due to political pressures to keep LIGs in an inferior position for the protection of rentiers (such as the positional premium in the English case). I have demonstrated that the massive expansion of FMAs post-1985, aided by the process of securitization engaged by banks, assisted increased levels of homeownership for LIGs. In addition, the United States played an even more positive interventionist role in low-income minorities' access to credit and property, as well as lowering their tax burdens, through the Community Reinvestment Act (CRA) of 1977.[76]

The CRA encourages banks to lend to LIGs. Put in place during Jimmy Carter's presidency (1977–81) from pressure from advocacy groups (especially the NPA) to stop "urban decline" and expand civil rights, the CRA requires banks to lend to low-income areas and not to engage in "redlining." The practice of redlining was where banks would accept deposits from a community but not lend back to them because of their low socioeconomic status, or for other reasons such as ethnicity. Banks would therefore figuratively, or literally, draw a red line around an area and disable it from credit access.[77] The qualitative importance of the CRA in the United States cannot

75. Interviews with staff from U.S. Federal Reserve, Washington, D.C., and staff from the National Community Reinvestment Coalition, Washington, D.C., November 2001.
76. While my focus so far has been on LIGs in general, this section deals explicitly with low-income earners.
77. Senator William Proxmire, sponsor of the CRA, Congressional Record, daily edition, 6 June 1977, S. 8958. See also the review of the first decade of the CRA in Robert C. Art, "Social Responsibility in Credit Decisions: The Community Reinvestment Act One Decade Later," *Pacific Law Journal* July (1987).

be overstated, if only because it repeatedly came under attack from banking interests and was repeatedly defended—and its powers expanded—by community groups and Democrats during the 1985–2000 period.

While Democrat dominance in the House and Senate from 1987 to 1994 led to a series of financial reforms that were socially progressive (including the RCDRIA's boost to the CRA), the entry of a hardening Republican House and Senate from 1995 (with the emergence of Newt Gingrich and his "Contract with America") provided a challenge to the legitimation of the U.S. financial reform nexus. Certainly there is a shift after 1995 represented even in the titles of financial reforms bills, with a change from "community development" to "regulatory relief."[78] Included in such reforms was an argument against state intervention in the U.S. financial system, which, according to Republican interests in Congress and the ABA, provided a tax on commercial banks that was a consequence of the "strong impulse to tar banks with the same brush as the S&Ls," making "credit less available to those who need it," and that the regulation was unfairly led, "aimed at redistributing resources [from commercial banks] to low-income neighborhoods."[79] These criticisms may have some financial, if not moral, footing. For example, one study of banks' tax burdens argued that when changes to TRA '86, the Tax Reform Act of 1993's increased corporate taxes, federal deposit insurance, Basle Accord provisions, and community-development regulation were totaled, the effective tax rates paid by U.S. commercial banks rose from 24 percent in 1986 to 41 percent in 1995.[80] As a consequence the American Bankers' Association and the Independent Bankers' Association (IBA) lobbied for regulatory relief through the weakening of the CRA but failed, at least up to the end of the Clinton administration.[81]

At the other end of the spectrum, collective anxiety about bank mergers and the prospect of "financial supermarkets" ignoring LIGs led to agitation for socially progressive financial reform.[82] The key progressive change was a shift in the assessment of credit going to LIGs from a process-based to a performance-based criteria. Rather than meeting with regulators and re-

---

78. See, for example, U.S. Senate Committee on Banking, Housing and Urban Affairs, "Economic Growth and Regulatory Paperwork Reduction Act of 1995," S. 650, 104th Congress, First Session, 1995; or the U.S. House of Representatives Committee on Banking and Financial Services, "The Financial Institutions Regulatory Relief Act of 1995," H. R. 1362, 104th Congress, First Session, 1995.

79. See, for example, Jeffrey M. Lacker, "Neighborhoods and Banking," *Economic Quarterly* 81, 2 (1995): 35–38.

80. Kuprianov, "Tax Disincentives," 67. TRA '93 increased the corporate tax rate to 35 percent on income above $10 million, as well as disallowing the tax shields mentioned earlier.

81. See the testimony of James Culberson Jr. of the ABA and Richard L. Mount of the IBA to the U.S. House of Representatives Committee on Banking and Financial Services, "The Financial Institutions Regulatory Relief Act of 1995," 63–93.

82. In 1996 alone, 359 banks were merged across state lines as commercial banks took advantage of the Riegle-Neal Interstate Banking Efficiency Act of 1994. See OECD, *OECD Economic Surveys, 1995–1996, United States* (Paris: OECD, 1996), 83.

viewing minutes from director's meetings, the CRA now forced banks to open their books to regulators and demonstrate that they were sufficiently lending to low-income groups and minorities.[83] The process of CRA accountability was overseen by groups such as the NCRC and NPA,[84] which raised funds to act as independent auditors and assess federal regulators' implementation of the CRA.[85] Other advocacy groups, such as local CDCs, continued to directly target errant financial institutions through the media and the courts (primarily on racial discrimination grounds) while NCRC and NPA formalized their involvement in the monitoring of financial institutions' performance in accordance with now rigorous economic social norms. Furthermore, groups like the NFHA continued to scrutinize HUD performance. The HUD, in turn, paid close attention to the behavior of FMAs, particularly through the establishment of the Office of Federal Housing Enterprise Oversight in 1992, which was charged with overseeing Freddie Mac and Fannie Mae. In this way the "checks and balances" of the U.S. system ensured the direction of credit to LIGs.

In addition to the change in assessment of the CRA, banks were required not only to open their books but use their expertise to assist with the training of local communities in financial knowledge. Post-1995, the development of the "Community Express" initiative led to a government guaranteed sponsorship of financial education for business start-ups in low-income areas, whereby a commercial bank would review a business's books on a fortnightly basis in return for additional CRA approval. Furthermore, the new CRA regulations allowed for a bank to decrease the frequency of the triannual tests by developing community programs on affordable housing. In particular, the new CRA regulations were arranged with banks such that they could rise to an "outstanding" rating if they engaged in extensive local community borrowing.[86] This was important for the banks because after 1995 they required CRA approval to engage in merger activity or to gain permission from the Fed to engage in insurance activities. The CRA therefore holds the "normative idea that compensation should be made for past in-

83. Under the provisions of the CRA, banks with more than $250 million in assets faced a lending test, service test, and investment test according to the information disclosed by applicants for loans and by actual recipients of loans. National Community Reinvestment Coalition (NCRC), "The New Community Reinvestment Act (CRA) Regulation," mimeo, Washington, D.C., 20 May 1997.
84. The NCRC formed out of sixteen community organizations, including ACORN and the Coalition Against Redlining, under the direction of Joe Kennedy. Under the direction of John Taylor since the mid-1990s, by 2000 it included 800 community organizations nationwide.
85. Representation by such groups in Congress was consistent throughout the 1980s and 1990s. For an early example, see the testimony given by Pauline Wilson, chairperson of the Coalition Against Redlining, at the U.S. Senate Committee on Banking, Housing, and Urban Affairs, "Competitive Equality in the Financial Services Industry, Parts I and II," S. Hrg. 98–629, 98th Congress, Second Session, 1984. See also Sidney, *Unfair Housing,* 163–66.
86. Interview with staff from NCRC, and with staff from Office of Thrift Supervision, November 2001.

equities . . . [by permitting the] transfer [of] resources to precisely the same groups that the earlier discriminatory policies transferred resources *from*— nearly creditworthy low-income home-owners."[87]

According to Fed data on the enforcement of CRA provisions, the number of home loans undertaken by minority groups increased following the emboldening of the CRA. While in 1993 loans to racial "minorities" were 16 percent compared to 84 percent for "non-minorities," in 1997 "minorities" received 21 percent compared to 79 percent for "non-minorities." This 5 percent increase over a four-year period reflected the regulatory power of the CRA in encouraging banks to demonstrate publicly that they did not racially discriminate. In sum, access to mortgages for low-income borrowers increased by 31 percent between 1993 and 1997. For low-income minority-group borrowers, the increase over the same period was 53 percent.[88]

There is evidence to suggest that the CRA is substantially linked to the role of FMAs in enchancing mortgage credit.[89] One study found that most providers of mortgage credit to low-income African American families used Fannie Mae to gain access to credit and add to the stock of capital within the U.S. financial system and, therefore, U.S. international financial capacity.[90] It has been estimated that lending under CRA provisions from 1992 to 2000 amounted to just under $1 trillion, outlining the importance of the regulation not only for social equity but the generation of credit within the U.S. financial system.[91] As a consequence of CRA strengthening, and community activism, U.S. financial institutions came under social scrutiny more than other sectors of corporate America.[92]

Pension Funds, Mutual Funds, and Progressive Taxation

While accounting for a dip following the stock market crash of 1987 and the recession in the early 1990s pre-Clinton, the financial wealth of U.S. fami-

---

87. Lacker, "Neighborhoods and Banking," 24.

88. Compared to an 18 percent rise for borrowers with over 120 percent of median income. See Robert B. Avery, Raphael W. Bostic, Paul S. Calem, and Glenn B. Canner, "Trends in Home Purchase Lending: Consolidation and the Community Reinvestment Act," *Federal Reserve Bulletin* 85, 2 (1999): 88.

89. Evanoff and Segal, "CRA and Fair Lending Regulations," 44–46.

90. Home ownership for African-Americans increased from 41.7 percent in 1989 to 46.3 percent in 1998. Edward N. Wolff, "Recent Trends in Wealth Ownership, 1983–1998," Working Paper No. 300 (Annandale-on-Hudson, N.Y.: Jerome Levy Economics Institute of Bard College, April 2000), 24, Table 7.

91. Testimony of John E. Taylor, President of the NCRC, to House Committee on Banking and Financial Services, Hearing on HR10, Financial Services Act 02 1999, 11 February 1999, ⟨http://financialservices.house.gov/banking/21199tay.htm⟩.

92. Thomas T. Holyoke, "Community Mobilization and Credit: The Impact of Nonprofits and Social Capital on Community Reinvestment Lending," *Social Science Quarterly* 85, 1 (2004): 202.

lies increased by 38 percent over the 1983 to 1998 period.[93] Undoubtedly most of this wealth gain went to wealthier rather than poorer households and raises an important question: if the United States increased its financial assets far and above the needs of the "real" productive economy, and people became more dependent on dividends from investments, then why did the United States not become a socially regressive rentier state?[94] As my argument is that the United States blocked a rentier shift post-1985, increased financial wealth may seem a little inconsistent with this logic since rentiers are by definition those who gain rents from "non-productive," "unearned," or "passive" income. However, there are two points to keep in mind here. First, increased investment in broad-based financial institutions like pension funds and mutual funds did add to the "productive" financing of corporate America domestically and internationally.[95] Increasingly this investment came mostly from the middle-income groups but also, increasingly, from the lower-middle income groups during the 1985–2000 period.

It is simply incorrect that financial elites are the only ones to profit from securitization and increased investment in mutual funds. U.S. households in the middle income brackets account for the bulk of mutual fund investment and are more likely to use mutual funds than those households earning over $100,000. Although there is a perception that mutual funds were only for the rich, over one-third of mutual funds' assets come from people on or below median household income.[96] According to the Fed, LIGs used mutual funds precisely because of the costs of investing in the stock or bond markets (brokerage fees, for example).[97]

Mutual funds increased sevenfold during the period under study and their growth was to a significant extent due to the use of retirement accounts. Individual Retirement Accounts (IRAs) were introduced under the first Reagan administration. During the 1985–2000 period, IRA assets increasingly went into mutual funds, with only 17 percent of them invested in mutual funds in 1985 compared to 49 percent in 1999. While TRA '81 allowed people to invest $2,000 per annum, with the returns holding a tax-

93. Wolff, "Recent Trends," 3.
94. In comparison, gross fixed capital formation only increased 2 percent between 1986 and 1996. Calculated from OECD, *OECD Economic Surveys, 1995–1996, United States*, vii; OECD, *OECD Economic Surveys, 1991/2, United States* (Paris: OECD, 1992), vii.
95. A contrary view is provided in Adam Harmes, *Unseen Power: How Mutual Funds Threaten the Political and Economic Wealth of Nations* (Toronto: Stoddart Publishing, 2001).
96. Household incomes below $49,000 have a greater share of mutual fund assets than those in the $50,000 to $74,000 bracket or those households with above $75,000, suggesting that mutual funds are used by the lower-middle classes to a massive extent. Obviously investors in mutual funds in this bracket are clustered toward the top of the bracket rather than households earning less than $25,000 (who account for 15 percent of mutual fund investment). Investment Company Institute, *Mutual Fund Shareholders* (Washington, D.C.: Investment Company Institute, 1996), 16, 23, 33. The Investment Company Institute is the U.S. national association of the investment company industry.
97. Engen and Lehnert, "Mutual Funds," 801.

free status, TRA '86 removed the tax-free status of IRAs for people on high incomes. The popularity of IRAs, particularly in the form of "401 (k)" accounts, continued regardless. Fifty-five percent of U.S. working households held some form of IRA in 1999, growing from 11.9 percent in 1984 and 30.7 percent in 1994.[98] One study suggests that 65 percent of people with 401 (k)s were in the lower-middle income group and account for 48 percent of the wealth within the system. Furthermore, this same study argues that while there was a serious decline in savings rates during the 1985–2000 period (from an average 9 percent of income from 1950 to 1985 to 0.5 percent of income in 2000), the use of IRAs in association with mutual funds led to significant new savings among LIGs for their retirement.[99]

Most of the investment from mutual funds, including through IRAs, went largely into U.S. corporate financing during the period. While mutual funds provided the capital for 20 percent of all traded stock in the United States, 63 percent of IRAs were invested in domestic equity.[100] Mutual funds and pension funds are not rentier-based because they do not lead to the extraction of rents from LIGs to prop up financial elites.

The figures presented above on LIGs' involvement with mutual funds are based on all pre-tax figures. If post-tax figures are taken into account to assess what means are available for LIGs relative to their wealthy counterparts, then our story becomes even cheerful. Under Clinton, the Tax Reform Act of 1993 (TRA '93) increased the top personal rate from 31 percent to 39.6 percent and created a new 36 percent tax bracket for upper-level incomes.[101] TRA '93 and the 1997 Taxpayer Relief Act also lowered the income tax rate for low-incomes and put in place a fourfold increase in tax subsidies to very-low income groups (permitting a subsidy of $3,756 for those below $15,000). Furthermore, a Republican-led charge for the re-emergence of the tax shields for banks, which were removed by TRA '86, was vetoed by Clinton.[102]

Direct taxation went up, not down. After examination of the statistics, there is no doubt that U.S. taxes on income and personal profits increased significantly during the 1985–2000 period. Calculated as a percentage of GDP, the OECD average increase in direct taxes on income and profits from 1985 to 1999 was 11 percent. The U.S. figure increased by 20 percent, while Japan decreased by 35 percent (which was partially compensated with so-

---

98. Ibid., 802; earlier figures from Investment Company Institute, "U.S. Household Ownership of Mutual Funds in 1999," *Fundamentals: Investment Company Institute Research in Brief* 8, 5 (1999): 1.
99. See Gary V. Engelhardt, "Have 401 (k)s Raised Household Saving? Evidence from the Health and Retirement Study," Social and Economic Dimensions of an Aging Population Research Paper No. 33 (Hamilton: SEDAP Research Program, McMaster University, October 2000), 14, 26–27. His answer is yes for low-income earners.
100. Engen and Lehnert, "Mutual Funds," 804.
101. Steuerle, "Tax Policy," 5–6.
102. Altshuler and Hubbard, "Effect of the Tax Reform Act," 13.

cially regressive consumption taxes, as discussed in the following chapter).[103] Capital gains tax as a proportion of all taxes collected in the United States increased from 2.5 percent to 3.8 percent over the period, while taxes on goods used more frequently by LIGs such as alcohol and tobacco decreased from 1.6 to 0.9 percent of total tax revenue between 1985 and 1999.[104] Thus while financial wealth for the rich increased at a faster pace, LIGs' tax burdens did not increase and their credit and property access grew. The very poor, however, were very much left behind.

The Grassroots versus Gramm

In 1990 the biggest commercial bank in the U.S. financial system was J. P. Morgan, with over $8 billion in market capitalization. By the end of the decade the biggest U.S. commercial bank was Citigroup with $144 billion in market capitalization. As stated earlier, by the mid-1990s, commercial banks in the United States could earn a quarter of their revenues from equity underwriting and could sell bonds. The Financial Services Modernization Act reformed the Glass-Steagall Act and provided commercial banks with an expanded range of activities under the regulatory watch of the Fed.

The concentration of assets in the commercial banking sector should come as no surprise. As we saw in England and, to a lesser extent, Germany, banking concentration occurs under periods of intense financial internationalization. In the United States, the number of banks dropped dramatically as mergers between banks flourished—from 18,700 in the mid-1970s, to 14,500 in the mid-1980s, to just over 8,000 by the end of the decade. Banking concentration was dramatic. While in 1985 the top 100 banks in the United States owned 52 percent of the industry's assets, the top 100 owned 75 percent of the industry's assets in 2000.[105]

Despite arguments about regulatory gridlock in the United States financial system in the early 1990s, and the need for risk-based capital adequacy regulations and nationwide banking, all this was formalized by 1999 with the GLBA.[106] The GLBA repealed the 1933 Glass-Steagall Act and the 1956 Douglas Bank Holding Company Act and permitted the formation of bank holding companies under the supervision of the Fed. These bank holding

103. OECD, *OECD Revenue Statistics, 1965–2000* (Paris: OECD, 2001), 19, Table B, 142–43, Table 56, 174–76, Table 71.
104. Ibid., 174–76, Table 71. This accounts for both federal and state taxes on alcohol and tobacco.
105. Bill Bassett and Tom Brady, "What Drives the Persistent Competitiveness of Small Banks," unpublished study, U.S. Federal Reserve, Washington, D.C., May 2002, 32–35, Charts 2–6.
106. Cerny, "Gridlock and Decline," 429–33.

companies could have branches across the United States and could engage in retail and commercial banking and also in securities underwriting.

In the discussions for the GLBA, a Republican-led movement, with strong, if qualified, support from the ABA, emerged to remove redlining provisions from the new regulatory framework. In the hearings Ralph Nader, among others, expressed concern that it would diminish the role of the CRA, which had "raised the hopes of citizens in areas where there was little hope and has brought untold numbers of volunteers into grass roots community efforts."[107] Similarly, John Taylor from the NCRC argued that the Republican-led changes would be "like rolling back the GI Bill or Social Security because too many veterans had received higher education or too many senior citizens had escaped poverty."[108] The NPA and NFHA also petitioned and lobbied to prevent a dilution of the act. The NPA, in particular, outlined how the CRA could be improved. Importantly, the proposed changes were blocked by Democrats in the committee process, who threatened to abolish the entire bill should the CRA weaken as a consequence.

The CRA stayed in the GLBA and was applied to all areas of bank holding companies' activities, although with a "sunshine requirement" to lighten the regulatory burden of the CRA on small financial institutions (assets less than $250 million; this is discussed further in the Epilogue). Furthermore, any banks with a CRA non-satisfactory rating were prevented from engaging in insurance and merger activities.[109] For example, in 2000 the merging of New England Bank Fleet with First Boston was blocked by the Fed until an agreement was made that the merged institution would provide one billion dollars in new loans to LIGs under CRA conditions.[110] The Fed argued in 1999 that, as a consequence of the emboldened CRA, lending to "lower-income and minority borrowers and neighborhoods" would increase.[111] By the mid-1990s U.S. banks were lending more than in 1985 and, due to their integration into the FHLB system and need to conform to CRA regulations, were lending more to LIGs than ever.[112]

During the signing of the GLBA, Texan Republican senator Phil Gramm argued, "We are here today to repeal Glass-Steagall because we have learned that government is not the answer. We have learned that freedom and competition are the answers."[113] Given the evidence presented here, Gramm was

107. Testimony of Ralph Nader to House Committee on Banking and Financial Services, 11 February 1999, 4.
108. John Taylor from the NCRC in "NCRC Reiterates Support."
109. Sections 48, 714 and 715 of the GLBA. See NCRC, *Advanced CRA Manual* (Washington, D.C.: NCRC, 2000), 2: 5–6; 4: 3–4.
110. Interview with staff from NCRC, November 2001.
111. Avery, Bostic, Calem, and Canner, "Trends in Home Purchase Lending," 85.
112. Bassett and Brady, "What Drives the Persistent Competitiveness," 32–35, Charts 2–6.
113. Available from Banking Senate Committee at ⟨http://banking.senate.gov/prel99/1112gbl.htm⟩.

clearly incorrect. Rather than winding back the role of the state, the GLBA extended it through its inclusion of the Federal Home Loan Bank Modernization Act of 1999 (FHLBMA).

The FHLBMA, which New York Republican senator Alphonse D'Amato railed against as "big government," encouraged the development of Community Financial Institutions (CFI) with less than $500 million in assets to join the system. The intent of this regulatory reform was to protect community banks during a period of "mega-mergers" in the financial services industry.[114] More broadly, the GLBA gave more powers to the FHLB system, which had more assets than Citicorp and issued more overnight debt than the U.S. Treasury in 2000, to issue mortgage credit to LIGs.

Due to state intervention through FMAs, mortgage credit increased dramatically during the 1990s to LIGs. Residential mortgages were of the lowest risk among all types of investments in the United States in the late 1990s and, as stated earlier, FMA mortgage-backed securities were useful for banks wishing to meet their Basle Accord obligations. Thus, while in 1990 *low-income* groups received 18.5 percent of all mortgage loans, they received 30.7 percent by 1999.[115] As LIGs gained access to mortgage credit with the assistance of CRA regulations and FMAs, the latter FMAs who saw their role, in part, as a "counter-point to the mega-mergers problem," imposed greater restrictions on banks that sought to acquire loans at sub-prime rates. Furthermore, studies for the Department of Housing and Urban Development revealed that for the 1990s, many minority group loan applicants would not have received loans without a) the applicant's awareness of Fair Housing legislation (more than half of adult Americans know of the legislation across income groups); b) the actual enforcement of the legislation; and c) the HUD's own scrutinizing of FMAs' practices.[116]

The GLBA assisted the rejuvenation of local finance within the United States by permitting S&Ls to join the FHLB system and allowing small commercial banks greater access to securities trading. By the late 1990s small banks were growing more rapidly than large banks thanks to their greater involvement with mortgage securitization. The GLBA imposed the Basle Ac-

114. Susan Hoffmann and Mark Cassell, "What Are the Federal Home Loan Banks Up To? Emerging Views of Purpose among Institutional Leadership," *Public Administration Review* 62, 4 (2002), 466–467.
115. African Americans' and Hispanic Americans' access to mortgages increased during the 1990s from 10 percent of all mortgages to over 16 percent. Testimony of the National Community Reinvestment Coalition, before the U.S. Senate Committee on Banking, Housing, and Urban Affairs, "Predatory Mortgage Lending: The Problem, Impact and Responses," S. 2405, 106th Congress, Second Session, Friday, 27 July 2001, 10–11.
116. Margery Austin Turner et al., *All Other Things Being Equal: A Paired Testing of Mortgage Lending Institutions* (Washington, D.C.: The Urban Institute, 2002); Martin D. Abravanel and Mary K. Cunningham, *How Much Do We Know? Public Awareness of the Nation's Fair Housing Laws* (Washington, D.C.: The Urban Institute, 2002).

cord on S&Ls and small banks to increase their use of Treasury debt and FMA mortgage-backed securities.[117]

In fact, in 1999 the funding of FMAs was equal to 103 percent of Treasury debt. A good proportion of this debt (28 percent) was financed by foreign investors, particularly Japanese and, increasingly, Chinese investors.[118] Funding by FMAs consistently represented between 18 and 24 percent of all federal government lending from 1990 to 2000.[119] At the same time, foreign investment in Treasury bonds increased from 14 percent in 1985 to 29 percent in 1999, alongside an increase in domestic household investment in Treasury bonds from 16 percent in 1985 to 23 percent in 1999.[120] Accordingly, more capital was in the system from foreign and safe domestic sources. Quite simply, the United States was able to increase its revenue to redistribute it effectively for the provision of credit to LIGs.

Conclusion: High Legitimation of the Financial Reform Nexus

Toward the close of the twentieth century the United States blocked a 1980–84 rentier shift and positively intervened post-1985 into its financial reform nexus for LIGs. By doing so it broadened and deepened its domestic pool of capital and international financial capacity. To make this possible, the U.S. government and financial regulators made changes across the financial reform nexus that enabled LIGs to access their social wants in accordance with economic social norms of creditworthiness to attain property and entrepreneurship. When the state did not do so, the reaction from U.S. LIGs was prominent.

Crucially, in the U.S. case I find that there is no significant or systematic extraction of rents from LIGs to support rentiers' financial interests as in the other cases under study. Furthermore, following the radical changes engendered by the 1980–84 rentier shift, institutional change in the U.S. case was most certainly incremental and accompanied by change in economic social norms at all times. Such activity relied on financial innovations becoming everyday conventions with state support. A punctuated equilibrium model, material or ideational, is therefore of little use here because it fails to capture the everyday dimension. Nor can we explain the United States

---

117. Interview with staff from Office of Thrift Supervision, November 2001.
118. In 1999, 51 percent of government sponsored enterprises and federally related mortgage pool securities were American household investors, 28 percent foreign investors and 21 percent American commercial banks. D'Arista, "Is a Mortgage Bubble," 1–2.
119. Ibid., 2–3.
120. Calculated from Board of Governors of the Federal Reserve, *Flow of Funds of the United States, 1985–1994*, 79; Board of Governors of the Federal Reserve, *Flow of Funds of the United States, 1995–2001*, 79; OECD, *OECD Economic Surveys, 1995–1996, United States*, 46.

through a conventional tale about "state capacity" because forms of state intervention are not sufficiently differentiated.

If we account for the massively increased role of the FMAs in enhancing mortgage loans to the LIGs, the fact that over one-third of mutual funds are held by those on median income and below, and the immense social importance of CRA provisions, then we have a good case for stating that LIGs play a causally significant role in supporting U.S. international financial capacity. By 2000 the FMAs were hailed in the United States for providing LIGs with increased access to housing and for permitting the "transformation of the local mortgage loan market into the global securities giant it is today."[121] FMAs presented a clear example of U.S. positive state intervention for LIGs that gained a high degree of legitimacy and enhanced international financial capacity as a consequence. The United States was also able to influence, to a large extent, the regulatory structure and normative environment in a manner that was highly legitimate domestically. The implementation of the Basle Accord as a consequence of the ILSA and U.S. public rejection of rentier activity is the exemplar.

The extent of U.S. positive state intervention has not been generally recognized in political economy literature, where the prevailing view is that the United States forces change on other states in the international financial order, and relies on its international power as a substitute for its weak domestic capacities. However, in the U.S. case the state was able to gain a high degree of legitimacy from LIGs in part because financial reforms were slowed or blocked until they could be "piggy backed" with a broader social interest under the scrutiny of advocacy groups. Seen this way, the U.S.'s apparently fragmented and gridlocked system actually provides room for the contestation of financial reforms and, through this process, allows redistribution that then propagates economic social norms on attaining credit and the use of financial innovations.

I do not agree, therefore, with the view that the "idea of business had completely triumphed" in the United States to the extent that state intervention was effectively minimized and Democratic innovation quashed.[122] With the exception of the Garn-St. Germain Act of 1982 and the Financial Services Modernization Act of 1999, major financial reforms in the United States during the 1985–2000 period have occurred under Democratic majorities in the House and Senate (1987–95). The United States was able to create an effective social source of financial power through positive state intervention. The depth and breadth of this social source of financial power was greatest under the Clinton administration and was built from everyday po-

121. Anthony M. Santomero and David L. Eckles, "The Determinants of Success in the New Financial Services Environment: Now That Firms Can Do Everything, What Should They Do, and Why Should Regulators Care?" *Economic Policy Review* (Federal Reserve Bank of New York) 6, 4 (2000): 11.

122. Blyth, *Great Transformations,* 200.

litical struggles that transformed the financial reform nexus. Accordingly, we should not understand the broadening and deepening of the U.S. financial system under Clinton as a result of "trickle-down" growth from a more favorable economic environment. That would be placing the cart before the horse. State intervention was required for institutional change. As we shall see in the Epilogue, the U.S.'s social source of financial power is under threat from the rentier shift of the George W. Bush administration. But that is later. For now we should ask: why did Japan fail to wrestle primacy in the international financial order away from the United States?

6

The Financial Reform Nexus in Japan

In the late 1980s Japan was hailed to soon be the next principal power in the international financial order following the displacement of U.S. dominance. Japan's imminent dominance was a consequence of its international creditor status, particularly due to its investments in U.S. government debt, and its more interventionist state. Backed by a united society, Japan's destiny was to become "equal, if not superior to, the West."[1]

The financial data from the late 1980s make it difficult to dismiss the above view. After all, by 1988 Japanese commercial banks filled the ranks of the world's top twenty-five banks and held 40 percent of all international bank assets, investing particularly in stock markets and commercial real estate.[2] During the mid-1980s the Japanese state propagated the idea that becoming a rentier state within the international financial order would assist it in developing "some kinder gentler middle ground between a centrally controlled economy and a laissez faire market-driven economy."[3] This plan did not go smoothly.

Japan's transition from an "embedded mercantilist" state to an "international investor" state from the mid-1980s led to a series of investments that burst with the "bubble economy" and initiated a decade-long crisis.[4] However, more than bad investments, a post-1985 Japanese rentier shift was supported with negative state intervention and led to the systematic extraction of rents from lower-income groupings (LIGs). If we investigate Japan's financial woes we soon discover that Japan diminished its international fi-

1. See Robert Gilpin, *The Political Economy of International Relations* (Princeton: Princeton University Press, 1987), 328.
2. Eric Helleiner, "States and the Future of Global Finance," *Review of International Studies* 18, 1 (1992): 40–41.
3. In the words of former Japanese foreign minister, Ōkita Saburō, cited in Chalmers Johnson, *Japan, Who Governs? The Rise of the Developmental State* (New York: W. W. Norton, 1995), 312.
4. T. J. Pempel, *Regime Shift: Comparative Dynamics of the Japanese Political Economy* (Ithaca: Cornell University Press, 1998), 16.

nancial capacity by undermining its social sources of financial power. The outcome of massive increases in Japanese capital outflows was not increased international financial capacity, but prolonged financial stagnation and domestic frustration. Bad international investments were a consequence of a negatively interventionist state.

Japanese LIGs suffered across the financial reform nexus. For example, despite persistent claims throughout this period about Japan's superior financial position due to its high volume of domestic savings, these savings were not used to assist LIGs. For example, the postal savings system, which was widely held to be a pillar of Japanese egalitarianism and exceptionalism, was used to fund unnecessary public works and subsidize cheap housing credit for rentiers rather than LIGs. Furthermore, LIGs' contestation of financial reforms was hampered by inequalities within the electoral system and the isolation of pilot economic agencies from public accountability. As the twentieth century came to a close, Japanese LIGs' belief-driven actions demonstrated a clear decline in the legitimacy of the financial reform nexus and frustration that state intervention did not redistribute credit and property access, or relieve increased tax burdens.

Despite the relatively static portrayal of asset change in Figure 6.1, the Japanese financial system changed rapidly during the 1985–2000 period from a model of competitiveness to, for the dramatically inclined, "quasi-Soviet."[5] This transition can be attributed to the Ministry of Finance's (MoF) long-standing "convoy" approach (*gosō sendan hōshiki*) to policy, by which financial reforms moved at the pace of the slowest financial institution. This approach retarded the development of the financial system because it spread rentiers' risks through the system.

As seen in Figure 6.1, at the head of the convoy were city banks and regional banks, which both acted as commercial banks.[6] City banks between 1985 and 2000 declined, as did regional banks. During this period, commercial banks failed to remove non-performing loans from their books. So while their share of the financial system (shown in Figure 6.1) remained strong, they were actually quite weak. Merger activity during the period was present but not particularly prominent among these institutions, with the thirteen city banks in 1985 falling to nine by 2000 as "mega-mergers" increased in the late 1990s. In 1985 there were sixty-three regional banks, while in 2000 there were sixty-four.[7]

---

5. "On a Wing and a Prayer," *The Economist*, 7 April 1999, 23.

6. I have classified *sōgo* banks (mutual savings banks) under regional banks following the guidelines provided by the Japanese Statistics Bureau. *Sōgo* banks are classified as "Regional Banks II" in government statistics, but only for some years and not others. I have consolidated different types of regional banks into one set simply because the data set is otherwise unworkable.

7. Statistics Bureau, *Japan Statistical Yearbook* (Tokyo: Ministry of Public Management, Home Affairs, Posts and Telecommunications, 2002), 454, Table 13–8.

Figure 6.1 Key Japanese financial institutions' assets as a percentage of total financial assets, 1985–2000.

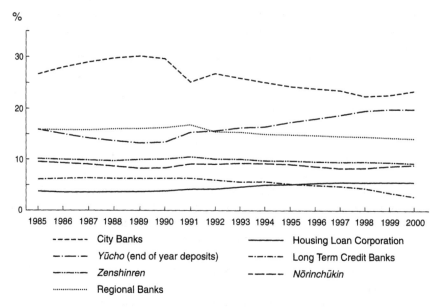

Source: Statistics Bureau, *Japan Statistical Yearbook* (Tokyo: Ministry of Public Management, Home Affairs, Posts and Telecommunications, various years 1985–2002), Tables 12.8–12.22, 13.8–13.22.

Next in line was the postal savings system (commonly called *yūcho*), an institution with which 80 percent of Japanese hold accounts and which is "the only purveyor of financial services that really cares about the people."[8] Indeed, the *yūcho* is commonly asserted as representative of Japanese egalitarianism.[9] However, while there is a broad base of savers, the top 10 percent of income-earning households account for 76 percent of total savings while the bottom 50 percent account for 5.5 percent.[10] Importantly, the *yūcho* provided funding for the Fiscal Investment and Loan Program (also known as the *zaitō*), the government's "second budget," which was used to fund public works and provide cheap housing loans.

8. Cited in Frances McCall Rosenbluth, *Financial Politics in Contemporary Japan* (Ithaca: Cornell University Press, 1989), 191.

9. Linda Weiss, *The Myth of the Powerless State: Governing the Economy in a Global Era* (Cambridge: Polity Press, 1998), 160.

10. David W. Campbell and Wako Watanabe, "Household Saving in Japan," unpublished study, Institute for Posts and Telecommunications Policy, Japan Society for the Promotion of Science, Tokyo, and the National Science Foundation, Grant # INT-9600308, May 1997, 3–5. It should also be noted that figures on participation in the *yūcho* can be misleading, as many Japanese hold multiple postal savings accounts due to the tax break given to "small savers" who are not differentiated by a social security number or similar identification. See Rosenbluth, *Financial Politics*, 206–7.

Further down the convoy were the *Zenshinren,* the central association and umbrella for small business credit cooperative associations (*Shinkin*), and the *Nōrinchūkin,* the central association and umbrella for agricultural cooperatives. Both underwent furious merger activity in the last quarter of the twentieth century.[11] The *Zenshinren* reflect the power of small business in Japan, while the *Nōrinchūkin* represent agricultural interests. Both were key supporters of the long-reigning Liberal Democratic Party (LDP, which held office consecutively from 1948 to 1993). The *Nōrinchūkin* were especially important in funding housing loan companies known as *jūsen.* With *positive* state intervention the *jūsen* began to provide competitive housing loans in 1971. With *negative* state intervention they became Japan's most prominent real estate speculators in the mid-1980s.[12] Toward the end of the convoy, Long-Term Credit Banks (LTCBs) and Trust Banks were also attracted to *jūsen* in the mid-1980s and are thought to provide "dedicated capital" to corporate Japan. However, like the *Großbanken* in the German case, the role of the LTCBs has been exaggerated, and we should downgrade their importance for the Japanese economy.

Finally at the caboose was the Housing Loan Corporation (*Jūtaku Kin'yū Kōko,* hereafter HLC), which increased its assets by less than 2 percent and provides a stark contrast with the example set by the U.S.'s FMAs. As I explain below, the source of this frustration was that Japanese LIGs effectively subsidized cheap housing loans for rentier landlords.

This chapter demonstrates that the Japanese "uniqueness" and "manifest destiny" should be strongly called into question,[13] as should the view that Japan represents a combination of strong state, strong culture, and strong savings. Japan's state strength, particularly in the recent past, has been contrasted with the U.S.'s fragmented political system, which is considered weak. Stephen Krasner, for example, argues that Japan is a strong state because "power is concentrated in the hands of a small number of actors in the executive branch who can set policy and secure, through coercion or incentives, the support of major groups in civil society."[14] The Japanese state, this story goes, had independence from political interests that could slash through red tape and committee processes to "achieve some larger social or political goal."[15] Such a view inclines us to explain away regressive state poli-

11. Yoshio Suzuki, *The Japanese Financial System* (Oxford: Clarendon Press, 1987), 223–27, 235–38. While in 1985 there were 4,244 agricultural cooperatives, there were but 1,362 by 2000. Not as dramatically, in 1985 there were 456 *Shinkin* cooperatives and only 376 in 2000.

12. Unlike other institutions, the Japanese government statistics provide only a very partial data set on *jūsen* assets, and after 1995 the category simply drops out of the statistics altogether when they became insolvent. I have therefore omitted *jūsen* from Figure 6.1.

13. Peter J. Katzenstein, *Cultural Norms and National Security: Police and Military in Postwar Japan* (Ithaca: Cornell University Press, 1996), 12–14. Contra Robert Gilpin, "Economic Evolution of National Systems," *International Studies Quarterly* 40, 3 (1996): 423.

14. Stephen D. Krasner, "The Accomplishments of International Political Economy," in Steve Smith, Ken Booth, and Marysia Zalewski, eds., *International Theory: Positivism and Beyond* (Cambridge: Polity Press, 1996), 121.

15. Gilpin, "Economic Evolution," 417, 420. See also John Zysman, *Governments, Markets, and*

cies as cultural differences rather than a violation of economic social norms. The Diet's lack of responsiveness to LIGs' contestation of the legitimacy of changes in the financial reform nexus should not be explained by cultural traits.

Furthermore, an apparent social consensus permitted the Japanese state to pursue the "politics of growth" over the "politics of distribution"—or at least this was a popular explanation for the success of East Asian developmentalism until it was unable to explain Japan's inability to recover from the mid-1990s.[16] A different understanding is that Japan undermined its social source of financial power by privileging the politics of growth for rentiers while ignoring the politics of redistribution for LIGs. Under such conditions Japanese LIGs increasingly withdrew from an evermore belligerent financial "bureaucratic dictatorship."[17]

Gaiatsu, Naiatsu, and Cheap Money

The United States has often pressured Japan to liberalize its financial services sector and, particularly, to provide monetary stabilization by appreciating the yen and to attract more Japanese investment into U.S. debt. The Japanese government has often blamed this foreign pressure (*gaiatsu*) to explain the "enforced liberalization" of the Japanese financial system.

During the high-growth period of 1952–71 (when GNP grew annually at 11 percent), state control over the Japanese financial system was enacted through the Foreign Exchange and Trade Control Act of 1949, which remained in effect until 1980. The controls prevented the export of Japanese capital and slowed both foreign direct investment and capital exports to a trickle during the postwar period. In addition, between 1950 and 1967 only seven foreign banks were given access to Japan, and all of them were from Asian states. Post-1967, Citibank, Chase Manhattan, and the Bank of America all had a presence in Tokyo, but their operations were strictly limited. Furthermore, only after 1972 did the MoF give Japanese banks permission to raise credit on markets in London and New York.[18] In short, Japan was a closed shop.

In 1983—during Reagan's rentier push in the United States—a creeping

---

Growth: Financial Systems and the Politics of Industrial Change (Oxford: Martin Robertson, 1983), 237, 243; William D. Coleman, *Financial Services, Globalization, and Domestic Policy Change* (Houndsmill: Macmillan Press, 1996), 73, 78; Weiss, *Myth of the Powerless State*, 28.

16. Weiss, *Myth of the Powerless State*, 155, 203.

17. Ikuta Tadahide "'Ōkurashō dokusai' bōkokuron" [The Ministry of Finance dictatorship], *Foresight* 4, 12 (1993): 6–10. My thanks to Shogo Suzuki for translating all the Japanese language material drawn upon in this chapter.

18. Louis W. Pauly, *Opening Financial Markets: Banking Politics on the Pacific Rim* (Ithaca: Cornell University Press, 1988), 67–68.

recognition of the need to devalue the U.S. dollar and attract creditors to fund U.S. debt led a partnership of U.S. government and private interests to encourage the Japanese to let their capital out through the "Yen-Dollar Agreement." Conventional accounts of this agreement emphasize that U.S. dominance prompted the Japanese government to give commercial banks permission to sell government bonds in a secondary market, to increase its use of commercial debt securities, and to allow foreign financial institutions potential membership to the Tokyo Stock Exchange.[19] Domestic financial reforms included encouraging Japanese investment in U.S. debt, which quickly increased in 1985. However, we should not dismiss the prominence of internal pressure (*naiatsu*) in understanding the beginnings of Japan's rentier state.

During the 1970s, corporate Japan's dependence on bank financing declined dramatically despite common perceptions of the Gerschenkron-like link between banks and corporations. Prior to 1975 the Bank of Japan (hereafter BoJ) had positively intervened into the financial system by purchasing government debt that had been purchased by city banks to finance loans to corporate Japan. Thus, the corporations were indebted to banks, which were indebted to the BoJ. From 1975 onward, the BoJ sought to lessen the dependence of corporate Japan on its funds, by reducing its repurchasing of government debt, and encouraged an internal secondary market for yen repurchase agreements (*gensaki*). Thus while banks provided 84 percent of corporate financing in the 1970–94 period, they accounted for only 60 percent in the 1980–84 period.[20]

In 1978 both Prime Ministers Fukuda Takeo and Ōhira Masayoshi promised to provide a more open financial system and, in particular, to reform the Foreign Exchange and Trade Control Act. In 1980 a revision of the act permitted more capital to leave Japan, but in reality the reform merely confirmed what had already occurred in the marketplace.[21] The new direction of Japanese finance was also confirmed with the New Banking Law of 1981, which encouraged commercial banks to develop more flexible savings accounts for customers, permitted banks to underwrite government debt, and removed interest rate ceilings on deposits (like the Regulation Q reform in the previous chapter). By the time of the Yen-Dollar Agreement, Japanese city banks already had 30 percent of their total assets invested abroad.[22] Importantly, in 1984, the MoF reformed the "real de-

19. Andrew C. Sobel, *Domestic Choices, International Markets: Dismantling National Barriers and Liberalizing Securities Markets* (Ann Arbor: University of Michigan Press, 1994), 32, 108.
20. Kent A. Calder, "Assault on the Banker's Kingdom: Politics, Markets, and the Liberalization of Japanese Industrial Finance," in Michael Loriaux, Meredith Woo-Cumings, Kent E. Calder, Sylvia Maxfield, and Sofia Pérez, *Capital Ungoverned: Liberalizing Finance in Interventionist States* (Ithaca: Cornell University Press, 1997), 19–23.
21. Ulrike Schaede, "The 1995 Financial Crisis in Japan," Working Paper 85 (Berkeley: Berkeley Roundtable on International Economics, February 1996), 4.
22. Indeed, by 1983 they accounted for 11 percent of all lending to British residents and ac-

mand" rule which had previously prevented Japanese financial institutions from engaging in wholesale speculative activities. Furthermore, in 1985, the MoF permitted banks to deal directly in yen-dollar trades rather than going through only MoF-approved Tokyo brokers, and allowed Japanese corporations to raise more of their capital on the stock market, thereby relying less on banks.[23] All these domestic actions encouraged international investment.

These domestic-driven changes were in line with Prime Minister Nakasone Yasuhiro's administration's explicit aim to transform Japan from a developmental state to a rentier state befitting a more mature economy.[24] The Plaza Accord of 1985, which realigned the yen-dollar exchange rate from ¥242:$1 in September 1985 to ¥153:$1 in September 1986, reinforced the benefits of a rentier shift. A higher yen would provide the yen for massive investment overseas by Japanese commercial banks and allow Japanese corporations to move offshore. Accordingly, the BoJ produced a "cheap money" policy that dropped interest rates to their lowest level in forty years and facilitated massive credit expansion. Japanese banks borrowed more and more from within Japan and recycled the funds to offshore financial centers, becoming an "unconstrained source of funds in terms of both price and quantity."[25] Furthermore, the MoF encouraged banks to use short-term debt in managing long-term international lending positions as part of a strategy to become the "world's banker."[26] While in the late 1970s Japanese financial institutions accounted for 15 percent of bond outflows and 12 percent of short-term bank outflows in the international financial order, by the late 1980s they accounted for, respectively, 55 and 50 percent.[27] Between 1981 and 1988 Japan's external financial assets increased from $10 billion to $279.7 billion, making Japan the largest exporter of long-term capital in the international financial order.[28] In short, under the high yen and cheap money, Japan had chosen to become the leading international creditor, and saw a rentier shift as the best means of international investment and domestic compensation.

---

counted for 40 percent of all foreign bank activity in the United States. See Pauly, *Opening Financial Markets*, 80–83.

23. Calder, "Assault on the Banker's Kingdom," 21, 28.

24. Pempel, *Regime Shift*, 189.

25. Henry S. Terrell, Robert S. Dohner, and Barbara R. Lowrey, "The Activities of Japanese Banks in the United Kingdom and in the United States, 1980–88," *Federal Reserve Bulletin* 76, 2 (1990): 44.

26. Yoichi Shinkai, "The Internationalization of Finance in Japan," in Takashi Inoguchi and Daniel I. Okimoto, eds., *The Political Economy of Japan: Volume 1, The Changing International Context* (Stanford: Stanford University Press, 1988), 266–67.

27. T. J. Pempel, "Structural *Gaiatsu:* International Finance and Political Change in Japan," *Comparative Political Studies* 32, 8 (1999): 916.

28. Eric Helleiner, "Money and Influence: Japanese Power in the International Monetary and Financial System," *Millennium: Journal of International Studies* 18, 3 (1989): 343, 352.

Landlord Subsidization for Shoddy Dwellings

We saw in the English case that an increased dependence on international portfolio investment occurred during a period when LIGs called for state intervention to improve their quality of housing and access to mortgage credit. While the dynamics are different, of course, Japanese LIGs during the 1985–2000 period faced similar problems.

The Maekawa Plan of 1986 (named after the Bank of Japan Governor Maekawa Haruo, and serving as an advisory council to Prime Minister Nakasone) outlined that Japan could avoid the problem of domestic underconsumption by using increasing rents from international investments to stimulate domestic consumption.[29] The Maekawa Plan would therefore assist all Japanese to build an "affluent life," including increased home ownership.[30] Following the Plaza Accord and the initiation of the "cheap money" policy, Japanese financial institutions' accumulated lending to the property sector increased by 14.1 percent per annum from 1986 until 1991.[31] But the increased investment was not for Japanese LIGs to attain an affluent life. During the mid-1980s to early 1990s, real estate investment for the owner-occupied household sector halved while the non-financial companies' share increased by a factor of 2.6.[32] And while the Japanese state had positively intervened to supply LIGs with mortgages in the 1960s and 1970s, this changed in the 1980s with increased rentier activity. So while nearly 100 percent of residential mortgages were offered to owner-occupiers in the mid-1970s, by 1990 22 percent of residential mortgages were granted to owner-occupiers with the rest going to real estate speculators.[33]

Deeply implicated in this regressive change was the HLC. In 1985 the HLC provided 36 percent of housing loans, city banks 17.7 percent, regional banks 14.4 percent, *Zenshinren* organizations 13 percent, and *jūsen* 3.4 percent.[34] The original purpose of the HLC was to legitimate access to

29. C. Randall Henning, *Currencies and Politics in the United States, Germany and Japan* (Washington, D.C.: Institute for International Economics, 1994), 174.

30. Takatoshi Ito, "Public Policy and Housing in Japan," in Yukio Noguchi and James M. Poterba, eds., *Housing Markets in the United States and Japan* (Chicago: University of Chicago Press, 1994), 217–18.

31. For example, as a percentage of their assets, between 1980 and 1991 city banks increased their lending for real estate interests from 8.1 to 18.9 percent. Regional banks increased their investment from 6.9 to 15.8 percent, Trust Banks from 17.5 to 40.5 percent, and Long-Term Credit Banks from 16.7 to 37.1 percent. See Kazuo Ueda, "Institutional and Regulatory Frameworks for the Main Banking System," in Masahiko Aoki and Hugh Patrick, eds., *The Japanese Main Bank System* (Oxford: Oxford University Press, 1994), 107.

32. Yukio Noguchi, "Land Prices and House Prices in Japan," in Noguchi and Poterba, eds., *Housing Markets*, 18.

33. Mayumi Otsuma, Ken Ellis, Todd Zaun, Andrew Morse, and Norie Kuboyama, "Japan's Housing Lenders' Crisis," *JPRI Critique* 3, 2 (1996): 1.

34. The only significant change from these percentages during the bubble period was an increase in the share of regional banks, which peaked with 22 percent of the market share in 1991. Schaede argues that by 1991 *jūsen* held 12 percent of the residential housing loan mar-

mortgage credit to Japanese LIGs. During the 1960s and 1970s, when Japan constructed the social foundations to provide it with international financial capacity, it fulfilled this role. In theory it could do so because the HLC provided mortgages below market rates, with the principal financed with *yūcho* savings and the interest rate differential paid for by taxpayers. Ideally this highly redistributive system would have extracted resources from dominant economic groups to provide cheap credit to LIGs. The reverse, however, is true. The HLC was, in fact, a key factor in undermining the legitimation of the Japanese financial reform nexus.

There is no doubt that there was sufficient demand for housing from LIGs in the 1985–2000 period, when the prevailing public opinion was that "if one wishes to live in a decent house," then one must acquire property.[35] There were good reasons to support this view, as in the late 1980s to early 1990s 60 percent of dwellings either just met or were below Ministry of Construction (MoC) standards. For the rental market, 92 percent of dwellings either just met or fell below MoC standards.[36] Drawing a parallel with the English case, Japanese LIGs lived in accommodation that was "shoddy and expensive."[37]

This problem was greatly exacerbated by the fact that mortgage credit through the HLC was difficult to acquire. One simple reason was that average down payments soon became 40 percent of the market value of the required property.[38] This provided a key source of frustration for LIGs who did not wish to wait for retirement to become homeowners. This frustration was particularly evident for LIGs as institutional impediments to property ownership were associated with a lack of social mobility.[39]

Keeping in mind that in Japan the value of housing loans was equal to about 60 percent of the market value of the property, in Figure 6.2 I illustrate the average value of loans from the main providers of housing loans.[40]

---

ket. However, my calculations place *jūsen* at 3 percent in 1991. Schaede, "The 1995 Financial Crisis in Japan," 13. See Statistics Bureau, *Japan Statistical Yearbook*, Tables 12.20, 13.20, various years between 1985 and 2002.

35. Noguchi, "Land Prices," 12.

36. Ito, "Public Policy," 224–25.

37. Avner Offer, *Property and Politics, 1870–1914: Landownership, Law, Ideology and Urban Development in England* (Cambridge: Cambridge University Press, 1981), 116. The quote refers to Edwardian England.

38. This contrasts heavily with the role of HUD in the previous chapter, from which U.S. LIGs could acquire mortgage approval with a down payment of 3 percent of the property value. The average housing deposit in the United States is approximately 5 percent, with some commercial banks requiring 10 percent. See David Miles, *Housing, Financial Markets and the Wider Economy* (New York: John Wiley and Sons, 1994), 99.

39. Tachibanaki Toshiaki and Keiko Shimono, "Wealth Accumulation Process by Income Class," *Journal of the Japanese and International Economies* 5, 3 (1991): 245–46.

40. The calculation is simply the total value of new loans made divided by the number of loans issued by the institution. Unfortunately statistical records on the number of new loans are only available up to 1995. Statistics Bureau, *Japan Statistical Yearbook*, Tables 12.20, 13.20, various years between 1985 and 1997.

Figure 6.2 Average value of new home loans from key Japanese financial institutions, value in millions of yen, 1985–95.

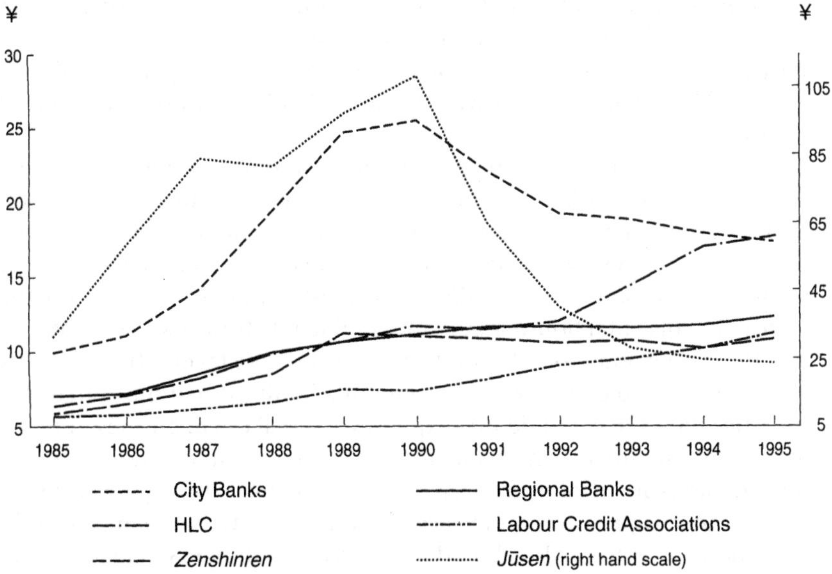

Note: All financial institutions are measured against the left-hand scale other than *jūsen,* which are measured on the right-hand scale.
Source: Statistics Bureau, *Japan Statistical Yearbook* (Tokyo: Ministry of Public Management, Home Affairs, Posts and Telecommunications, various years 1985–2002), Tables 12.20, 13.20, various years.

While the HLC could reasonably make a claim to serve LIGs in 1985, it could by no means do so in 1995. By 1990 the HLC's issue of loans was, on average, of greater market value than those issued by regional banks and *Zenshinren.*

With the exception provided by *jūsen* (which I discuss further below), by 1995 the HLC was issuing the most expensive of all housing loans.[41] Because the HLC took capital from the *yūcho* to fund cheap loans and then paid off the remainder with tax revenue, LIGs effectively subsidized landlords. Kent Calder estimates tax subsidies to the housing sector to be ¥341.3 billion in 1995, a 19.2 percent increase from the 1984 figure, noting that "the press was particularly critical of the high proportion of high-income people borrowing for housing loans, noting how such activity was subverting the redistributive purpose of the programs."[42]

How did the HLC become so removed from LIGs? First, the HLC had no income limit on its borrowers (one study found that 13.4 percent of HLC

41. It was necessary to be a member to acquire a loan from the *Zenshinren* system or Labour Credit Association. The most accessible of institutions, as can be seen in Figure 6.2, were the regional banks.
42. Calder, "Assault on the Banker's Kingdom," 36.

borrowers in the 1986–89 period were in the top income bracket).[43] Second, the HLC favored loans for the construction of new properties, particularly rental accommodation, for borrowers with extant property assets as collateral.[44] While in 1986 there were 140,000 new condominiums under construction, by 1990 there were over 220,000 with the expansion of HLC activities.[45] Third, the HLC provided loans to landlords who then received favorable tax conditions.

As noted in the previous chapter, mortgage interest payments could be deducted from assessable income tax, greatly reducing the tax burden on U.S. LIGs. In the Japanese case an owner-occupier could deduct mortgage repayments from his income tax to a maximum of 1 percent of the value of the loan. At the same time, landlords' interest payments on loans for the construction of rental housing were fully deductible from assessed rental income for tax purposes—and prior to 1991 it could be taken off income tax if the payments exceeded rental income. If a landlord had more than ten properties then she could deduct expenses as a real estate business, including salary payments to family members. On top of these generous provisions, the assessment of a property for property taxes was reduced by 30 percent if the property was rented accommodation.[46] Other than landlords, the property taxes were also abused by agrarian landholders in urban areas, who paid as little as 1/57th of the equivalent urban residential tax rate on chronically undervalued properties.[47] This privilege for "urban farmers" was reward for their support for the LDP.

In 1990, following public contestation from LIGs on their subsidization of landlords and the poor quality of housing, the MoF placed a cap on the number of residential mortgages that could go to any one individual, but not the capacity for individuals with more than ten properties to reclassify as a real estate company, who were exempt from the policy change. Under

---

43. The 1989 average income for a person receiving a mortgage was ¥9.7 million. Even from 1999 figures this is the fourth quintile of income ranges (the first and second are, respectively, those earning less than ¥5 million and those between ¥5 million and ¥6.5 million). Yearly income for people not planning to buy a house is ¥4.96 million (nearly half of ¥9.7 million). See Tachibanaki Toshiaki, "Housing and Saving in Japan," in Noguchi and Poterba, eds., *Housing Markets*, 175, 179; Nakagawa Shinobu, "Why Has Japan's Household Savings Rate Remained High Even During the 1990s?" unpublished study, Research and Statistics Department, Bank of Japan, July 1999, 2, note 2.

44. Miki Seko, "Housing Finance in Japan," in Noguchi and Poterba, eds., *Housing Markets*, 50–51, 60.

45. See the chart "*Shinsetsu bunjō jūtaku chakkō kosū no suii*" [Changes in the construction of new dwelling projects] in Ministry of Construction, *Jūtaku chakkō tōkei* [Housing construction statistics] (Tokyo: Ministry of Construction [*Kensetsushō*], 1997), 47.

46. Thomas Dalsgaard and Masaaki Kawagoe, "The Tax System in Japan: A Need For Comprehensive Reform," Economics Department Working Papers No. 231 (Paris: OECD, 2000), 17.

47. Kiyohiko Nishimura, Fukujyu Yamazaki, Takako Idee, and Toshiaki Watanabe, "Distortionary Taxation, Excessive Price Sensitivity, and Japanese Land Prices," NBER Working Paper No. 7254 (Cambridge, Mass.: National Bureau of Economic Research, July 1999), 2–5.

further contestation the Japanese government introduced a non-residential land-value tax (*chika zei*). However, like the People's Budget's gains, the rate and increased revenue was negligible. The introduced rate was 0.2 percent of land value and by 1995 it was dropped back to 0.15 percent and then abolished in 1997.[48] To make matters worse the evasion of general property taxes continued to the extent that while the official property tax rate was 1.4 percent for the 1985–2000 period, the effective tax rate was between 0.1 and 0.3 percent.[49] During the period the government sought to make up for revenue leaks from property tax evasion by introducing a consumption tax.

The Consumption Tax: Shaking the Peppercorn Tree

As discussed in other cases, there are often direct links between inequities in electoral and tax systems and problems in sufficiently legitimating a financial reform nexus. Due to the concessions given on capital interest, interest income, and paucity of property tax implementation, one Japanese scholar referred to the post-1989 tax system as "the most unfair in the world."[50] While this is surely an exaggeration, the important factor here is not the level of tax burdens but the perceptions of inequality in comparison to how LIGs believed the economy should work. The proposed introduction of a consumption tax was met with anger by LIGs, who reacted in 1993 by challenging the LDP and removing their control in the House of Councillors of the Diet for the first time since 1955. As the Japanese saying goes, "A mountain peppercorn may be small but creates a hell of a lot of trouble."[51] The LDP's repeated actions to introduce a consumption tax were akin to shaking the peppercorn tree for LIGs.

Before discussing the consumption tax, it is important to note that the Japanese electoral system provided an unfair advantage to rural constituencies, and that its multi-member district system encouraged particularistic rather than broad-based political representation. First, while the drawing up of electoral boundaries in the immediate postwar period reflected the fact that half of Japan's population lived in rural areas, by the late 1980s fewer than 8 percent of the population lived in rural areas but the boundaries stayed the same. As a consequence, by the 1980s one agrarian vote effectively came to equal four times the value of an urban vote.[52] Second, in the

48. Yamasaki Yoshisaburo and Robert V. Andelson, "The Unearned Increment in Japan," *American Journal of Economics and Sociology* 59, 5 (2000): 362; OECD, *OECD Revenue Statistics, 1965–2000* (Paris: OECD, 2001), 142, Table 56.

49. Dalsgaard and Kawagoe, "Tax System in Japan," 15–16.

50. Sumi Tomoyoshi, *Nihon no Kokka Zaisei* [Japan's State Finance] (Shin Nihon Shuppankai: Tokyo, 1992), 84.

51. My thanks to Shogo Suzuki for passing on this phrase.

52. Mary G. McDonald, "Farmers as Workers in Japan's Regional Economic Restructuring, 1965–1985," *Economic Geography* 72, 1 (1996): 51.

pre-1994 multi-member district electoral system, up to six seats for the House of Representatives were allocated per district, with voters choosing only one member. Under the provisions of this system, one party could place four candidates for the same seats, with the hope of having them all voted in (which commonly occurred for the LDP). As a consequence it was in the interests of prospective members to build a coalition of dedicated corporate supporters rather than face the prospect of voters simply voting for their preferred party. The system therefore led members to pursue narrow political goals rather than a broad social interest.[53]

Representative of such politics, the LDP promised not to introduce a consumption tax following a failed attempt to do so in 1979, which cost the LDP half its seats in the House of Representatives in the election of the same year and forced the party to scramble together a coalition government by bringing in independent MPs.[54] In the mid-1980s the LDP floated the idea of a consumption tax once more and was met with similar criticism. While the tax reform was packaged as a means to bring greater "fairness" and "justice" to the tax system, only those earning more than ¥6 million would receive a tax cut and, as a consequence, the "majority of taxpayers felt betrayed and did not support Nakasone's reform."[55] A 1986 *Asashi Shimbun* survey found only 9 percent of Japanese thought that the tax would increase social fairness and that 57 percent of Japanese strongly opposed the introduction of any form of consumption tax. In the face of such opposition, Nakasone reaffirmed the promise "not to introduce a large-scale indirect tax" in the 1986 election campaign.[56] However, only a few months later Nakasone proposed that Japan should put in place comprehensive tax reforms which would cut income tax and introduce a consumption tax. This attempt was again dressed up on the grounds of fairness and, importantly, Nakasone's promises to address two principle causes of tax inequality, the *kuroyon* and *maruyū* systems.

It had long been recognized that Japanese taxation was under a *kuroyon* system, which literally means "9-6-4." Salaried workers paid taxes on assessments equivalent to 90 percent of their incomes, small business owners were taxed on 60 percent of assessable income, and farmers were taxed on 40 percent of assessable income. Whereas small businesses were given the ability to self-assess their tax liability, salaried workers were taxed at the source of their income and could therefore not evade taxation.[57] Furthermore, the

53. Frances McCall Rosenbluth and Michael F. Thies, "The Electoral Foundations of Japan's Banking Regulation," *Policy Studies Journal* 29, 1 (2001): 25.

54. Junko Kato, *The Problem of Bureaucratic Rationality: Tax Politics in Japan* (Princeton: Princeton University Press, 1994), 305.

55. Homma Masaaki, "Tax Reform in Japan," in Takatoshi Ito and Anne O. Krueger, eds., *The Political Economy of Tax Reform* (Chicago: University of Chicago Press, 1992), 76–77.

56. Kato, *Problem of Bureaucratic Rationality*, 156, 164–65, 306. See also Junko Kato, *Regressive Taxation and the Welfare State: Path Dependence and Policy Diffusion* (Cambridge: Cambridge University Press, 2003), 173–81.

57. Pempel, *Regime Shift*, 62, 197.

maruyū system permitted "small savers" to claim a tax exemption. Like the "9-6-4" tax system, it was widely known that the *maruyū* system encouraged tax evasion: this was facilitated by an abuse of a social security number system that enabled people to open up numerous accounts and claim multiple small saver exemptions. Nakasone and his successor, Takeshita Noboru, argued that the abolition of the *maruyū* system would require the introduction of a consumption tax.[58] The "9-6-4" system, however, would not be altered.

A consumption tax of 3 percent was introduced in 1989 despite continued public opposition. While 3 percent may not seem like much, once more it is the violation of LIGs' beliefs on how the economy should work that is important politically. The tax was also socially regressive when placed in the context of other tax reforms pushed through at the same time.

From my calculations there was an effective decrease to the overall tax revenue base. As a proportion of tax revenue, personal income tax was reduced by just under 9 percent, corporate tax reduced by 10 percent, and inheritance tax by 16 percent.[59] Tax cuts from the reform led to a 10 percent reduction in taxes paid by families in the ¥7 million to ¥10 million range (lower-middle income groups are ¥4 million to ¥6 million). There were no significant reductions for people earning from ¥2 million to ¥6 million, meaning that the tax reform effectively increased the real tax burden on LIGs and especially upon the poor.[60] Furthermore, the tax reform effectively worsened the "9-6-4" informal tax division because it exempted small businesses from paying consumption tax but allowed them to retain their collection of consumption taxes up to ¥400 million, effectively permitting a public subsidy of small businesses.

As forewarned by the Japanese public, should a consumption tax be introduced the LDP would suffer electoral losses. They did so in the 1989 House of Councillors (Upper House) and 1990 House of Representatives (Lower House) elections and it "was apparent that the consumption tax was a major reason for this result."[61] The LDP suffered serious losses in both houses, with the Upper House falling out of the LDP's hands. However, despite the weakening legitimacy of the Japanese financial reform nexus, the LDP and MoF continued to increase the extraction of rents from Japanese LIGs.

Buoyant Bubbles and the Basle Brush

In the previous chapter we briefly discussed the Basle Accord and the U.S.'s capacity to attract Japanese investment to its government debt. These

58. Homma, "Tax Reform," 72–74.

59. Calculated from the figures provided in Kato, *Problem of Bureaucratic Rationality,* 211, 274, n. 34; and OECD, *OECD Revenue Statistics, 1965–2000,* 142, Table 56.

60. Homma, "Tax Reform," 86.

61. Kato, *Problem of Bureaucratic Rationality,* 216–17; Kato, *Regressive Taxation,* 180–81.

changes coincided with increasingly large outflows of capital from Japan. On the back of a cheap money policy, with low interest rates that allowed massive credit expansion (the BoJ official interest rate in 1987 was 2.5 percent), real estate prices, stock prices, and international investments skyrocketed in value. Not all investments were in U.S. Treasury bonds, as Japanese banks subsequently shifted further into real estate speculation and made inroads into lending to other states, particularly to the United States. As a consequence, Japan increased its assets within the U.S. domestic financial system from $177.9 billion in 1985 to $420.5 billion by 1989, making up 12 percent of the total U.S. domestic loan market.[62] In retaliation U.S. business commentators argued that the "vulnerable financial houses of the West are slowly but steadily being eaten away by the Japanese."[63]

Domestic opposition to the Japanese international rentier investments deepened from a belief in lost opportunities. As suggested by Yukio Noguchi, although one-third of all Japanese savings went into international investments during the bubble period, the rentier strategy led to ignorance of Japanese LIGs' social wants: "Domestic savings were directed not into improvements of domestic infrastructure but into the acquisition of assets abroad. The Japanese, with their low levels of social capital, may be compared to a family living in a dilapidated house who have worked very hard and scrimped to save money and have used it not to improve their own home but to lend to others."[64] In addition to international rentier investments, domestic credit went to "less fiscally sound firms, land speculators, real estate companies, nonbank financial intermediaries, politicians, and members of organized crime."[65] Japanese scholars complained that the MoF's permissive regulation was creating a "Japanese disease" that would create massive problems when the bubble burst, including the potential use of taxpayers' monies to bail out Japanese commercial banks' non-performing loans.[66] Indeed, the Bank for International Settlements' (BIS) Basle Accord was required to impose stringent capital adequacy rather than permitting banks to consistently "overlend" and overexpose themselves to financial shocks.

LIGs were right to be concerned about the use of their tax monies to bail out Japanese financial institutions given the MoF's treatment of the debt crisis. While Japanese banks were not as heavily indebted to Latin American states as their U.S. equivalents, a handful were massively overexposed. For example, at the time of the crisis, the Bank of Tokyo had lent 83 percent of

62. Brian Wallace Semkow, "Foreign Financial Institutions in Japan," *Law and Policy in International Business* 23, 2–3 (1992): 361–64.

63. Richard W. Wright and Gunter A. Pauli, *The Second Wave: Japan's Global Assault on Financial Services* (Exeter: A. Wheaton, 1987), 98, 111.

64. Yukio Noguchi, "The 'Bubble' and Economic Policies in the 1980s," *Journal of Japanese Studies* 20, 2 (1994): 298.

65. Pempel, "Structural *Gaiatsu*," 918.

66. See Ozawa Terutomo, "The New Economic Nationalism and the 'Japanese Disease': The Conundrum of Managed Economic Growth," *Journal of Economic Issues* 30, 2 (1996).

its capital to Latin American states.[67] We might recall that in the United States, restrictions were placed on commercial banks to absorb bad debts or suffer a domestic premium on their borrowing. However, reflecting the MoF's "profit-padding" approach to financial regulation, the MoF allowed Japanese commercial banks to claim losses as tax deductions.[68] In fact, the MoF's inaction on raising the capital adequacy of Japanese banks led the United States to push for the Basle Accord.

Between 1984 and 1988, the activities of Japanese banks fueled over half the growth of all international banking activity and increased their international assets by 75 percent more than U.S. commercial banks.[69] This was also due to the fact that U.S. commercial banks were undergoing restructuring through the securitization of assets and boosting their capital adequacy ratios to 8 percent under the careful watch of the Federal Reserve. Japanese banks' capital adequacy ratios at the time were still around the 2 percent mark.[70]

As discussed in the previous chapter, the Basle Accord was presented as a *fait accompli* to the Japanese by the United States and the United Kingdom. We also noted that, in assessing the risk of different kinds of assets that could be included in the Basle Accord, the U.S.'s domestic implementation gave preference to Treasury debt followed by FMA securities. Similarly, Japan's domestic implementation of the Basle Accord included debates over what kinds of assets could be used to meet the new 8 percent capital adequacy requirement. The critical element here was that the Japanese state bargained for the inclusion of unrealized capital gains from real estate and stock investment. Following demands from the All Japan Banking Federation (*Zenginkyō*) to use 70 percent of unrealized capital gains as "supplementary capital," the Japanese were able to forge a compromise with the United States at 45 percent.[71] As most of these investments were speculative, the success of Japanese banks therefore depended on the continued success of a rentier strategy at home and internationally.

By 1988—the time of the announcement of the accord—capital adequacy ratios for U.S. banks were between 8 to 10 percent, and easily in accordance with the BIS's 8 percent, while most Japanese banks were still in the range of 2 to 4 percent. To meet Basle Accord standards by the end of 1992, Japanese banks were required to purchase massive amounts of low-risk securities. Even with the provision for unrealized gains from investment

67. Saori N. Katada, "The Japanese Government in Two Mexican Financial Crises: An Emerging International Lender-of-Last-Resort?" *Pacific Affairs* 71, 1 (1998): 65, 71.

68. Frances McCall Rosenbluth, "Japanese Banks in Mexico: The Role of Government in Private Decisions," *International Journal* 46, 4 (1991): 684.

69. Terrell, Dohner, and Lowrey, "Activities of Japanese Banks," 39.

70. John D. Wagster, "Impact of the 1988 Basle Accord on International Banks," *Journal of Finance* 51, 4 (1996): 1323.

71. Wolfgang H. Reinicke, *Banking, Politics, and Global Finance: American Commercial Banks and Regulatory Change, 1980–1990* (Aldershot: Edward Elgar, 1995), 172.

included, Japanese banks had to purchase between $31 billion and $46 billion of non-risk government debt. As mentioned in the previous chapter, Japanese banks spent $21.8 billion on U.S. Treasury notes and bonds between 1988 and 1992. Bank profitability plummeted as a consequence.[72]

However, as earlier, we should not exaggerate the influence of *gaiatsu* because the Basle accord was supported by the Japanese public.[73] Frances Rosenbluth and Ross Schaap, for example, argue that public support for the Basle Accord came from the perception that Japanese commercial banks were investing recklessly and that "Japanese voters do not want to prop up banks with any more tax money and regulatory forbearance than they had already delivered."[74] The Japanese public wished to hobble the international competitiveness of their banks to reduce their tax burden through the public funding of bailouts for private non-performing loans. Despite their opposition, however, Japanese taxpayers did pay out when the bubble burst in 1990 (discussed below). Indeed, the decision to include unrealized capital gains as part of the accord was a disaster for both Japanese banks and the Japanese taxpayer. While in 1988 capital gains represented 93 percent of "supplementary capital," by 1992 capital gains represented only 40 percent.[75] Japan's bet on a rentier strategy was not successful.

Jūsen and Electoral Reform

The bursting bubble exposed the fact that the assets that Japanese financiers had so readily adopted were grossly unrealistic. Accordingly, following his appointment in December 1989, the governor of the BoJ, Mieno Yasushi, tightened monetary policy in 1990 and burst the bubble. Due to Mieno's actions, interest rates increased from 2.5 percent to 6 percent between 1989 and 1991, placing pressure on returns from investments made in the extremely low-interest rate environment.

A collapse on the Tokyo Stock Exchange was the immediate reaction to the bursting of the bubble, as it lost 45 percent of its value and required intervention from the MoF to stop trading. While intervention in the stock ex-

72. Brian J. Hall, "How has the Basle Accord Affected Bank Portfolios?" *Journal of the Japanese and International Economies* 7, 4 (1993): 421–22. See also Leonard Seabrooke, *U.S. Power in International Finance: The Victory of Dividends* (Basingstoke: Palgrave, 2001), 136–39.

73. Thomas Oatley and Robert Nabors, "Redistributive Cooperation: Market Failures, Wealth Transfers and the Basle Accord," *International Organization* 52, 1 (1998): 37.

74. Frances McCall Rosenbluth and Ross Schaap, "The Domestic Politics of Financial Globalization," Leitner Working Paper 2001–04 (New Haven: Leitner Program in International and Comparative Political Economy, Yale University, 2001), 12.

75. Eric Helleiner, "Still an Extraordinary Power, but for How Much Longer? The United States in World Finance," in Thomas C. Lawton, James N. Rosenau, and Amy C. Verdun, eds., *Strange Power: Shaping the Parameters of International Relations and International Political Economy* (Aldershot: Ashgate, 2000), 232; Hall, "How Has the Basle Accord," 408.

change was successful, the MoF was unable to constrain Japan's city banks—
which lost ¥29 trillion ($325 billion) in falling stock prices between 1990
and 1992—from rapidly selling investments, leading one MoF official to
comment at the time that he was "shocked, shocked, that banks should have
been so selfish and uncooperative in the face of a national crisis."[76] On top
of stock losses, real estate losses accounted for two years' national output, or
¥566 trillion ($6.37 trillion).[77]

The MoF's reaction to the bursting of the bubble was to give financial institutions greater freedoms so that they could trade their way out of a non-
performing loan crisis (recalling the U.S. strategy for savings and loans
associations [S&Ls] in the early 1980s). The 1992 Financial System Reform
Act removed barriers between commercial and investment banking, and allowed banks and securities companies to enter each other's businesses to
achieve this aim. While the United States had adopted a similarly doomed
strategy with the Garn-St. Germain Act for S&Ls, the MoF's solution exacerbated international rentier activity while hiding domestic losses from the
public and from the international financial order.[78] As pointed out by Jennifer Amyx, when the MoF investigated Japanese financial institutions with
non-performing loans, the ministry "permitted such institutions to adjust
accounting procedures and thereby mask their problems."[79] Furthermore,
the MoF's acknowledgment that the use of taxpayer monies would lead to a
public outcry to bail out failing institutions led them to use informal ties between banks to create mergers rather than double their supervisory efforts.
And, as can be seen in Figure 6.1, despite the massive non-performing loans
problem, there was not a sharp reduction in city banks' or regional banks'
assets. Rather than removing malignant cysts, the MoF allowed the cancer
to spread.

The financial crisis among *jūsen* exemplified the inadequacies of the MoF.
While *jūsen* had been created in the early 1970s with the aim of increasing
competition in the Japanese housing loan market to permit, in theory,
cheaper credit to LIGs, they became, in reality, the leading real estate speculators during the 1980s bubble economy. If we look back to Figure 6.2, the
right-hand side of the scale represents the average size of home loans from
the *jūsen* between 1985 and 1995 (when they were dismantled). *Jūsen* certainly did not provide housing loans for Japanese LIGs. Rather, in 1986 the

76. Cited in Rosenbluth and Schaap, "Domestic Politics of Financial Globalization," 31.
77. Peter Hartcher, *The Ministry: How Japan's Most Powerful Institution Endangers World Markets*
(New York: Harvard Business School Press, 1998), 87.
78. The MoF also created a Cooperative Credit Purchasing Company to deal with Japan's
mass of non-performing loans, but it was largely ineffectual until the mid-1990s. Thomas F.
Cargill, Michael Hutchison, and Takatoshi Ito, "Japan's 'Big Bang' Financial Deregulation:
Implications for Regulatory and Supervisory Policy," Working Paper (Washington, D.C.: Japan Information Access Project, June 1997), 6.
79. Jennifer A. Amyx, *Japan's Financial Crisis: Institutional Rigidity and Reluctant Change* (Princeton: Princeton University Press, 2004), 162.

average loan from a *jūsen* was already ¥58 million, rising to ¥108 million in 1990, before falling to ¥23.6 million in 1995.[80]

The main sources of funding for the *jūsen* came from agricultural cooperatives (42 percent), city banks (38 percent), and regional banks (8 percent).[81] They were, therefore, supported by the most powerful actors in the Japanese financial system and *jūsen* were not included in the MoF's attempt to curb real estate speculation in the late 1980s.

While officially under the guidance of the Ministry of Agriculture, Forestry and Fisheries (MoA), *jūsen* were in fact under the unofficial guidance of the MoF. Due to political pressure in 1991, the MoF froze all real estate transactions pending an investigation into the role of the *jūsen*. This first investigation into the activities of *jūsen* found that 40 percent of their loans were already non-performing.[82] The MoF's response was to "socialize" the risk and in 1992 when the largest of the *jūsen*, *Jūtaku Kin'yū*, was about to collapse, the MoF arranged for a joint bailout with the Sanwa bank to ensure that the *jūsen's* interest payments were made. In 1993 the MoF redistributed *Jūtaku Kin'yū's* non-performing loans burden to nine city banks. Although *jūsen* losses were essentially hidden from the public, the MoF 1993 suggestion for a taxpayer funded complete bailout of the *jūsen* "brought long-simmering public unease over the ministry's vast powers to a rolling boil."[83] The revelation that the chairmen of five of the seven *jūsen* were former elite bureaucrats from the MoF also went down badly. Despite the efforts of LDP politicians to persuade the people that the management of the crisis was consistent with Japanese norms, an electoral revolt led to the removal of the LDP from its thirty-eight-year reign in the Diet following the perception that the MoF and the LDP were too autonomous from society.[84]

The LDP's electoral defeat was thus a consequence of the withdrawal of public consent over changes to the Japanese financial reform nexus and support for a reformist political party that would represent the interests of urban Japanese LIGs. Supporters of the Japan New Party that led the coalition that replaced the LDP were "genuinely disturbed by the deep-seated corruption" of the LDP and sought economic deregulation.[85] A breakdown of

80. Statistics Bureau, *Japan Statistical Yearbook*, Tables 12.20, 13.20, various years between 1985 and 1997.

81. Takatoshi Ito, "The Stagnant Japanese Economy in the 1990s: The Need for Financial Supervision to Restore Sustained Growth," in Takeo Hoshi and Hugh Patrick, eds., *Crisis and Change in the Japanese Financial System* (Norwell: Kluwer, 2000), 89.

82. Curtis J. Milhaupt, "Japan's Experience with Deposit Insurance and Failing Banks: Implications for Financial Regulatory Design?" *Washington University Law Quarterly* 77, 2 (1999): 414–18.

83. Hiwatari Nobuhiro, "The Reorganization of Japan's Financial Bureaucracy: The Politics of Bureaucratic Structure and Blame Avoidance," in Hoshi and Patrick, eds., *Crisis and Change*, 114–15; Jon Choy, "New Financial Watchdog Faces Uphill Battle," *JEI Report*, 25, 3 July (1998): 4.

84. Amyx, *Japan's Financial Crisis*, 166–67.

85. Pempel, *Regime Shift*, 203.

the votes demonstrated that it was young urban Japanese who had voted against the LDP and who "were less susceptible to the politics of personal favors because they want second bedrooms, not an extra *tatami* mat."[86]

One problem for LIGs who sought voice through the electoral system was a highly fragmented political party system (as opposed to the views of Japan as a "strong state" discussed above). From my count there were no less than twenty new or renamed political parties (not factions) formed, splintered, and realigned between 1992 and 1997. The only party to retain its identity throughout this period was the LDP.

Political party fragmentation hampered the development of a cohesive representative party for LIGs and led to the following scenario. The new coalition government began under the leadership of the Japan New Party and its new leader, Hosokawa Morihiro. However, due to financial scandals and leadership changes, the prime ministership was soon handed over to Hata Tsutomu of the Renewal Party (*Shinseitō*). Hata's government collapsed in 64 days, and the LDP was soon back in the corridors of power, this time under a coalition government with the Japan Socialist Party (the *Shakaitō*, which then changed its name to the Social Democratic Party of Japan in January 1996). The opposition parties were too busy bickering amongst themselves to mount an effective opposition. Former prime minister Hata, for example, had split from his party to form the *Taiyōtō* party in 1996, which then became the *Minseitō* party in 1998. *Minseitō* then merged with the Democratic Party of Japan (*Minshutō*). The LDP-Social Democratic coalition government was initially led by "socialist" Murayama Tomiichi, but he was soon replaced by the LDP's Hashimoto Ryūtarō. So within eleven months of the LDP's electoral defeat, it was back in charge under a LDP-Socialist coalition!

The only positive element of this period was electoral reform, which all non-LDP parties insisted upon. The new 1994 electoral reform shifted the Japanese system from a multi-member district system to a mix of single-seat and proportional representation. This change would ideally permit the voting public to punish politicians' use of "public money to rescue unworthy causes."[87] However, despite electoral reform, rural votes were still worth twice the value of urban votes. As a consequence the LDP won office in the 1996 election while failing to win over 30 percent of the vote in any urbanized area.[88] It was back to the old-style Japanese politics.

---

86. Peter F. Cowhey, "Elect Locally—Order Globally: Domestic Politics and Multilateral Cooperation," in John Gerard Ruggie, ed., *Multilateralism Matters: The Theory and Praxis of an Institutional Form* (New York: Columbia University Press, 1993), 178. A *tatami* mat is a traditional Japanese mat, measuring about two meters by one meter, used as a standard by which to measure a residence's floor space.

87. Frances Rosenbluth and Ross Schaap, "The Domestic Politics of Banking Regulation," *International Organization* 57, 2 (2003): 332.

88. Matthew Carlson, "Consequences of Electoral Reform in Japan: The Changing Costs and Quality of Competition," paper presented to the Annual Meeting of the American Political Science Association, San Francisco, 30 August–2 September 2001, 16–20.

Extrastructure and the *Dai-Hinmin* Game

In Japan during the 1990–95 period, the funding of public works—what Gavan McCormack calls "extrastructure"—was larger, as a percentage of GDP, than the total value of defense contracts in the United States during the height of the Cold War period.[89] This "extrastructure" represented a massive burden on Japanese LIGs and the weakening legitimacy of the Japanese financial reform nexus because it was paid for out of tax revenue and postal savings. It restricted LIGs' access to credit for property, since the funds came out of the same source. Compounding this problem for LIGs was the implementation of a consumption tax. Akin to the famous Japanese card game *dai-hinmin*, where the poorest player gives her/his two best cards to the richest player at the start of the game, LIGs were increasingly worse off.

Japan's growth in extrastructure depended upon the issuing of public debt to the extent that by 1995 Japan's public indebtedness was 7.6 percent of GDP, compared with 2.8 percent in the United States.[90] More important than extent of indebtedness is who it was for. Of the bonds issued in 1985, ¥8 trillion (57 percent) were "construction bonds." In 1990 nearly all of the issued debt was in construction bonds and in 1995 it comprised ¥17 trillion of the ¥22 trillion issued (77 percent).[91] Even without considering the economic stimulus packages implemented to boost domestic consumption in the 1990s, Japanese public investment was two to three times larger than that of other G7 states and there was widespread "public recognition that the public works budget is the most significant source of political corruption."[92] By the mid-1990s one-third of all Japanese river beds were concreted, cool climate freeways were heated, bullet trains sped to sparsely inhabited but politically important rural destinations, and plans were underway for the construction of an artificial "Island City."[93] At the same time, one-fifth of Japan's roads were not suitable for vehicular traffic and massive problems existed with the quality of public housing.[94]

Rather than an example of strong state intervention to boost domestic consumption and near-full employment, extrastructure was clearly indica-

89. Gavan McCormack, "Afterbubble: Fizz and Concrete in Japan's Political Economy," JPRI Working Paper 21 (Washington, D.C.: Japan Policy Research Institute, June 1996), 2.
90. Pempel, *Regime Shift*, 147–48.
91. Financial Systems Council, "Final Report of the Special Committee for Financial Structural Reform: Conditions for a Vigorous Twenty-First Century" [*Zaisei kōzō kaikaku tokubetsubukai saishū hōkoku: katsuryoku aru nijūisseiki heno jōken*] (Tokyo: Ministry of Finance, 12 December 1996), 22.
92. Mishima Ko, "The Changing Relationship Between Japan's LDP and the Bureaucracy: Hashimoto's Administrative Reform Effort and its Politics," *Asian Survey* 38, 10 (1998): 974. See also Brian Woodall, *Japan under Construction: Corruption, Politics, and Public Works* (Berkeley: University of California Press, 1996).
93. Gavan McCormack, "Breaking the Iron Triangle," *New Left Review* 13, January/February (2002): 14.
94. Fukui Haruhiro and Shigeko N. Fukai, "Pork Barrel Politics, Networks, and Local Economic Development in Contemporary Japan," *Asian Survey* 36, 3 (1996): 269–70.

tive of rentier interests and a source of declining state capacity. This is more so if we consider the source of funds for extrastructure, the *zaitō*. While the *zaitō* can be seen as a source of long-term funds for key industries,[95] it does draw upon *yūcho* savings while LIGs continued to be frustrated by their lack of access to credit. Between 1992 and 1995 the *zaitō* provided ¥60 trillion to public works, of which at least 70 percent came from the *yūcho*, allowing rentier interests to "channel the population's life savings into a wide range of debt-encrusted public bodies."[96] To make matters worse, it has been estimated that the costs of collusion for extrastructure were 33 percent of the industry's revenues in the 1990s, and that the Japanese state could abolish the socially regressive consumption tax and still enhance state revenues if firm antimonopoly laws were put in place.[97]

There are good reasons to link the growth in extrastructure to the increase in consumption tax. The LDP supported consumption tax increases in the 1980s to permit income tax cuts, but also to provide direct support to the development of public works. The increase in consumption tax from 3 percent to 5 percent passed through the Diet in 1994 and was introduced in 1997. Ironically it was not an LDP leader but the "socialist" prime minister Murayama Tomiichi who supported the rise in consumption tax under the banner of the "people's welfare tax" (*kokumin fukushizei*).[98] The Japanese public did not agree. Surveys from a range of newspapers between 1994 and 1996 illustrates that 72 percent of those surveyed called for an abolition of the consumption tax altogether.[99]

The 1994 2 percent increase in the consumption tax, as in 1989, was also accompanied by ¥2 trillion in income tax cuts. While the increase may seem small, by 1995 consumption taxes made up one-third of all tax revenue. During the 1985–2000 period, while taxes in the United States were becoming increasingly direct, in Japan they were becoming evermore indirect. In the United States during the 1985–99 period, income tax as a percentage of total tax revenue increased from 45 to 49 percent, while indirect taxes decreased from 18.8 to 16.3 percent. In Japan during the same period income tax dropped from 45 to 31 percent, while indirect taxes (primarily the consumption tax) increased from 14 to 20.1 percent.[100] Furthermore, my cal-

95. Weiss, *Myth of the Powerless State,* 140.

96. Estimates on how much the *yūcho* provides to the *zaitō* vary. McCormack argues that it is 100 percent, while Dick Beason and Jason James cite a 1998 figure of 72 percent. I have taken the lower figure. See McCormack, "Afterbubble," 4; Dick Beason and Jason James, *The Political Economy of Japanese Financial Markets: Myth versus Reality* (Basingstoke: Macmillan Press, 1999), 181.

97. Johnson, *Japan, Who Governs?* 77–78.

98. Junko Kato, "When the Party Breaks Up: Exit and Voice among Japanese Legislators," *American Political Science Review* 92, 4 (1998), 861–64; Adam S. Posen, *Restoring Japan's Economic Growth* (Washington, D.C.: Institute for International Economics, 1998), 50.

99. From 1994–96 surveys in the following newspapers: *Tōkyō Shimbun, Asahi Shimbun, Nikkei, Mainichi Shimbun,* and *Sankei.*

100. OECD, *OECD Revenue Statistics, 1965–2000,* 142, Table 56, 174–75, Table 71.

culations on the impact of the 1997 consumption tax hike indicate that the effective increase in the tax bill for household incomes above ¥8 million was up by approximately 25 percent, while the effective tax bill on household incomes below ¥6 million increased by approximately 33 percent. The elderly, who paid 34 percent more, were the worst affected by the tax reform among LIGs.[101]

The increased tax burden on LIGs also meant that they had less access to home ownership simply because they had less money to spare for the necessarily exorbitant deposit. In contrast to the United States, the percentage of Japanese households with mortgage debts actually declined from 33 percent in the late 1980s to 28 percent in the late 1990s, while at the same time overall Japanese household indebtedness increased by 13 percent.[102]

Bearing in mind that land prices in Japan by 1995 had returned to 1985 levels in terms of affordability, the question remains why did the HLC not return to lending to Japanese LIGs and alleviate LIGs' "tremendous pent-up demand for better housing"?[103] The answer is that by the mid-1990s the HLC had clearly become an institution to subsidize cheap housing loans for upper-income groups and landlords. Accordingly, the OECD commented in 2000, "Unlike many other countries which target support on social housing, the [HLC] scheme in Japan . . . is quite regressive."[104]

Once more LIGs sought to punish the state at the ballot box. In 1998, the LDP lost the Upper House again when the Fiscal Structural Reform Act of 1998 proposed an increase in public works, further cuts in income taxes, and no revision of consumption tax rates. The electoral defeat was attributed to the consumption tax and discontent among Japanese urban LIGs.[105] They were also angry about taxpayer monies being used to bail out financial institutions.

Crocodile Tears and Wardrobe Deposits

In 1995 the world's top ten banks were still Japanese but they were only one-third as profitable as U.S. banks, and they had not embraced securitiza-

---

101. Japanese Consumer Cooperative Union, *Senkyūhyaku kyūjūnananen no kazokukōseibetsu szōshishan* [Calculations of tax burdens according to family characteristics] (Tokyo: Japanese Consumer Cooperative Union, 1997), 1.

102. Mortgage indebtedness figures from Ministry of Internal Affairs and Communications, "Results for Survey of Saving Trends 2000" [*Heisei jūninen chochiku dōkō chōsa kekka*] (Tokyo: Ministry of Internal Affairs and Communications, 15 March 2001), 1.

103. Johnson, *Japan, Who Governs?* 76; Tachibanaki and Shimono, "Wealth Accumulation Process," 244–47. Tachibanaki and Shimono suggest that by the mid-1990s "renter households in Tokyo and other metropolitan areas [were] giving up on the hope of ever being able to afford a home."

104. OECD, *OECD Economic Surveys, Japan* (Paris: OECD, 2000), 141–43.

105. Ihori Toshihiro, Doi Takero, and Kondo Hiroki, "Japanese Fiscal Reform: Fiscal Reconstruction and Fiscal Policy," *Japan and the World Economy* 13, 4 (2001): 353.

tion.[106] The main reason for the slow turn to securitization was that banks carried masses of non-performing loans on their books from losses on the "bubble economy." In 1997 the MoF estimated the value of non-performing loans to be ¥30 trillion ($230 billion), while private estimates were ¥93 trillion ($700 billion).[107] The extent of the non-performing loan problem led Japanese banks to try desperately to earn revenue in order to retire bad debt. It also placed more pressure on the MoF, although the ministry was slow in responding.

Once again, the handling of the *jūsen* problem was illustrative of the weakening legitimacy of the financial reform nexus and the bungling of the MoF, as "public criticism of the MoF reached a pitch unparalleled in postwar history."[108] By 1995 all of the *jūsen* were insolvent and had non-performing assets to the tune of ¥5.3 trillion ($42.4 billion). The losses were so severe that the MoF made it clear that should *jūsen* fail, the agricultural cooperatives that had lent to them would also fail, and therefore taxpayer funds would have to be made available to support these politically sensitive interests. As a consequence, and despite MoF assurances that taxpayer monies would not be used to bailout *jūsen*, ¥685 billion ($7.71 billion) from tax revenue went directly into a Jūsen Resolution Corporation to bail out bad *jūsen* loans and to compensate agricultural cooperatives.[109] In a poll conducted by the newspaper *Asahi Shimbun*, 90 percent of the respondents objected to the idea that Japanese taxpayers' monies should be used to soak up bad loans from *jūsen*.[110]

There was growing frustration over the MoF's inaction on financial reform. While in 1995 the MoF had established a Financial System Stabilization Committee and furthered the work of the Cooperative Credit Purchasing Company (CCPC), the extent of their operations was "little more than doing nothing."[111] Furthermore, in 1995 the collapse of the Hyōgo Bank and Cosmo and Kizu Credit Cooperatives completely drained the Japan Deposit Insurance Corporation, leading to increased public anxiety about the safety of their deposits. But they had little means of finding out as the MoF continued to restrict information to the public on the extent of bad loans and used a "settlement of accounts approval system" (*kessan shōnin seido*) for troubled banks that kept external auditors from assessing the extent of the non-performing loan problem.[112]

106. McCormack, "Breaking the Iron Triangle," 8.
107. To provide a comparison this figure is equal to seven-eighths of all commercial and industrial loans made in the United States. See Edward J. Lincoln, "The 'Big Bang'? An Ambivalent Japan Deregulates its Financial Markets," *Brookings Review* 16, 1 (1998): 37.
108. Amyx, *Japan's Financial Crisis*, 171.
109. Rosenbluth and Thies, "Electoral Foundations," 30.
110. Ibid., 14.
111. See Thomas F. Cargill, "Deposit Guarantees, Non-Performing Loans and the Postal Savings System in Japan," Working Paper 93–14 (Sydney: Centre for Japanese Economic Studies, Macquarie University, 1993), 6.
112. Figures provided by *Kyōdo saiken kaitori kikō* [Cooperative Credit Purchasing Company], cited in *Imidas '98* (Tokyo: Shūeisha, 1997), 75.

Public concern allowed the minority parties in the Diet to campaign, during the 1996 election year, for an overhaul of the MoF and the entire financial system. In response, the Hashimoto administration also announced a "Biggu Bangu" plan to deregulate the financial system over the next five years (akin to England's 1986 "Big Bang").[113] But the most publicly significant change for mid-1990s financial reform was that the MoF's standard policy of not permitting banks to fail but merging them instead itself failed. In 1997 the tenth largest city bank, the Hokkaidō Takushoku Bank (known as *Takugin*), was about to collapse and the MoF arranged a merger with the Hokkaidō Bank to ensure that *Takugin* could dispose of its non-performing loans.[114] The Hokkaidō Bank, however, rejected the merger (and the prospect of masses of non-performing loans) and *Takugin* subsequently collapsed, clearly indicating that MoF intervention systems had also collapsed, sparking a short-lived run on banks from depositors.[115] Also of concern to the public—and other states in the international financial order—was the surprise that, while the MoF had stated that *Takugin* had a capital adequacy ratio of 9.34 percent, it was soon revealed that its real capital adequacy was zero. *Takugin* was not alone in failing to meet Basle Accord standards, for during 1997–98 more than thirty Japanese banks withdrew from international operations to avoid the Basle Accord's 8 percent capital adequacy requirement in favor of the Japanese government's more relaxed 4 percent.[116]

Such cover-ups and withdrawals increased public anxiety and frustration over financial reform. This was compounded by seemingly endless revelations of scandals from MoF bureaucrats and the resignation of Finance Minister Mitsuzuka Hiroshi over bribery charges. In dramatic fashion those implicated in scandals publicly apologized and wept, but little changed. The public opposed, unsuccessfully, the ¥7.45 trillion ($61 billion) of taxpayer monies used to offset bad loans in 1998, including the first nationalizations of financial institutions in the postwar period.[117] Once more the LDP was punished with significant electoral losses in the House of Councillors (winning only 35 percent of seats) in the 1998 election.[118] Following the elec-

113. Henry Laurence, *Money Rules: The New Politics of Finance in Britain and Japan* (Ithaca: Cornell University Press, 2001), Chapter 6.

114. Matsushita Yasuo, "Recent Monetary and Economic Conditions in Japan and the Reform of Financial Markets," *Bank of Japan Quarterly Bulletin*, August (1997): 9; Edward J. Lincoln, "Japan's Financial Mess," *Foreign Affairs* 77, 3 (1998): 62. The collapse of Yamaichi securities during the same period is obviously also important, but my focus here is on changes to banks.

115. Amyx, *Japan's Financial Crisis*, 182.

116. David Woo, "In Search of the 'Capital Crunch': Supply Factors Behind the Credit Slowdown in Japan," Working Paper 99/3 (Washington, D.C.: Monetary and Exchange Affairs Department, International Monetary Fund, 1999), 4, 15.

117. The Nippon Bank and the Long-Term Credit Bank. See "Troubled Bank is Nationalized by Japanese," *New York Times*, 24 October 1998: C1.

118. Statistics Bureau, *Japan Statistical Yearbook*, Table 22–7, 2002.

tion the LDP introduced a Financial Revitalization Law, which established a Financial Revitalization Commission (FRC), and plans for a "bridge bank" to assist industrial financing (without consulting the MoF). While the FRC was a lackey of the MoF, a new regulatory body, the Financial Supervisory Agency (FSA, renamed the Financial Services Agency in July 2000), was established with some real clout. The new overseer was given a budget of ¥60 trillion ($500 billion) and was responsible to the Diet, providing greater means for public contestation of financial regulation.[119]

While the FSA was a positive development to allow greater public influence over financial reform, Japanese LIGs were actively fleeing the system due to the Japanese state's incapacity to legitimate the financial reform nexus. The continuing fragility of the financial system led ordinary Japanese savers to withdraw their savings from the depository financial institutions and to place them in the *yūcho*, or into "wardrobe deposits" (*tansu yokin*, storing the cash at home).[120] In 1998, runs on smaller banks and credit unions led to ¥5 trillion of flows out of smaller depository financial institutions and into the *yūcho*.[121] Thus, although in Figure 6.1 we see a marked increase in investment in the *yūcho*, it was largely due to increased anxiety about the government's capacity to implement real financial reform.[122] Other than the *yūcho*, the growth of "wardrobe deposits" meant that the growth of cash in circulation was five times greater per capita than in the United States and indicative of a "country where banks are not lending to people and people are not spending."[123]

Interestingly, for those who could afford it, U.S. banks operating in Japan provided some relief. Following a 1995 agreement that gave permission for U.S. banks to attract retail business in Japan, Citicorp was able to attract ¥1.5 trillion ($12.5 billion) in deposits due to its capacity to generate personal credit, including mortgages.[124] The success of U.S. banks in Japan underlined the fact that the revenue of U.S. banks weighed against their assets was a ratio of 15:1 compared to Japanese banks of 80:1. U.S. banks were simply more willing to lend to the Japanese public than Japanese banks. More to the point, Japanese banks were still intensely interested in rentier activity.[125]

119. See Amyx, *Japan's Financial Crisis*, Chapter 9.

120. My thanks to Shogo Suzuki for passing on this newly emerged phrase.

121. "Japan's Long Winter," *Economist*, 17 April 1999: 25; Woo, "In Search of the 'Capital Crunch,'" 17.

122. A 1997 BoJ survey found that in 1991 30 percent of Japanese invested their money according to profitability and 37 percent according to safety. By 1997 only 15 percent of Japanese people deposited for profitability and 50 percent for safety. The third category was fungibility. See Bank of Japan, *Chochiku to shōhi ni kansuru seron chōsa* [Public survey on savings and consumption] (Tokyo: Bank of Japan, 1997), ⟨www.boj.or.jp/ronbun/97/ron9709a.htm⟩.

123. R. Taggart Murphy, "Japan's Economic Crisis," *New Left Review* 1, January/February (2000): 44.

124. To place this in context, Japan's largest bank, the Bank of Tokyo-Mitsubishi, had in 1997 ¥82 trillion in assets. "Japan's Long Winter," 24.

125. Ibid.

The *Hara-Kiri* Trade and the Asian Monetary Fund

In the late 1990s market actors in the international financial order actively punished states it considered to be retarding financial reform or which excessively engaged in "lending long and borrowing short." Under a continuing rentier strategy Japan did both. While many scholars blamed the United States for creating the Asian financial crisis of 1997–98, Japan was the primary culprit.[126]

Ten years after the Plaza Accord the yen had appreciated to ¥80:$1 and encouraged further international investment by Japanese financial institutions. In 1995 bilateral negotiations between the United States and Japan over a "New Economic Partnership" led to the revaluing of the yen at ¥145:$1, but the revaluation did not slow the exporting of capital. The rapid outflow of capital from Japan was also supported by a continuation of the BoJ's "very cheap money" policy. While in the mid-1980s interest rates within Japan were around the two to 3 percent range, in 1995 the BoJ lowered interest rates to a historical low of 0.5 percent.

As mentioned above, the Japanese state's response to the non-performing loan crisis was to allow banks to try and invest their way out of trouble. This environment soon produced what became known as the "yen-carry" trade (and later as the *"hara-kiri"* or self-disembowel trade), which constituted borrowing at very low interest rates in yen and then investing in Southeast Asian states. In most Southeast Asian states, where domestic interest rates were twenty times the Japanese equivalent, the practice was extremely profitable. As a consequence, in 1990–96 Japanese banks lent more to Southeast Asia than they had in the previous three decades. In 1996–97, 30 percent of international loans to Southeast Asia were from Japanese sources, up from 26 percent in 1995, and much of it for commercial real estate interests.[127] The sheer volume of the "yen-carry" trade placed huge inflationary pressures on the recipient states and caused concern in the international financial order over why the Japanese state, unable to reform itself, was encouraging such financial stresses.

In particular, punishment for Japan's domestic and international financial practices came from the "Japan premium." A premium on Japanese banks' international lending activities was first put in place in 1992, following the bursting of the bubble. However, it was in the mid-1990s that it exerted the most influence. At its peak in 1997, the Japan premium added 1.2 percent interest on Japanese banks' international lending (adding an additional $1.7 trillion to the cost of lending in 1995).[128] The "Japan premium"

126. Richard Leaver and Leonard Seabrooke, "Can the IMF be Reformed?" in Walden Bello, Nicola Bullard, and Kamal Malhortra, eds., *Global Finance: New Thinking on Regulating Speculative Capital Markets* (London: Zed Press, 2000), 99. See also Michael J. King, "Who Triggered the Asian Financial Crisis?" *Review of International Political Economy* 8, 3 (2001): 446–47.
127. OECD, *OECD Economic Surveys, 1997–1998* (Paris: OECD, 1998), 59.
128. Hanajiri Tetsuro, "Three Japan Premiums in Autumn 1997 and Autumn 1998: Why did

recognized the dangers of Japan's banks rapidly exporting capital while at the same time having masses of non-performing loans, but it did not sufficiently slow lending.

In the 1990s Japanese banks' investments in Southeast Asia outweighed U.S. banks by a ratio of six to one.[129] Japanese banks lent the most to Thailand and it was therefore no surprise that the Asian financial crisis began there. At the time of the crisis Japanese banks were heavily exposed to Thailand ($37.5 billion), South Korea ($24.3 billion), Indonesia ($22 billion), and Malaysia ($8.2 billion). Accordingly, in 1998 Japan's nine biggest commercial banks put aside ¥300 billion ($2.6 billion) for non-performing loans from Southeast Asia. However, the extent of non-performing loans actually amassed to ¥750 billion ($6.5 billion).[130] Worse still, Japanese banks were soon trapped in a "Catch-22." For most of them, writing off non-performing loans would have placed their capital adequacy ratios below Basle Accord standards, forcing them to withdraw from the international financial order. If they did not write off the loans they faced the continuing prospect of the "Japan premium."

It is in this context that the Japanese state put forward an alternative framework through a proposal for an Asian Monetary Fund (AMF) that advertised itself as a "friendly neighborhood bank" in contrast to the apparently draconian U.S.-led International Monetary Fund (IMF). The proposed fund would provide $100 billion to assist Asian states in crisis, with fewer conditionality rules than the IMF and with repayment of loans over a longer period. Funding for the institution would come primarily from Japan, but also from China, Hong Kong, Taiwan, and Singapore.[131] However, one problem with this framework was that it rested on Japan's financial system, which had proven not only to be slow to respond to crises, but was suffering from a serious non-performing loan problem.

While the AMF proposal outlined that the institution would provide "administrative guidance" for crisis-stuck states and that as long as they had "complied with the good practice guidelines, there would be an assured line of credit," critics pointed to Japan's inability to perform the same task.[132] Indeed, this was precisely the criticism made by Michel Camdessus, the managing director of the IMF, who argued that Japan should drop the proposal

Premiums Differ Between Markets?" Financial Markets Department Working Paper Series 99-E-1 (Tokyo: Bank of Japan, August 1999), 4–5; Bank of Japan, *Annual Review 1998 for Fiscal 1997* (Tokyo: Bank of Japan, 1998), 122.
129. Seabrooke, *U.S. Power,* 181, Figure 6.1.
130. Jennifer A. Amyx, "Political Impediments to Far-Reaching Banking Reforms in Japan: Implications for Asia," in Gregory W. Noble and John Ravenhill, eds., *The Asian Financial Crisis and the Architecture of Global Finance* (Cambridge: Cambridge University Press, 2000), 143–46.
131. Leaver and Seabrooke, "Can the IMF be Reformed?" 97, 102–3, 107–8.
132. Graham Bird and Ramkishen Rajan, "Is There a Case for an Asian Monetary Fund?" *World Economics* 1, 2 (2000): 141.

and that if it wanted to assist the region then it should deal with its own financial system reform first. More important, the Clinton administration opposed the formation of an AMF on the grounds that it would lead to "reform shopping" from Southeast Asian states and would not impose the necessary market discipline.[133] The Japanese government soon dropped the proposal, blaming U.S. pressure.

Following the withdrawal of the AMF proposal, the plan was repackaged in 1998 as the "New Miyazawa Initiative" under former Prime Minister and Minister of Finance Miyazawa Kiichi, which provided $30 billion ($15 billion in short-term funds, $15 billion in medium-to-long-term financing) for similar purposes as the proposed AMF, but on a bilateral rather than multilateral basis.[134] Clearly Japan was not able to adopt a multilateral leadership role that could provide an alternative framework for the international financial order without reforming domestically.[135] To augment Japanese international financial capacity, Japan needed to heighten the legitimation of its domestic financial reform nexus.

Conclusion: Moderate Legitimation of the Financial Reform Nexus

Japan in the last quarter of the twentieth century underwent a rentier shift that led to the extraction of rents from LIGs and the declining legitimacy of the financial reform nexus. Across the financial reform nexus, on tax, property, and credit, Japanese LIGs received the short end of the stick. In particular, the use of *yūcho* provided an extra tax on LIGs as it was then used to prop up rentiers through funding public works, "extrastructure," and subsidizing the cheap housing loans for the wealthy. In contrast, Japanese LIGs were alienated from access to credit for homeownership, providing a clear difference between Japan's HLC and the U.S.'s FMAs. On top of these sources of frustration was the imposition of a consumption tax and incapacity to reform the "9-6-4" system, both of which harmed Japanese LIGs and supported rentier's interests. Japanese LIGs' access to credit and property was therefore effectively blocked while their tax burdens continued to increase.

Japan's once championed "strong state" economic agencies, like the MoF, proved to be heavily implicated in rentier activity (as with the *jūsen*) and will-

133. See Leaver and Seabrooke, "Can the IMF Be Reformed?" 96–101.
134. Helleiner, "Still an Extraordinary Power," 242–43.
135. An alternative framework was designed by the Manila Framework Group, which developed under the Association of Southeast Asian Nations (ASEAN) to provide monitoring of financial conditions but not to provide an independent body. Coordinated with the Chiang Mai initiative that links ASEAN to China, Japan and South Korea (the ASEAN+3) both sought to provide regional forms of financial governance explicitly not under Japanese leadership. See Worapot Manupipatpong, "The ASEAN Surveillance Process and the East Asian Monetary Fund," *ASEAN Economic Bulletin* 19, 1 (2002): 111–23.

ing to use taxpayer monies to bail out their surveillance failures. The LDP's failure to represent LIGs in preference for landlords, "urban farmers," elites within the construction sector, and electorally powerful rural constituencies belies the common tropes about Japan having a firm social consensus on how the economy should run, and that Japan is a fundamentally egalitarian society. This chapter demonstrates that not only should forms of state intervention be disaggregated into positive and negative types, but that doing so reveals that we should not conflate institutional change and social change.

While institutional rigidity prevailed among Japanese financial institutions and assisted the stagnation of the financial reform nexus, Japanese LIGs frequently contested changes in how the economy should work, seen most clearly in the multiple dethronings of the LDP following a period of stable rule from 1948 to 1993. During the 1985–2000 period the Japanese state's broad use of negative intervention was increasingly out of step with LIGs' expectations about how state intervention should lead to redistribution throughout the financial reform nexus that would enhance their lifechances.

Instead, the Japanese state extracted rents from LIGs for rentier interests. By the end of the decade, the amount of taxpayer funds already committed to the bailout of Japanese commercial banks and the *jūsen* was already five times greater than the amount paid out by the U.S. government for the commercial banking and S&L crises of the 1980s. But, as argued by Eugene Dattel, the key distinction between U.S. and Japanese financial reform is that in the United States "the public learns the extent of the damage and who is to blame; individuals are held accountable; the problems are not systemic; and institutions adjust."[136] As suggested above, discovering the extent of the non-performing loan problem was a source of greater anxiety for Japanese LIGs as they acted on their beliefs and increasingly withdrew their money from financial institutions to place it in the *yūcho,* or in the wardrobe.[137] The Japanese state's propagation of a "wait and see" social consensus norm on the handling of financial crises weakened the legitimacy of the financial reform nexus.

---

136. Eugene Dattel, "Cultural Captivity: Japan's Crippled Financial System," *World Policy Journal* 13, 1 (1996): 35.
137. In addition, in 2000 the Housewives Association raised concerns about the prevalence of redlining within the Japanese financial system and access to housing loans for LIGs. *Shufu rengō kai* [Housewives Association], *Jūtaku kinyū ni tsuite no iken* [Suggestions concerning housing loans], 2000, ⟨www.mlit.go.jp/jutakukentiku/house/dainikai/3-2watanabe.pdf⟩. There have been, however, discussions initiated by the U.S. Department of Housing and Urban Development and the Japanese Ministry of Posts and Telecommunications on the need for a CRA-like agreement. See Fukumitsu Hiroshi, "*Reddorainingu ron kara Kinyū haijo ron he—yūshi sabetsu ron no tenkai to sono igi*" [From the argument of redlining to finance], unpublished study, Ministry of Posts and Telecommunications, 2000, ⟨www.fbc.keio.ac.jp/~kaneko/JSME/01s106-fukumitsu.pdf⟩. Since November 2002 the Democratic Party of Japan has been pushing a *Kinyū asesumento hō* [Financial Assessment Act] similar to the U.S. CRA ⟨www.dpj.or.jp/english/policy/plan.html⟩.

Recent estimates of Japan's non-performing loan problem suggest that in the closing years of the twentieth century it was intensifying rather than diffusing. Estimates range between ¥80–100 trillion ($600–750 billion) by the U.S. government, ¥111 trillion ($840 billion) by the IMF, and up to ¥240 trillion ($1.8 trillion) by financial market analysts. At worst, the non-performing loan problem in 2000 was equal to half of Japan's GDP and represented over three times the amount of bad loans the Japanese financial system had been able to retire in the 1990 to 2000 period.[138]

In addition to the private crisis in Japan, in 2000 it was revealed that the Japanese state was possibly up to ¥780 trillion (or $5.89 trillion) in the red. In the English case the Liberal Party was a "party of thrift." In the Japanese case the long-ruling Liberal Democratic Party was a "party of gluttons." By 2000 Japan was the most indebted state in the OECD despite persistent claims concerning the massive private financial wealth in Japan as a source of financial power. As a consequence it has been predicted that the Japanese government will soon not be able to meet its welfare obligations to LIGs.[139]

Despite the rise of Japan's financial institutions to the top-twenty lists of world's largest banks and brokerage houses in the late 1980s, and despite the massive outflows of investment during the 1990s, Japanese international financial capacity rested on a shaky domestic foundation. As discussed in the first chapter, international financial capacity is not simply volumetric but also involves the capacity to influence the regulatory and normative environment of the international financial order. Such influence, in turn, is based on a state's domestic legitimation of its financial reform nexus. The Japanese state's post-1985 negative state intervention assisted a rentier shift that led to bad international investment choices and weak regulatory and normative influence. The frequent violations of public expectations undermined the massive potential Japan had to broaden and deepen the domestic pool of capital through positive state intervention. In sum, considering the Japanese state's systematic extraction of rents from LIGs, its incapacity to reform the financial system, and overwhelming failure of its rentier strategy, one might conclude that Japanese international financial capacity was effectively hoist on its own petard.

138. McCormack, "Breaking the Iron Triangle," 7–8.
139. As commented by McCormack, the previous record for indebtedness was set by Britain, which in 1947 had debt equivalent to 707.57 percent of tax revenues. In Japan in 2000 the equivalent figure was 1,548.5 percent. McCormack, "Breaking the Iron Triangle," 10–11, 21; Beason and James, *Political Economy,* 129–33.

7

The Social Sources of International Financial Orders

The key proposition of this book is that if a state intervenes positively to legitimate its financial reform nexus for lower-income groupings (LIGs), it can provide a sustainable basis from which to increase its international financial capacity. A state does so by deepening and broadening the domestic pool of capital and by propagating economic social norms that generate financial innovations and strengthen a state's influence on the regulatory and normative character of the international financial order. However, as the previous chapters demonstrate, most states do not intervene positively into their financial reform nexuses for LIGs and impede their international financial capacity by instead supporting rentier interests. And in some cases they directly support a "rentier shift."

I have elected not to examine how states adapt to changes within the international financial order to compete more effectively. In fact, I have actively avoided the competitive-adaptation models often discussed within "state capacity" and "varieties of capitalism" literature, and instead have concentrated on specifying how domestic dynamics, particularly the state's legitimation of its financial reform nexus to LIGs, affects the domestic basis from which the state engages the international financial order. Rather than mapping the "national trajectories" of England, Germany, Japan, and the United States, the aim has been to understand how the social sources of financial power were undermined or augmented. Here I concentrate on the international effects of fundamentally domestic choices, and particularly how we can see links between behavior within the principal state to the character of the international financial order, and any challenges to that order posed by a rival.

As discussed in the first two chapters, my intention is not to provide a general theory on the domestic sources of international financial orders. My theoretical ambitions are much more modest and linked to the ideal type of how state intervention may link the pocketbooks of LIGs through a chain of financial institutions to the global financial marketplace. In discussing different financial orders at the international level my aims are also humble. I do not assert that a state's influence on the international financial order led to claims to legitimacy that are then conferred by other states. Assessing such claims and their conferral or denial within an international financial order would require another book. My interest here is to understand how variation in the domestic legitimacy of states led to different social constructions of international financial orders. To do so requires us to consider how domestic changes within the principal financial power lead to an entirely different normative and regulatory character of the international financial order. We can provide such an analysis by examining differences in types of investment and regulatory and normative standards held as benchmarks and focal points in different historical periods.[1] The main aim in this chapter is to differentiate the international financial orders of the periods under study by their domestic social sources. At all times, what happens abroad relates to what happened in the legitimation of the financial reform nexus at home.

In the first period under study, English primacy led to the construction of an international rentier economy. The main rival to English primacy, Germany, was unable to influence the character of the international financial order. It is undisputed that England had greater international financial capacity than Germany between 1890 and 1915. By 1914, London was undeniably seen as the focal point for the management of the international monetary system, with 40 percent of securities issued globally emerging from the City's financial institutions and exchanges.[2] While Germany was perceived as the key rival to English primacy in the international financial order, it was not able to extract credit from the international financial order (as demonstrated by problems in obtaining war loans), nor did it export capital to any great degree. Germany also had little influence over the regulatory and normative structure of the international financial order. As also discussed in Chapter 4, England would not have benefited from adopting Germany's model of state intervention, as professed by a number of English and German scholars of the period, because German state intervention was primarily negative. Rather, England's problem lay in its inability to legitimate its financial reform nexus sufficiently. This was because while the Liberal Party's rhetoric on social reform recognized that contestation was alive and well among LIGs, it did not implement policy changes to redistribute

1. See, more generally, Randall D. Germain, *The International Organization of Credit: States and Global Finance in the World Economy* (Cambridge: Cambridge University Press, 1997), and Paul Langley, *World Financial Orders: An Historical International Political Economy* (London: Routledge/RIPE Series in Global Political Economy, 2002). See also Leonard Seabrooke, "Civilizing Global Capital Markets: Room to Groove?," in Brett Bowden and Leonard Seabrooke, eds., *Global Standards of Market Civilization* (London: Routledge/RIPE Series in Global Political Economy, forthcoming).
2. See Ranald Michie, *The London and New York Stock Exchanges, 1850–1914* (London: Allen & Unwin, 1987), 91.

the financial reform nexus in LIGs' favor and block a rentier shift. As a consequence, the state was increasingly out of step with the economic social norms held by LIGs, and the propagation of norms on the benefits of rentier investment increased LIGs' frustration and left England financially vulnerable to the shock of World War I.

In the latter period, U.S. primacy led to the construction of an international creditor economy. Japan attempted to influence the character of the international financial order but was undermined by its domestic rentier shift that undercut its international financial capacity. We may be surprised by this finding were we to base our conclusions on a volumetric study of capital exports. Indeed, when considering the massive export of capital from Japan following the Plaza Accord of 1985 (discussed in Chapter 6), one could suggest that it is more difficult to argue that the United States had greater international financial capacity than Japan during the 1985–2000 period. Certainly the growth in foreign assets and liabilities for Japanese commercial banks—the key financial institution in Japan—was enormous. Between 1985 and 1990 Japanese commercial banks' assets increased nearly sixfold (from $126.2 billion to $719.8 billion), and continued to grow past the bursting of the bubble economy ($1 trillion), until returning to below 1992 levels in 1999 ($760 billion).[3] But, as argued in the previous chapter, the choice of assets was poor and exacerbated the problems in reforming the Japanese financial system. Greater resources do not necessarily lead to greater influence on the regulatory and normative character of the international financial order.[4]

The U.S.'s influence, however, was strong. As indicated in Chapter 5, U.S. commercial banks attained record profits in the 1990s from the benefits of the securitization process and from resurgence in lending activity, including increased mortgage credit. The role of Federal Mortgage Agencies (FMAs) as a "global securities giant" in securitizing mortgage credit in excess of $1 trillion by the mid-1990s generated a source of capital to be used by U.S. financial institutions and corporations in the international financial order.[5] Accordingly, when one accounts for the U.S.'s key financial institutions, the

---

3. Calculated from International Monetary Fund (IMF), *International Financial Statistics, November 1990* (Washington, D.C.: IMF, 1990), 308–9, lines 21 and 26c; IMF, *International Financial Statistics, November 1995* (Washington, D.C.: IMF, 1995), 330–31, lines 21 and 26c; IMF, *International Financial Statistics, June 2000* (Washington, D.C.: IMF, 2000), 428–29, lines 21 and 26c. I have adjusted the figures from yen to dollars in accordance with yearly exchange rate fluctuations. Furthermore, Japanese commercial banks' foreign liabilities increased nearly fivefold between 1985 and 1990 (from $203.9 billion to $1 trillion) before reducing to nearly half their size by 1999 ($533.1 billion).

4. Eric Helleiner, *States and the Reemergence of Global Finance: From Bretton Woods to the 1990s* (Ithaca: Cornell University Press, 1994), 203. Compare with Germain, *The International Organization of Credit,* 166.

5. Anthony M. Santomero and David L. Eckles, "The Determinants of Success in the New Financial Services Environment: Now That Firms Can Do Everything, What Should They Do, and Why Should Regulators Care?" *Economic Policy Review* 6, 4 (2000): 11.

Untied States had both greater foreign assets and liabilities than Japan. In particular, U.S. foreign holdings of equity and foreign direct investment were significantly larger than Japan's ($2.14 trillion in foreign direct investment in 1998 for the United States, compared with Japan's $270 billion in the same year, or the U.S.'s $1.4 trillion in equity securities, compared with Japan's $209 billion).

The only category of foreign financial assets in which Japan held more than the United States was in debt securities ($561 billion for the United States in 1998, compared with the $852 billion for Japan), most of which were U.S. Treasury debt. In fact, during the closing decade of the twentieth century the United States was able to enhance its capacity to extract capital from the international financial order and into its debt as the percentage of U.S. Treasury debt held by non-residents increased from 16.9 percent in 1988 to 35.7 percent in 1999.[6] Undoubtedly, the United States had greater international financial capacity than Japan, especially when we consider how the United States dominated the regulatory and normative environment of the international financial order (which I discuss below).

These findings conflict with standard views of U.S. power within the international political economy, including those that emphasize "hegemony" and "state capacity."[7] Within such literature U.S. influence is viewed as perverse. From this perspective, U.S. elites exercise international power at the expense of their poorer fellow Americans and the U.S. relies on its international power to compensate for its fragmented political and regulatory structure, and consequent lack of state intervention in the economy.[8] It follows, according to this logic, that if a more interventionist and apparently egalitarian state were the principal in the system, such as Japan, we would have had a more stable international financial order in the 1985–2000 period. I address this question below.

The problem here is that most studies do not sufficiently disaggregate state intervention into positive and negative forms, and that they view the state-society complex as a functional rather than a contested space. As discussed in Chapter 2, if we are to have a serious treatment of how legitimacy affects the creation of social sources of financial power, then we need an approach where economic social norms can influence the state from the bottom up. We would then be able to see, for instance, that Japan intervened negatively during the 1985–2000 period: that the Japanese state ignored contestation from LIGs, that it redistributed assets to rentiers, and that its

---

6. During the period overall, Treasury debt held by U.S. residents increased 1.35 times, while non-resident holdings increased 3.6 times. Calculated from IMF, *International Financial Statistics, November 1995*, 604–5, lines 59ta–59tb, 79aad–79aed; IMF, *International Financial Statistics, June 2000*, 432–33, 804–7, lines 59ta–59tb, 79aad–79aed.
7. Germain, *International Organization of Credit;* Linda Weiss, *The Myth of the Powerless State: Governing the Economy in a Global Era* (Cambridge: Polity Press, 1998).
8. Linda Weiss, "State Power and the Asian Crisis," *New Political Economy* 4, 3 (1999): 331.

propagation of economic social norms that encouraged the concealment of financial problems alongside international rentier investment frustrated LIGs and led to the weakening legitimacy of the entire financial reform nexus. In stark contrast, the United States demonstrated positive state intervention for LIGs and was able to broaden and deepen the domestic pool of capital, encourage financial innovations, and increase its international financial capacity. In short, if we wish to understand the domestic sources of why international financial orders differ, then treating legitimacy as an important social source of financial power is a vital step.[9]

Figures 7.1 and 7.2 summarize the case studies and link the legitimation of domestic financial reform nexuses to the structure of the international financial order in the historical periods under study (on which I expand below). All cases but the United States are examples of relative failure, of which Germany was the worst. Despite Germany's perceived ability to rival English international financial capacity, Germany was effectively a "non-starter" due to the low legitimation of its financial reform nexus. It was trapped in a fiscal struggle between the Reich and *Länder* that prevented the formation of a coherent financial system. The subsequent abuse of the *Sparkassen,* the exaggerated power of the *Großbanken,* the blocking of financial reforms to protect the interest of large landowners, and the feudal-like structures within the cooperative system, were all reflections of Germany's low legitimation of the financial reform nexus for LIGs. While there was state intervention across the financial reform nexus, it was for the benefit of the Prussian landed interests, and for the protection of local conservative elites (who also had access to the *Sparkassen*), both of whom extracted rents from LIGs. This negative state intervention, at both the Reich and *Länder* levels, led to socially regressive changes across the financial reform nexus for LIGs. As can be seen in Figure 7.1, taxes increasingly became indirect (for example, "the dear loaf"); LIGs were disabled from property ownership; and their access to credit was captured within the fiscal struggle described above. The political impediments of the mixed electoral system blocked the contestation of financial reform and avenues that would ameliorate the low legitimation of the financial reform nexus. There were insufficient grounds upon which to build German international financial capacity, and when English primacy was challenged by World War I, Germany did not provide an alternative framework for the international financial order, but was caught up in a struggle to finance a war effort with only minor assistance from a society of financially powerful states from which it had effectively isolated itself.

The English case demonstrated that English international financial capacity was built on a sufficiently legitimated foundation between 1840 and

---

9. An alternative conception is to study democratic transition. Democracy often enhances legitimacy but the two are not necessarily parallel. See Kenneth Schultz and Barry R. Weingast, "The Democratic Advantage: Institutional Foundations of Financial Power in International Competition," *International Organization* 57, 1 (2003).

Figure 7.1 Domestic legitimacy of financial reform nexuses and the character of the international financial order, 1890–1915

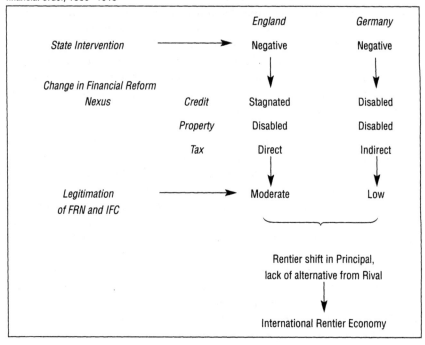

1890. By 1900 England still had the highest legitimation of a financial reform nexus among the states under examination (recall that state intervention is positive until 1890). The increase in rentier activity that accompanied the post-1890 construction of gentlemanly capitalism and the Liberal government's decision not to intervene against the rentier shift led to its weakening legitimacy. England was effectively pulled in two directions: first, toward the state playing a positive interventionist role through increasing direct taxation on rentiers, and thereby recognizing changing economic social norms in England that agitated for greater political representation; and, second, the Bank of England's (BoE) support for bank concentration and financial impoverishment of the provinces, and the City of London's support for international rentier investment. As shown in Figure 7.1, the second direction won the tug of war. As discussed in Chapter 3, the increase in People's Budget taxes on rentier's interests was only of symbolic value, as it did not significantly add to the state's coffers or capacities. In addition, LIGs were not permitted access to property ownership, despite their frequent complaints, and their credit systems stagnated or were used to supplement government revenue.

Figure 7.2 Domestic legitimacy of financial reform nexuses and the character of the international financial order, 1985–2000

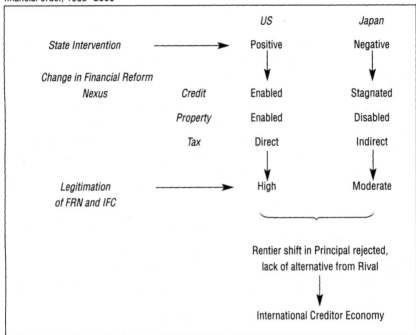

In short, the English state did not sufficiently legitimate the financial reform nexus for LIGs. As a consequence, as noted in Figure 7.1, the combination of the principal state's only moderate domestic legitimation and the rival state's low domestic legitimation led to an "international rentier economy." By 1915 the only moderate legitimation of the English financial reform nexus provided an insufficient resource upon which to generate ongoing English international financial capacity and, as a consequence, England was unable to sustain primacy in the international financial order following the financial shock of World War I.

It is commonly assumed that the Japanese case most closely resembles the German case because both states are viewed as heavily interventionist. But, as this book demonstrates, Japan more closely resembles the English case, important differences notwithstanding. The similarities are most evident in changes to property and credit relations. In both Japan and England, LIGs were effectively disabled from accessing property and their credit systems stagnated or were used to supplement government revenue. The English case differs by being more socially progressive on taxation. We may recall that in contrast to England's Liberal Party, which was a "party of thrift," Japan's Liberal Democratic Party (LDP) was a "party of gluttons" that actively supported rentier activity.

With the "cheap money" policy that followed the Plaza Accord of 1985, the Japanese LDP supported a shift to rentier activity. This led to regressive changes across the financial reform nexus with an increased extraction of rents from LIGs to support rentier activity at home and abroad. While financial institutions such as the Japan Housing Loan Corporation (HLC) had fulfilled a positive social role in earlier decades, by the mid-1980s they became socially regressive. The development of the *jūsen* housing loan companies, originally formed to enable LIGs' access to mortgage credit through a more competitive domestic system, is the most dramatic example. As seen in Figure 7.2, taxes became increasingly indirect (consumption tax), access to property ownership was increasingly disabled (while LIGs subsidized dominant economic groups' access to cheap mortgages through the HLC), and credit systems stagnated or were used to extract rents from LIGs, such as the use of *yūcho* savings to support "extrastructure." As a consequence, rather than sufficiently legitimating the financial reform nexus to LIGs, the Japanese state's redistribution in favor of rentiers led Japanese LIGs not only to withdraw their consent for the legitimacy of the financial reform nexus, but to withdraw from the use of financial institutions (the growth in "wardrobe deposits").

The pre-1994 Japanese electoral system encouraged the LDP's gluttony and favored the interests behind the Japanese state's rentier shift. Effectively, the lack of political representation under the electoral system and the autonomy of the Ministry of Finance (MoF) from societal interests removed any voice for LIGs to contest financial reforms within Japan. Even after the 1994 electoral reform, urban Japanese LIGs were still effectively blocked from altering the financial reform nexus in their favor. Furthermore, although Japanese banks were able to increase their international banking assets post-1985, the Japanese state proved incapable of reforming its financial system when the bubble burst. In lieu of reform, the burden fell on taxpayers to bail out bad investments. The Japanese case emphasizes the importance of disaggregating forms of state intervention to understand why its international financial capacity weakened despite its high volume of international assets and liabilities.

The U.S. case provides the exception and allows us to differentiate the international financial order in the late nineteenth/early twentieth centuries from the late twentieth century. Under the first Reagan administration there was a rentier shift that led to a series of calamities, both domestic (savings and loans associations [S&L] and commercial bank crises) and international (the debt crisis). But by the mid-1980s there was a movement to block the rentier shift. This movement was strongly influenced by community activism from groups such as the National Community Reinvestment Coalition and National People's Action, and by the Democrats in Congress, which led to a restructuring of the U.S. financial system. Contestation therefore directly aided redistribution that enabled LIGs with greater access to credit for property ownership through the emboldened role of Federal Mortgage Agencies, which coincided with the growth and propagation of the securitization process. At the same time, tax changes also favored LIGs in 1986, 1993, and 1996, and were complimented by the U.S.'s encouragement of the Bank for International Settlement's (BIS) Basle Accord, which effectively represented a tax on the world's commercial banks—especially Japanese banks—to boost U.S. government revenue through the sale of Treasury debt. Furthermore, despite perceptions concerning a slow, "gridlocked," socially regressive process of financial reforms, private financial institutions lent increasingly to LIGs, particularly on residential mortgages supported with positive state intervention.

As noted in Figure 7.2, LIGs benefited from increasingly direct taxes (taxing upper-income groups and banks), from a system for property ownership that directly enabled LIGs to acquire property (and then use their securitized mortgage payments to provide capital to corporate America), and from a credit system that strongly encouraged financial institutions to lend to LIGs despite earlier misgivings about creditworthiness. The United States was therefore able to legitimate its financial reform nexus to LIGs to a high degree. As a consequence, the expansion of the U.S. financial system provided a more sustainable basis from which to project international financial capacity and give itself a buffer against international financial shocks. As noted in Figure 7.2, the combination of the principal state's high domestic legitimation and the rival state's moderate domestic legitimation led to an "international creditor economy."

The International Rentier Economy, 1890–1915

In 1909 John A. Hobson wrote that as the state positively intervened to enhance social liberal freedoms, it would ideally take over the provision of credit to legitimate access for all LIGs. For Hobson, while the "interests of the individual borrower lies in secrecy, that of society lies in publicity . . . as credit is an essential element to liberty."[10] Hobson argued that the international financial order would be inherently unstable if the state was not able to perform this role.

As we now know, the English state was unable to play the role Hobson wished for it because the Liberal Party did not sufficiently attack the power

---

10. John A. Hobson, *The Crisis of Liberalism: New Issues of Democracy* (London: P. S. King and Son, 1909), 105–6.

of the rentiers and the construction of gentlemanly capitalism.[11] Credit relations within England reflected how those with high economic, social, and political status sought to defend their "positional premium" and suppress the life-chances of LIGs as changes to economic social norms intensified their frustrations at the lack of access to credit and property. As a consequence of the English rentier shift, assessments of creditworthiness were increasingly tied to gentlemanly capitalists, which in turn required the establishment of face-to-face communication in order to maintain one's reputation.[12] Georg Simmel, for example, provides some insight into the distinctions of the time by arguing that in England "the common man is one who buys goods by cash payment; a gentleman is one to whom I give credit and who pays me every six months by cheque."[13] As discussed in Chapter 3, this situation worsened following banking concentration, as provincial local bank managers were disempowered from using their local information to enable credit access to customers they knew.

The international financial order increasingly reflected these dynamics in the decade preceding World War I. The consequent "international rentier economy" became dependent upon the domestic legitimation of a financial reform nexus that was increasingly shaky and a state that was effectively disengaged. The reflection of domestic rentier characteristics in the international financial order can be seen in England's treatment of the Gold Standard, its treatment of international finance regulation, and in the types of investment predominant throughout the period. All three reflected aspects of the domestic legitimation of the financial reform nexus and problems in assessing creditworthiness at the international level.

While some political economy scholars have pointed to England's apparent "hegemony" in orchestrating the Gold Standard, the key characteristic of England prior to World War I was its hands-off approach.[14] The society of states participating in the Gold Standard effectively supported the monetary order in coordination with, rather than under the direction of, the BoE. Indeed, according to Patrick O'Brien, England took no responsibility for "maintenance of convertibility, for price and exchange rate stability," and "offered no advice to other monetary authorities about the management of national supplies of money, credit and loans."[15] This approach also carried

11. Hobson recognized the failings of the Liberals and redirected his calls for state intervention to the Labour Party during World War I. See Leonard Seabrooke, "The Economic Taproot of US Imperialism: The Bush *Rentier* Shift," *International Politics* 41, 3 (2004): 300.

12. Nigel Thrift and Andrew Leyshon, "A Phantom State? The De-Traditionalization of Money, the International Financial System and International Financial Centres," *Political Geography* 13, 4 (1994): 316.

13. Georg Simmel, *The Philosophy of Money* (London: Routledge and Kegan Paul, 1978), 479.

14. On England's need to coordinate with other states in the maintenance of the gold standard see Giulio Gallarotti, *The Anatomy of an International Monetary Regime: The Classical Gold Standard, 1880–1914* (Oxford: Oxford University Press, 1995), Chapter 1.

15. Patrick Karl O'Brien, "The Pax Britannica, American Hegemony and the International

across to the types of investment used by English investors, and their view of international financial regulation. English rentiers relied on the English state to overcome problems in assessing the creditworthiness of others, while dismissing any international financial regulation that would increase scrutiny on the creditworthiness of English investors. As discussed in Chapter 3, English rentiers relied on an imperial naval defense system to defend their financial interests (the dreadnoughts issue exploited by Lloyd George in 1909). At the same time, the rentier rejected increased direct taxation to pay for social reform, or even for a military build-up that could stave off international antagonisms.[16]

In the 1890–1915 period, developing states received 63 percent of global foreign direct investment, whereas in the 1985–2000 period they received only 28 percent.[17] Due to problems in assessing the creditworthiness of states receiving investment, 85 percent of English overseas portfolio investment was in moderate-to-high risk debt securities, which financed governments that could be pressured or punished, and industries such as railways, mining, metallurgy, and telephony that were under English control.[18] As such, English investors argued that a "creditor nation cannot afford to be weak" in the enforcement of its contracts, and required the corresponding naval power to do so.[19] The most profitable of foreign investments during the 1890–1915 period were Argentinean railways bonds, for which the capital came from English investors and where English naval intervention into Argentina was explicitly stated, should there be a default on investment. English rentiers called upon their state to threaten the use of force to guarantee financial returns.[20] Groups such as the English Corporation for Foreign Bondholders provoked the English state into threatening debtor states to enforce the payment of private loans, or face international "blacklisting."[21]

Economic Order, 1846–1914 and 1941–2001," paper presented at Thirteenth Congress of the International Economic History Association, Buenos Aires, 23 July 2002, 26. This view is also supported in John H. Clapham, *The Bank of England: A History*, Vols. 1 and 2 (Cambridge: Cambridge University Press, 1944).

16. John M. Hobson, "The Military-Extraction Gap and the Wary Titan: The Fiscal-Sociology of British Defence Policy, 1870–1913," *Journal of European Economic History* 22, 3 (1993): 504–5.

17. Richard E. Baldwin and Philippe Martin, "Two Waves of Globalization: Superficial Similarities, Fundamental Differences," NBER Working Paper No. 6904 (Cambridge, Mass.: National Bureau of Economic Research, 1999), 20.

18. Michael D. Bordo, Barry Eichengreen, and Jongwoo Ki, "Was There Really an Earlier Period of International Financial Integration Comparable to Today?" NBER Working Paper No. 6738 (Cambridge, Mass.: National Bureau of Economic Research, 1998), 17.

19. Hanford J. Mackinder, *Britain and the British Seas* (London: MSG Haskell House, 1906), 346.

20. Lance E. Davis and Robert Huttenback, *Mammon and the Pursuit of Empire: The Political Economy of British Imperialism, 1860–1912* (Cambridge: Cambridge University Press, 1987), 263–64.

21. Trish Kelly, "Ability and Willingness to Pay in the Age of Pax Britannica, 1890–1914," *Explorations in Economic History* 35, 1 (1998): 31–36, 42.

These were not idle threats, and were realized in Venezuela in 1903 and Peru in 1907. Luis Drago, the Argentinean jurist and foreign minister in the early 1900s, argued that "Britain's normal, if not absolutely invariable practice has been to take coercive military or naval measures, or to threaten them, in defence of her citizens, only when these were wronged by the seizure of their property or by personal injuries."[22] English influence on the regulatory and normative character of the international financial order favored coercion over assessments of creditworthiness, and therefore military might rather than regulatory right. For English rentiers the only alternative to the face-to-face establishment of creditworthiness was denial of credit (in the domestic context for English LIGs) or the use of negative state intervention through force (in the international context).

But England found its use of force to ensure return on investments difficult to sustain in the international financial order. At the Hague Conference of 1907, the United States persuaded England to sign onto the Drago Doctrine (named after the Argentinean jurist and foreign minister mentioned above) that limited the use of force against defaulters and, instead, recommended international arbitration. While in 1906 England rejected the doctrine on the grounds that it reserved the right to intervene to protect the property of English citizens in "countries of doubtful honour," by 1907 it could no longer justify its use of force to the society of states in the international financial order, especially when English LIGs were railing domestically against the use of dreadnoughts to support rentier activity.[23]

While England eventually signed the Drago Doctrine, it would not sign onto international financial regulation that would scrutinize the creditworthiness of English investors. For example in 1912, with the idea of taming international finance, European states championed an "International Uniform Law on Bills of Exchange and Promissory Notes." Although thirty of the thirty-eight attending states signed the convention, it was rejected by England and the United States and subsequently failed.[24] England rejected it on the basis that it had always maintained a *laissez-faire* approach to the international financial order and that, as the proposed regulatory framework law would keep a register of personal investors' activities, it was an infringement on personal liberties.[25] This attitude reflected the domestic construction of gentlemanly capitalism where, despite the supposed rationalization of credit access that accompanied bank concentration, creditworthiness was assessed through the medium of informal social settings, not farmed out to an international regime.

22. Cited in Charles Lipson, *Standing Guard: Protecting Foreign Capital in the Nineteenth and Twentieth Centuries* (Berkeley: University of California Press, 1985), 54.
23. Kelly, "Ability and Willingness to Pay," 43.
24. Institute of Bankers, Correspondence Relating to Conference on Bills of Exchange and Cheques at The Hague, June 1912, BoE Archives, CCO 1094.
25. Ibid.

The types of investment favored by English investors, the rejection of external international financial regulation, and the attitude toward the use of force to secure returns on investment typified the international rentier economy. As argued in Chapter 3, English international financial capacity rested on increasingly dubious domestic foundations, particularly as LIGs railed against rentier behavior, and English middle class "superloyal schizoids" came to question their strange combination of state liberalism with imperialism.[26] Worse still, the City of London and rentiers' attitudes toward the war was that they "did not believe in its coming" despite their hand in escalating conflict among imperial powers.[27]

Furthermore, because Germany was fundamentally a "non-starter" due to its reluctance "to peer below the horizons of Europe" and its domestic incapacities, the decline in English international financial capacity left the immediate post–World War I international financial order in a regulatory and normative vacuum that greatly exacerbated international financial instability.[28] As a consequence, World War I shattered the Gold Standard, and England was not able to reestablish itself as the principal in the international financial order following the conflict. In part this was, once more, a consequence of England's choice of investments, as states with large investments abroad were most damaged by the financial shock of World War I. England's problems in assessing creditworthiness at home and abroad led to the development of an "international rentier economy" in which the use of force was associated with the potential for increased investment. This link between militarism and rentier interests proved unsustainable.

The International Creditor Economy, 1985–2000

Within the United States, positive state intervention was extended domestically between 1985 and 2000. Rather than relying on the threat of force to combat uncertainty surrounding creditworthiness, or concentrate overwhelmingly on portfolio investment, the international financial order under U.S. primacy reflected regulatory initiatives to enhance creditworthiness assessments.[29] This objective was entirely in accordance with entrepreneurial

26. Michael Mann, *The Sources of Social Power, Vol. 2: The Rise of Classes and Nation-States, 1760–1914* (Cambridge: Cambridge University Press, 1993), 292, 583. Compare with Rudolph Hilferding, *Finance Capital: A Study of the Latest Phase of Capitalist Development* (London: Routledge and Kegan Paul, 1981), 322, in which this contradiction is recognized as generated by finance capital.
27. Clapham, *Bank of England*, 2: 415.
28. Avner Offer, *The First World War: An Agrarian Interpretation* (Oxford: Clarendon Press, 1989), 404.
29. This conclusion is also supported in Layna Mosley, *Global Capital and National Governments* (Cambridge: Cambridge University Press, 2003). Mosley finds that financial market traders go easy on developed states, but place much greater scrutiny on developing states in assessing their capacity to handle foreign debts. See also Timothy J. Sinclair, *The New Masters of Cap-*

economic social norms within the United States, although it did *not* reflect a redistributive domestic norm that permitted LIGs access to credit for property ownership.

As a consequence, U.S. investment, in contrast to English investment in the 1890–1915 period, was more heavily involved with direct investment than in debt securities. And unlike the English case, increased credit generation to the international financial order did not decrease domestic credit generation. During the 1985–2000 period, credit generation was not tied to the "ideological fiction" of a metallic standard, and the ongoing generation of credit, at home and abroad, was possible provided there were means of assessing and enforcing creditworthiness.[30]

A driving force of the changing structure of the "international creditor economy" during the 1985–2000 period was the legitimation of the U.S. domestic financial reform nexus for LIGs. In Chapter 5 we saw that there was a rejection of the first Reagan administration's rentier shift. Following the debt crisis, public opposition to U.S. commercial banks' risky loans to Latin American states led to the International Lending Supervisory Act of 1983, and support for the implementation of the Basle Accord.[31] Additionally, the cleanup following the S&L and commercial bank crises led to regulations that required banks to disclose information on their lending activities according to gender, race, geographic location, and socioeconomic status. Further reforms under the Clinton administration bolstered regulation to assess who was receiving credit, including the 1994 augmentation of the Community Reinvestment Act that placed commercial banks' lending to LIGs under heightened scrutiny.

In the "international creditor economy" of 1985–2000, the United States encouraged assessments of creditworthiness by encouraging international institutions that at least had formal, if not substantive, legitimacy among sovereign states who were members, and institutions that were at least officially—even if not actually—separate from direct U.S. control.[32] The United States encouraged assessments of creditworthiness among a society of states, within which recalcitrants were punished with premiums or were forced to withdraw from global finance. The imposition of a "Japan pre-

ital: American Bond Rating Agencies and the Politics of Creditworthiness (Ithaca: Cornell University Press, 2005).

30. There are numerous accounts of the de-linking of credit from the supposed "gold-dollar standard" of the Bretton Woods system to the "paper dollar" standard following the collapse of Bretton Woods. See, in particular, Fred Block, *The Origins of International Economic Disorder: A Study of United States International Monetary Policy from World War II to the Present* (Berkeley: University of California Press, 1977). My own attempt is Leonard Seabrooke, *US Power in International Finance: The Victory of Dividends* (London: Palgrave, 2001), Chapters 3 and 4.

31. We also noted that the Japanese state reacted very differently to the debt crisis, using taxpayer funds to bailout Japanese banks' non-performing loans.

32. Louis W. Pauly, *Who Elected the Bankers? Surveillance and Control in the World Economy* (Ithaca: Cornell University Press, 1997), 18–19.

mium" and thirty Japanese banks' withdrawal from international operations due to a failure to meet Basle Accord standards in 1997–98 alone provides an important example. Of course, our best example can be seen in the Basle Accord of 1988 (1992), which represents the most significant international financial regime during the 1985–2000 period and demonstrates that the United States encouraged regulation that would enhance the assessment of creditworthiness, as well as increase the extractive capacity of the U.S. government.[33] In contrast, the United States did not support an international financial regime to increase scrutiny on securities trading. Thus while banks' lending operations were under greater public scrutiny, particularly in the domestic realm, securities companies were left comparatively untouched.[34] Rather, responsibility for creditworthiness assessments of debt securities increasingly fell upon credit rating agencies such as Moody's and Standard and Poor's.[35]

From the mid-1990s the United States increasingly encouraged the growth of international financial regimes that would improve the assessment of creditworthiness. In the late 1990s, for example, the BIS increasingly allowed more "crisis prone" states to sign on to the Basle Accord, demonstrating the continuing movement to assess creditworthiness. From the late 1980s the Group of Seven (G-7—the United States, Japan, United Kingdom, France, Germany, Canada, and Italy) met with the International Monetary Fund (IMF) to coordinate financial information and augment the IMF's surveillance capacities to become the "very core of the institution."[36] But surveillance did not result in an expanded financial capacity for the IMF because the United States holds 17 percent of votes within the institution that requires 85 percent of votes for a "special decision." The U.S. veto over some IMF actions in times of financial crisis, such as the U.S. Congress's rejection of an IMF loan to Mexico in 1995 and refusal to approve an $18 billion IMF loan during the Asian financial crisis, has led the Fund to expand its scope of activities with little formal official institutional change.[37] So while the IMF's surveillance powers were heightened during the 1985–2000 period, its working capital was seriously run down over the post–World

33. Thomas Oatley and Robert Nabors, "Redistributive Cooperation: Market Failures, Wealth Tranfers and the Basle Accord," *International Organization* 52, 1 (1998): 37–41. See also Ethan B. Kapstein, *Governing the Global Economy: International Finance and the State* (Cambridge, Mass.: Harvard University Press, 1994), Chapter 5.

34. Despite the establishment of the International Organization of Securities Commissions in 1984 and its increased membership from 80 in 1990 to 159 in 1998, there is scant evidence to suggest that the regime has any teeth. See Geoffrey R. D. Underhill, "Keeping Governments Out of Politics: Transnational Securities Markets, Regulatory Cooperation and Political Legitimacy," *Review of International Studies* 21, 3 (1995).

35. See, in particular, Sinclair, *The New Masters of Capital.*

36. Pauly, *Who Elected the Bankers?* 41, 129.

37. Barry Eichengreen and Richard Portes, "Managing the Next Mexico," in Peter Kenen, ed., *From Halifax to Lyons: What Has Been Done About Crisis Management?* (Princeton: International Finance Section, Department of Economics, Princeton University, 1996), 29.

War II period (from being equivalent to 12.8 percent of the value of world imports in 1948 to 3.5 percent in 1998).[38] Again, this is entirely consistent with the U.S. economic social norms of entrepreneurship to enhance the assessment of creditworthiness without an economic social norm of redistribution to enhance property ownership for LIGs. As J. Lawrence Broz's research demonstrates, LIGs encourage Congress to vote for legislation that betters their life-chances across the financial reform nexus, but they are adamant that foreign states should not receive assistance paid for by the U.S. taxpayer.[39]

U.S. influence on the regulatory and normative structure of the international financial order has been understood as the enforcement of western "universal" financial norms upon states that discourages different interpretations of standards of creditworthiness or financial practices according to domestic economic social norms.[40] While this allegation holds some water, Layna Mosley's study demonstrates that Organisation for Economic Co-operation and Development (OECD) states have more "room to move" under financial market scrutiny than previously thought. Mosley found that in assessing creditworthiness, financial markets are interested in the stability of monetary policy, not in who governs the state under examination or how much and—importantly for the domestic legitimation of a financial reform nexus—in what ways governments spend their budgets.[41] Furthermore, while states considered to be emerging market economies are undoubtedly under more scrutiny than OECD states, as long as they "talk the talk" of conforming to international financial regulation and market practices—particularly by providing financial data and signaling the presence of institutions that meet with global standards—financial actors that assess creditworthiness will allow them more flexibility in how they "walk the walk" of everyday political and economic governance.[42]

38. Michael D. Bordo and Harold James, "The International Monetary Fund: Its Present Role in Historical Perspective," NBER Working Paper No. 7724 (Cambridge, Mass.: National Bureau of Economic Research, 2000), 53, Figure 1; Richard Leaver and Leonard Seabrooke, "Can the IMF be Reformed?" in Walden Bello, Nicola Bullard, and Kamal Malhotra, eds., *Global Finance: New Thinking on Regulating Speculative Capital Markets* (London: Zed Press, 2000), 102.

39. J. Lawrence Broz, "Congressional Politics of International Financial Rescues," *American Journal of Political Science* 49, 3 (2005).

40. Jacqueline Best, "Civilizing through Transparency: The International Monetary Fund," in Bowden and Seabrooke, eds., *Global Standards*.

41. Layna Mosley, "Room to Move: International Financial Markets and National Welfare States," *International Organization* 54, 4 (2000): 748, Table 1. From Mosley's interviews, only 5.6 percent of participants cited "who governs" as important in their assessments, while 11.8 percent cited how much governments spend, 31 percent on how they spend their budgets, 92.6 percent on inflation, and, finally, 96.6 percent on the size of the government deficit.

42. Piggy-backing on Mosley's argument, I refer to emerging market economies having "room to groove" within the boundaries of market signals that suggest institutional isomorphism in accordance with a global standard of market civilization. See Seabrooke, "Civilizing Global Capital Markets."

The proliferation of common standards within the society of states in the "international creditor economy" ballooned in number in the 1990s. For example, from the mid-1990s the BIS and the IMF put in place data dissemination standards for their members. From the mid-1990s the G-7 leaders met to discuss plans for a new "Global Financial Architecture," and in 1999 the G-10 created a Financial Stability Forum in coordination with the BIS, IMF, and World Bank.[43]

In June 1999 the G-7 promoted the use of the IMF's new *Code of Good Banking Practices in the Area of Monetary and Financial Transparency*, which recognized the need for capital controls in times of emergency and sought to improve universal standards of transparency to increase the capacity to anticipate crises.[44] The G-7 also expanded to a G-20 in order to increase the number of developing states involved in determining the new structure of financial regulation. While we have good grounds to be skeptical, the international financial order in the late 1990s became characterized by a regulatory and normative structure with an increasing focus on creditworthiness that permitted the increased participation of developing states—an "achievement of historic proportions, even if much remains to be worked out."[45]

Furthermore, small or weak states have demonstrated that they do have power in the international financial order even in cases in which international organizations have moved strongly against, such as the OECD's Harmful Tax Practices Regime and the Financial Action Task Force's "blacklisting" of tax havens believed to provide illegal tax services. Tax havens have been able to shine the light of transparency and creditworthiness back upon the developed states, effectively using both the regulatory and normative character of the international financial order as a means of protection and empowerment.[46] Thus, while developing states in the 1985–2000 period were under far more international regulatory scrutiny than during 1890–1915, they were largely removed from the threat of force to guarantee returns on

---

43. Bank for International Settlements, *Bank for International Settlements 69th Report* (Basle: BIS, 1998), 154–55. Although it has eleven members, the G-10 is the G-7 plus Belgium, the Netherlands, Sweden, and Switzerland. See also Layna Mosley, "Are Global Standards the Answer? National Governments, International Finance, and the IMF's Data Regime," *Review of International Political Economy* 10, 2 (2003).

44. Eric Helleiner, "Regulating Capital Flight," *Challenge* 44, 1 (2001): 26–27; Jacqueline Best, *The Limits of Transparency: Ambiguity and the History of International Finance* (Ithaca: Cornell University Press, 2005).

45. Randall D. Germain, "Global Financial Governance and the Problem of Inclusion," *Global Governance* 7, 4 (2001): 422. The G-20 includes Argentina, Australia, Brazil, Canada, China, the EU, France, Germany, India, Indonesia, Italy, Japan, South Korea, Mexico, Russia, Saudi Arabia, South Africa, Turkey, the United Kingdom, and the United States.

46. See Jason C. Sharman, "Small States and Weapons of the Weak in the Global Governance of Tax and Financial Services," in John M. Hobson and Leonard Seabrooke, eds., *Everyday International Political Economy: Non-Elite Actors and the Transformation of the World Economy* (forthcoming).

investment, and were becoming a more consultative force. Despite the massive amounts of private capital in the system, the regulatory and normative framework of the "international creditor economy" is a reflection of the extent of state intervention in financial systems, not its absence.

Finally, it is also interesting to consider the prospect of Japan fulfilling the role of principal in the international financial order during the 1985–2000 period. As noted in Chapter 6, Japan's international financial capacity was undermined by its rentier shift after 1985, leading to a failing capacity to influence the regulatory and normative character of its international financial order. Despite its massive financial wealth, Japan was unable to provide any significant challenge to the U.S.'s international emphasis on entrepreneurial creditworthiness. International financial power cannot be understood as simply volumetric, and once more we return to the point that international financial capacity is built upon a domestic social source of financial power. In turn, we can understand the construction of such financial power only by disaggregating state intervention and investigating the legitimation of the financial reform nexus for LIGs.

8

Liquid Conventions, Saturating Norms

Max Weber argues that it is "the 'interests' of individuals rather than the 'ideas' of an economic administration which will rule the world."[1] The pronouncement of economic ideas, and their embodiment in institutions, will always be secondary to actors' *"economically oriented social actions"* as they struggle with others in pursuit of their life-chances.[2] It is through these very struggles that individuals construct their interests. Individuals are saturated by economic social norms prior to determining their interests, but may also selectively recombine "liquid" conventions to influence these norms.[3] Ideas about how the economy should work—about how money and credit should be used, regulated, and distributed—provide weapons for actors to battle over resources. And such everyday battles over how the economy should work inevitably become centered on questions of legitimacy.

The construction of a social source of financial power must incorporate an understanding of legitimacy because financial relations are based on promises—intersubjective understandings that people will act on their professed beliefs—that mitigate the uncertainty actors face when indirectly placing their capital and trust in the hands of strangers.[4] At the most basic level, financial systems require legitimacy because financial institutions do not transfer money from one particular individual to another, or otherwise capital would be left to stagnate in "innumerable small puddles."[5] Of course, to whom financial institutions choose to lend credit, and under what con-

1. Max Weber, *Economy and Society: An Outline of Interpretive Sociology*, vol. 1 (Berkeley: University of California Press, 1978), 183–84.
2. Ibid., 85–86.
3. Max Weber, *Gesammelte Aufsätze zur Wissenschaftslehre* (Tübingen: J. C. B. Mohr, 1973), 129–30, 579 (hereafter *GAW*); Weber, *Economy and Society*, 1: 32.
4. Geoffrey Ingham, "'Babylonian Madness': On the Sociological and Historical 'Origins' of Money," in John Smithin, ed., *What Is Money?* (London: Routledge, 2000), 36.
5. Joseph A. Schumpeter, *History of Economic Analysis* (Oxford: Oxford University Press, 1954), 319–20; see also Max Weber, *General Economic History* (New York: Collier Books, 1961), 172, 191–92.

ditions, then becomes the key question for the legitimation of any financial institutional and social change.

Weber warned that during his lifetime the increased power of rentier interests within the modern capitalist system was a source of "unfreedom" (*Unfreiheit*) for the broader population as rentiers narrowed domestic financial systems to defend their often ill-gotten political, economic, and social position.[6] Finance during this period was increasingly becoming a "sport" for outer-worldly possessions removed from inner-worldly values.[7] The solution to this problem was for the state to intervene positively in the economy to assist people in lower-income groupings (LIGs) to not only obtain credit, but to have greater access to property and lower tax burdens.[8] Through doing so, LIGs would have more capital at their disposal, a greater potential to build equity, and an increased capacity to participate in a cumulative process of credit creation that could permit more people to achieve their life-chances and also build national financial wealth. Because credit, property, and tax politics—which I have referred to as the "financial reform nexus"—are everyday concerns, they reflect the legitimation of power between the state and social groups. This book has provided a comparative analysis of these concerns to detail what is unique about state-society relations that fosters or hinders the generation of social sources of financial power within different historical and social contexts.[9]

My view that legitimacy is central to the construction of a social source of financial power is at odds with most of the literature on how states generate financial power. As discussed in Chapter 1, most of the literature provides quantitative studies of the factor endowments and institutional logics that provide states with the right opportunity to generate financial power, or stresses path-dependent political structural constraints and "veto players" that hinder financial power.[10] Nearly all of this literature focuses on elites and assumes that they universally seek to maximize their economic utility. This literature has a weak conception of legitimacy and provides only part of the story because while we can explain the fact that State A had certain types of political institutions and therefore financial markets in period X, these approaches provide little understanding of how the state relates to social groups.

6. Max Weber, *Gesammelte Politische Schriften* (Tübingen: J. C. B. Mohr, 1988), 63–64 (hereafter *GPS*). A useful social-economic distinction here is John A. Hobson's use of socially regenerative "wealth" as opposed to socially degenerative "illth." See Leonard Seabrooke, "The Economic Taproot of U.S. Imperialism: The Bush Rentier Shift," *International Politics* 41, 3 (2004): 295–98.
7. Max Weber, *The Protestant Ethic and the Spirit of Capitalism* (London: George Allen and Unwin, 1976), 182.
8. David Beetham, "Max Weber and the Liberal Political Tradition," *Archives Européenes de Sociologie* 30, 2 (1989): 314; Weber, *GPS*, 19.
9. I derive this general aim from the analysis of credit, property, and tax relations in Max Weber, *The Agrarian Sociology of Ancient Civilizations* (London: Verso, 1998).
10. For example, Daniel Verdier, *Moving Money: Banking and Finance in the Industrialized World* (Cambridge: Cambridge University Press, 2002).

I have argued that understanding how states can produce a social source of financial power requires a substantive conception of legitimacy that is currently absent from approaches in political economy and institutional theory. I have outlined how rationalist institutionalists view norms as error terms in explaining institutional change, and how historical institutionalists rely too heavily on path dependent national trajectories. I also criticized economic constructivism for relying too heavily on radical uncertainty and the role of elites to explain institutional change, thereby producing a view of legitimacy by proclamation.

To augment economic constructivism's well-needed focus on how actors use ideas in battles over institutional and social change, I suggested that we turn to Weberian economic sociology and Max Weber's conception of legitimacy. As the previous chapter outlined how the case studies relate to the character of different international financial orders, this concluding chapter discusses the case material in light of the above theoretical points. I also restate the case for how Weberian economic sociology can augment economic constructivism.

Ideal Types, Social Mechanisms, and Institutional Change

This book provides a comparative historical investigation of the legitimation of domestic financial reform nexuses between states, rentiers, and LIGs. My claim here is that the interpretation of these relationships I provide helps us understand the social source of a state's domestic financial power and also its international financial capacity, understood as the capacity to export and extract credit from the international financial order, and to influence the order's regulatory and normative structure. In comparing the cases I used an ideal type and, as with all ideal types, its purpose is not to replicate reality but to posit an abstracted scenario that helps us understand it.[11]

According to the ideal type, positive state intervention in the economy in the interests of LIGs, and against rentiers, will legitimate a financial reform nexus to a high degree, deepen and broaden the domestic pool of capital, and increase the state's international financial capacity. Ideally, positive state intervention encourages financial institutions to lend to LIGs and enables public and private financial institutions to allow a chain of investment that links the LIGs' pocketbook through local and then national institutions to the global financial marketplace. The state can then enhance LIGs' capacity to pursue their life-chances in accordance with their economic social norms, as well as increase its international financial capacity through competitive home-borne financial innovations that both attract international investors to home institutions and permit greater export of capital. It can also

11. Max Weber, *The Methodology of the Social Sciences* (Glencoe, Ill.: Free Press, 1949), 106.

establish a "world's best practice" that influences the regulatory and normative character of the international financial order. As discussed in the preceding chapter, the difference between the international rentier economy of the late nineteenth/early twentieth centuries and the international creditor economy of the late twentieth century can be traced to the domestic legitimation of financial reform nexuses in principal and rival states.

I have posited a social group that can spoil this ideal-typical scenario. Rentiers have been understood in this book as high or very high income individuals who financially profit from what in the old language was called "unearned income" but today is referred to as "passive income" and "portfolio income"; that is, income derived from investments in which the investor has no active participation and which does not "produce" a good: income from rental properties, inappropriate tax subsidies, or dividends and interest from portfolio investment. In this study rentiers are typically passive portfolio investors, landlords, and large agrarian property holders. They can also be politicians who seek to enhance their personal rents, as one key means of providing a stable source of unearned income is to take control of the fiscal purse. Rentiers wish to protect and enhance their economic, political, and social status by redistributing resources within the financial reform nexus (credit and property access and tax burdens) away from LIGs and concentrating them among themselves.[12] To do so, I suggest, they enact a "rentier shift" to influence forms of state intervention and institutional change to alter the financial reform nexus in their favor. A rentier shift, as discussed in the case studies, raises not only the ire of LIGs but also serious questions about the legitimacy of the financial reform nexus.

In comparing the cases against the ideal type, a number of social mechanisms have been identified. The first is contestation, that social groups will contest the legitimacy of state intervention into the financial reform nexus through their belief-driven actions, which can vary from the withdrawal from a particular type of financial institution to open public protest. Contestation then leads the state to reassess its interventions into the economy and engender the second mechanism, the redistribution of political and economic assets and access. The material and ideational consequences of redistribution will assist, prevent, or reverse a rentier shift. The state then makes a claim to the legitimacy of its actions through propagation of ideas on how the economy should work, providing resources for groups to grab onto as they restart the process with further contestation.[13] Important focal points within this dynamic are provided by credit access, property owner-

12. This aim is constant among rentiers in both periods of study and has implications for credit, property, and tax politics. The extraction of rents from LIGs helps us identify rentier behavior in the contemporary period when, as discussed in Chapter 5, LIGs are now also greatly involved in "passive" investments like mutual funds.
13. Paul Pierson, *Politics in Time: History, Institutions, and Social Analysis* (Princeton: Princeton University Press, 2004), Chapter 2.

ship, and relative tax burdens. In the preceding chapters we saw how the so-cial mechanisms played out within England and Germany in the late nine-teenth/early twentieth centuries, and in the United States and Japan in the late twentieth century.

In the English case an earlier period of positive state intervention into the financial reform nexus during the mid-nineteenth century was contested by both LIGs and rentiers after 1890. As seen through the activities of groups such as Liverpool's Financial Reform Association, LIGs heightened their ex-pectations on their right to access to credit and property, as well as a shift to free trade that would lower their effective tax burdens. In contrast, rentiers incrementally constructed the idea of "gentlemanly capitalism" to assist the concentration of capital from once thriving and profitable provincial fi-nancial institutions into the City of London. Both LIGs and rentiers called upon the state to intervene on their behalf, particularly LIGs through the party political system and rentiers through the Bank of England, which im-plemented a redistributive "locks-up" policy on capital going back to the provinces.

We also saw that while the Liberal Party's ascension to power prevented a Conservative-rentier-led return to tariff protectionism, the party's actions to address the rentier shift were largely symbolic. Despite proclamations of the legitimacy of the new "social reform" by Liberal leaders, particularly David Lloyd George, there was a lack of action to redistribute access and assets away from rentiers. LIGs' frustrations translated into an active withdrawal from profitable financial institutions, particularly the Post Office Savings Bank system, and reflected a challenge to the Liberal Party's propagation of the idea that it was taking rentiers into hand. At the same time the Bank of En-gland and interests in the City of London propagated ideas of financial soundness and personal creditworthiness that aided the redistribution of as-sets and access toward short-sighted rentiers. These rentiers were so myopic, in fact, that their narrowly concentrated state-subsidized (the dreadnought argument) forms of international investment fell apart once World War I ar-rived. The lack of positive state intervention in the English case provided only moderate legitimation and weakened its international financial capac-ity. As such, there was no singular English national trajectory. Rather, there was a significant fork in the road with impediments to taking either route.

In Germany we saw how a state that was too autonomous from LIGs and too connected to rentiers prohibited the development of a social source of financial power. This finding problematizes both the notion that Germany's Great Banks (*Großbanken*) were well on the way to becoming world-beating financial powerhouses, and that Germany was on a special path (*Sonderweg*) that legitimated authoritarian state behavior to suppress social liberalism. As we saw, most of the political activity was around the public savings banks (*Sparkassen*) rather than the *Großbanken*. The German state also negatively intervened against LIGs despite increased contestation about their lack of access to credit and property, and unfair tax burdens (which, as we saw, determined voting rights in some regions), culminating in public rallies that ended with military force being used against civilians.

In Germany the conflict between the Reich and the *Länder* provided significant obstacles toward the development of direct taxation and encouraged local elites to use public financial institutions, particularly the *Sparkassen* and public agrarian large-landholder banks (*Landschaften*) for personal profit. Redistribution therefore went from LIGs to rentiers across the financial reform nexus, and credit access was concentrated among local elites. Legitimacy for the systematic extraction of rents from LIGs was claimed through the propagation of ideas about the need to fight "anonymous speculation" and Jewry, and to provide tariff protectionism and cheap credit to German large agrarian landholders on the grounds of national security. The constructed crises of speculation and Polish and Russian "land hunger" did not represent exogenous shocks to institutions, but were endogenously created by Prussian elites and large agrarian landholders attempting to legitimate their rentier shift. The widening gulf between, on the one hand, the German state's proclamations regarding the legitimacy of the financial reform nexus and, on the other, what LIGs viewed as legal and just resulted in a failure to generate a social source of financial power. This weakness was reflected in Germany's problems in coping with the financial strain of World War I.

In the Japanese case we found that contestation from LIGs largely fell on deaf ears. Despite numerous electoral challenges to the Liberal Democratic Party's long-held dominance, Japanese LIGs were increasingly frustrated by a lack of access to credit and property ownership. They were especially angered by the implementation of an economically very small but unpopular consumption tax that violated economic social norms. LIGs were also enraged by the use of taxpayer monies for both "extrastructure" and the bail out of rentier-like financial institutions. Proclamations about the legitimacy of government assistance for private banks did not gain consent from LIGs.

Unlike the English and German cases, however, the Japanese case did not reflect a significant split between different levels of the state—indeed, in 1985 the idea of a rentier shift was propagated by the ruling party, government ministries, and public financial institutions as a key component of a national trajectory of sustainable economic growth into a mature economy. The consequence of such policy convergence, however, was not an increased legitimation of the financial reform nexus. On the contrary, institutional change increased the extraction of rents from LIGs. Changes to the Housing Loan Corporation provide a good example, particularly its transformation from an institution built with the purpose of using its tax monies to subsidize loans to LIGs, to one that instead subsidized loans to rentier landlords. More generally, the Japanese post-1985 rentier shift led to international investments that were enormous in volume but increasingly precarious and which had little comparative influence on the character of the international financial order.

The closest case to the ideal type that emerges from our comparative historical study is the United States. While we should certainly not don rose-colored glasses about the capacity of the United States to naturally intervene in the economy in the interest of LIGs (take, for example, Reagan's first administration, or the George W. Bush administration in the epilogue to follow), the state did engender a social source of financial power that allowed it to boost its international financial capacity. This generation of financial power was at its strongest point under the Clinton administration, where institutional change and financial innovations in accordance with LIG's's economic social norms permitted a significant expansion in LIGs' property ownership, the sustained growth of Federal Mortgage Agencies (FMAs) to become a global debt securities giant, and assisted the rejuvenation of U.S. commercial banking. The U.S. domestic financial system became broader and deeper as it drew in actors from across the income spectrum and generated financial innovations. This change was not simply a consequence of low interest rates and "trickle-down" economic outcomes. Rather, political struggles between groups over how the economy should work led to institutional changes that broadened the social source of financial power and both benefited from and contributed to a more stable economic environment.

In the U.S. case, LIGs' contestation of the legitimacy of the financial reform nexus was particularly prominent. Advocacy groups such as the National Community Reinvestment Coalition and National People's Action contested potential changes to institutions against a backdrop of "civil rights," "fair housing," and "community reinvestment."[14] Such contestation became especially prominent in the wake of the attempted rentier shift during the first Reagan administration, and assisted its reversal from 1985 onward. Furthermore, the contestation also came from overlapping regulatory oversight between government agencies. The Department of Urban Housing and Development (particularly its Office of Federal Housing Enterprise Oversight), for example, kept its eye on FMAs' compliance with fair housing and community reinvestment legislation, while the Office of Thrift Supervision acted in a similar manner and the Federal Reserve oversaw everybody. The attention given to the prevention of "redlining" of LIGs (particularly minority LIGs), the tax breaks given to owner-occupiers rather than landlords, and the creditworthiness data obligations (such as the Home Mortgage Disclosure Act requirements) placed upon private financial institutions all helped to redistribute assets and access to LIGs.

An important lesson is that state centralization, such as through pilot eco-

---

14. Mara S. Sidney, *Unfair Housing: How National Policy Shapes Community Action* (Lawrence: University Press of Kansas, 2003), 17–18.

nomic agencies, is not necessarily the best means to build state capacity. The Democratic Party also played an important role in Congress in slowing and blocking legislative changes that would free up private financial institutions from their fetters of social responsibility.[15] Accordingly, the propagation of economic social norms focused less on kicking government out of private finance and more on increasing institutional capacity for creditworthiness assessment. As such we should take the proclamations of institutional entrepreneurs with a pinch of salt and not see them as auto-legitimating, including Republican senator Phil Gramm's trumpeting that "we have learned that government is not the answer" at the signing of the Financial Services Modernization Act that broke decades of apparent "gridlock" on financial institutions reform (as discussed in Chapter 5). Rather, financial institutions reform in the United States was stalled until it could be sufficiently legitimated.

The conferral of such legitimacy, however, does not necessarily mean that all LIGs were better off economically. Legitimacy cannot be assessed by a profit/loss calculation, just as we cannot sensibly talk about a social phenomenon being absolutely legitimate or illegitimate. We know, for example, that economic inequality in the United States increased during the period under study as those at the top of the income distribution increased their wealth at a faster rate than those at the bottom.[16] The point here, however, is that new conventions on how the economy should work (such as the increased awareness of fair housing laws) became rigorous economic social norms. What is important here is that legitimacy came from a perception of increased social mobility that many LIGs could see in different ways across the financial reform nexus.[17] And even if we think that LIGs may have been better off by following a different course of action, we are equipped with 20:20 retrovision. Processes of legitimation, however, are not decided *ex post*.

From the cases under examination, the United States was able to produce the constellation closest to the ideal type. We need only look at mortgage securitization as an example. In the United States in the late 1990s, LIGs were enabled with greater access to credit for mortgages for property ownership. Their mortgage repayments were channeled and repackaged through FMAs as lines of credit that U.S. corporations and financial institutions eagerly adopted. The FMAs were also able to attract significant foreign investment, as discussed in the previous chapter. While it is strange to think that Japa-

---

15. In the 1985–2000 period the most active representative of community banking concerns was Texas Democrat Henry B. Gonzalez, who led the restructuring of the Federal Deposit Insurance Corporation in the late 1980s.

16. Asena Caner and Edward D. Wolff, "Asset Poverty in the United States, 1984–1999: Evidence from the Panel Study of Income Dynamics," *Review of Income and Wealth* 50, 4 (2004).

17. See, in particular, Mérove Gijsberts, "The Legitimation of Income Inequality in State-Socialist and Market Societies," *Acta Sociologica* 45, 4 (2002).

nese and Chinese institutions were increasingly investing in public and quasi-public U.S. agencies that then used the same capital to enhance mortgage provision to LIGs, this is precisely what occurred. Certainly the generation of this financial power came from causes that one would not expect from the U.S. national trajectory of liberal market capitalism discussed in the "varieties of capitalism" and "state capacity" literature. As discussed in the previous chapter, the domestic legitimation of the U.S. financial reform nexus also led to an emphasis on creditworthiness within the international financial order that created an "international creditor economy." The legitimation of U.S. influence within the international financial order, however, is a topic beyond the scope of this book.

The cases demonstrate that everyday struggles between social groups over how the economy should work inform institutional and social change. The emergence of liquid conventions, such as increased consumption of foodstuffs in England in preference to saving money in financial institutions with waning legitimacy, or a similar new convention in Japan with the emergence of "wardrobe deposits," reflected LIGs' frustrations that their collectively shared expectations about how the economy should work were being violated. The selection of such conventions does not follow a pure economic logic but follows reflection upon economic social norms. Such influences must be interpreted and specified and we should not stray into treating norms as error terms that push actors off an otherwise utility-maximizing behavioral path, as is the tendency in rationalist institutionalism.

The cases also show that most institutional change is incremental and highly contingent on struggles between social groups and the state. This requires that we disaggregate forms of state intervention into positive and negative types and resist viewing states as following an institutional national trajectory that will only select ideas about institutional change that "fit," as often found in historical institutionalism. Such a structural explanation of institutional change permits little room for agency, and even less for the influence of LIGs.

My emphasis on everyday struggle also requires us to downplay, but not disregard, the role of radical uncertainty in explanations of institutional change. Within the cases, there are few moments when actors have no idea how to deal with a crisis. Even in the U.S. savings and loans crisis of the early 1980s, we saw a managed decline where the reform process took years and spurred contestation from LIGs that did influence institutional reforms. As discussed in Chapter 2, such struggle over ideas and economic social norms in everyday life is missed by economic constructivists and their focus on ideational entrepreneurs in times of radical uncertainty. As a consequence, economic constructivism has put forward a thin conception of legitimacy by proclamation that excludes a conception of society, and social influence, separate from institutions.

Weberian Economic Sociology and Economic Constructivism

The key contribution of economic constructivism to political economy and institutional theory is an emphasis on how ideas provide weapons in struggles over institutional change. This literature therefore takes a significant step from earlier work on how ideas must fit into an institutional logic of appropriateness to matter.[18] Economic constructivism has also taken the positive step of challenging the need for a general theory of institutional change and calls instead for comparative historical analysis in association with social mechanisms.[19]

In this book I have argued that Weberian economic sociology can augment economic constructivism with a focus on everyday struggle within which *axiorational* actors select liquid conventions to influence economic social norms. Weberian economic sociology also provides us with a strong focus on how economic social norms saturate individual choice by positing a society that is separate from institutions. We require such a conception to avoid the notion that everything is an institution, thereby collapsing social change into institutional change. Such a mistake encourages us to overemphasize institutional form and miss how actors draw upon non-institutional resources to influence their everyday political and economic environment. As such, explanations inevitably then fall back on picking "triggers" or "critical junctures" of significant changes to institutional form, thereby replicating punctuated equilibrium models. Instead, there is a dynamic relationship between institutional and social change that is informed by struggle between individuals seeking to fulfill their life-chances. Weberian economic sociology holds the six following assumptions as starting points for analyzing legitimacy in institutional and social change:[20]

    i) Individual belief-driven action is the root of institutional and social change, even when individuals act within social groups. Such actions are not held to be governed by universal laws of behavior but are informed by conventions and norms that become axiorational behavior.

   ii) All actors rationalize their environments to order and operate within them. Such rationalizations include instrumental aims but are certainly not reducible to them, as economic social norms saturate individual choice.

---

18. Mark Blyth, *Great Transformations: Economic Ideas and Institutional Change in the Twentieth Century* (Cambridge: Cambridge University Press, 2002); Craig Parsons, *A Certain Idea of Europe* (Ithaca: Cornell University Press, 2003).

19. Parsons, *A Certain Idea*, 238–42.

20. These principles are drawn from Weber, *Economy and Society*, Vol. 1, Chapters 1 and 2. Compare with Richard Swedberg, *Max Weber and the Idea of Economic Sociology* (Princeton: Princeton University Press, 1998), 163. On legitimacy see David Beetham, *The Legitimation of Power* (London: Macmillan, 1991), 31–35.

iii) When engaging the economy actors take into consideration the meaning of their actions for others. Actors reflect on not only pure economic phenomena, but also how economic behavior affects non-economic phenomena and vice versa.

iv) Actors are engaged in an everyday struggle with others in pursuit of their life-chances. In this pursuit they select conventions, which are liquid and recombinant, to influence economic social norms. Over time the frequent use of a convention establishes an economic social norm.

v) All economic social behavior is engaged in an ongoing process of legitimation. This process takes place between actors who claim that their actions have legitimacy, and actors who are affected by the actions and assess to what extent claims to legitimacy should be conferred with consent.

vi) We can understand all of the above only through interpreting the specific social context of the period.

These assumptions underpin the analysis in this book. While some of these points may be seen as of theoretical importance only, they are important for economic constructivism, in particular, and political economy and institutional theory, in general, because they call us to problematize rationality, to afford agency to actors often considered to have no causal significance to political and economic change, and to treat legitimacy as a dynamic process rather than ignoring it or treating it as a state's resource or condition.

The above assumptions, as discussed in Chapter 2, also call us to reconcile ourselves with an idiographic rather than nomothetic methodological individualism as the source of institutional and social change. Legitimacy must be understood, at its very base, as individual-level phenomena, since belief, and belief-driven actions that may follow, is necessarily subjective before becoming intersubjective. This view allows us to move away from rationalist institutionalism's individual, self-interested utility maximizer as the abstract unit of analysis, without turning to a view that all social phenomena are relative and not grounded in the material world. Rather, by acknowledging that individuals give meaning to their belief-driven actions *a posteriori* rather than *a priori* we can understand axiorational behavior as the basis for economic social action.[21] Through the Weberian interpretive (*Verstehen*) method of placing individual action in historical context, we may also understand how norms saturate decision making rather than viewing them as error terms. Reconciling ourselves to idiographic methodological individualism also allows us to provide actors with greater agency and to shrug off

---

21. Raymond Boudon, "The Social Sciences and the Two Types of Relativism," *Comparative Sociology* 2, 3 (2003): 437.

the excessive structuralism of some historical institutionalist and economic constructivist scholarship that views actors as almost overwhelmingly responding to a logic of appropriateness.

I have stressed that actors choose liquid conventions and are saturated by economic social norms. The key point here is that individuals involved in legitimation processes often select elements of extant conventions to influence economic social norms and therefore the behavior of rulers if they seek to claim that their actions have sufficient legitimacy. It is in this sense that conventions are liquid and always entwined with legitimation processes.[22]

The conception of selection (*Auslese*), as suggested in Chapter 2, is also important to recognize, particularly given its similarity to recent literature within institutional theory on "bricolage" and "translation."[23] It is only in this sense that economic social change is evolutionary, that through struggle actors innovate and recombine ideational and material resources.[24] Winston Churchill's tinkering with the normative force of a past "dear food" and changing it into a contemporary "dear houses" argument to reflect LIGs changing economic social norms, and accordant frustrations, provides a good example of a liquid selection of conventions. It also provides a good example of how social change "backgrounded" potential institutional change. This behavior, unlike recent economic constructivism, takes place among a range of social actors, including LIGs, and not only ideational entrepreneurs and elites. The selection of "civil rights" norms by U.S. advocacy groups to argue for new conventions on how financial institutions should behave is another example, particularly its persistence in providing a new economic social norm based on "community reinvestment." As we will see in the epilogue to follow, this economic social norm is now under attack by Republicans and rentier interest groups on the grounds of "regulatory relief" to improve the sound allocation of credit.

With the aid of Weberian economic sociology we can move away from the idea of legitimacy by proclamation and seek to understand struggles not only over claims to legitimacy but also their conferral. Furthermore, this approach emphasizes the need to study dynamic processes and move away from a reliance on exogenous shocks in understanding institutional and social change.[25] In short, economic constructivism can learn from Weberian economic sociology and from Max Weber's conception of legitimacy in seek-

22. Weber, *GAW,* 575–80.

23. Weber, *Economy and Society,* 1: 38–40; John L. Campbell, *Institutional Change and Globalization* (Princeton: Princeton University Press, 2004), Chapter 3.

24. W. G. Runciman, *The Social Animal* (London: HarperCollins, 1998).

25. As recently argued by Kathleen Thelen, *How Institutions Evolve: The Political Economy of Skills in Germany, Britain, the United States and Japan* (Cambridge: Cambridge University Press, 2004), 291–94; Mark Blyth, "When Liberalisms Change: Comparing the Politics of Deflations and Inflations," in Arthur T. Denzau, Thomas C. Willett, and Ravi K. Roy, eds., *Neoliberalism: Ideas, Interests, and the Changing International Economy* (London and New York: Palgrave, 2005).

ing to understand how ideas are enmeshed in everyday struggles over institutional and social change.

Prospects and Purpose

This book has sought to provide a qualitative "middle range theory" of the social mechanisms that can build or undermine the construction of a social source of financial power. The case studies compare states against an ideal type and seek to outline, through three social mechanisms, why states did or did not deepen and broaden their domestic pool of capital through their legitimation of financial reform nexuses for LIGs and, then, how this constellation informed their influence in the international financial order. Throughout this analysis I have emphasized the importance of disaggregating state intervention to reveal everyday struggle between the state and social groups.

Any analysis, of course, can be improved. While I do not think that a large-n statistical analysis would permit the detailed interpretation of institutional and social change from the small-n comparisons provided here, further research could certainly turn its attention to providing greater quantitative evidence. We cannot simply mark a dollar bill and see how far it goes up the chain of financial institutions, but access to detailed breakdowns of financial data from the types of institutions discussed here would improve our process tracing and lend greater support for the propositions in addition to the strong, albeit counterintuitive in many cases, logic of the argument. Still, as discussed, legitimacy is not derived only from economic performance, particularly decided *ex post,* and actors often willingly incur personal economic costs to fulfill economic social norms.

All of the above leads to the question as to whether studies of legitimacy are transferable to other issue areas, particularly as I have emphasized interpretation, historical contingency, and a conception of legitimacy that embraces a form of methodological individualism—all propositions thought to stand in bad odor in much social science. The answer is that legitimacy and belief-driven action among LIGs are relevant in any area of broad political and economic concern, and comparative historical analyses of how LIGs have agency in the domestic and international political economies are sorely needed.[26]

The legitimation of institutional change for LIGs on issues as diverse as labor retraining, labor casualization, the burden of consumption taxes, the connection between monetary policy and political conservatism among new propertied groups, and the relationship between national identity, eco-

---

26. John M. Hobson and Leonard Seabrooke, eds., *Everyday International Political Economy: Non-Elite Actors and the Transformation of the World Economy* (forthcoming).

nomic social norms, and agricultural trade policy all spring to mind.[27] This is particularly the case as the literature on varieties of capitalism and state capacity deals poorly with issues of broader political representation. As Reinhard Bendix reminds us, while we may speculate how states are most likely to become internationally competitive, this knowledge is of little use if the state does not have sufficient legitimacy to harness support from its broader population.[28] Understanding legitimation dynamics, particularly through the disaggregation of state intervention, is therefore very important.

Another area is the relationship between corporations and society. While much economic sociology is devoted to understanding conceptions of corporate control, there is little on the politics of corporate behavior in relation to their legitimation claims made to the broader public. On the contrary, much of this recent literature views legitimacy as a condition bestowed on markets and market actors by states.[29] In contrast, for this book the state is simply the prism through which struggles between social groups over legitimacy refract.

We also need a better understanding of legitimacy *within* the international political economy beyond the view that the legitimacy of international organizations comes from following their own rules, supplying technical know-how, and providing positive outcomes.[30] It is vital to move beyond the view of legitimacy by proclamation from international and national policy elites, as discussed earlier. In this area, understanding the "legitimacy gaps" between what international organizations claim as legitimate and what member state governments are willing to provide their consent for in front of their own populations presents a research challenge.[31]

In all these areas my view is that Weberian economic sociology and Max Weber's conception of legitimacy can greatly enhance economic constructivism's pertinent focus on ideational struggles that inform material life. In doing so we can provide a rich account of institutional and social change in which the broader population does not take a back seat, and where we recognize the capacity of a range of actors and social groups to transform their own political and economic environments by contesting the legitimacy of power. This reminds us that institutions, particularly state institutions, op-

27. Recent remedies to this include Pepper D. Culpepper, *Creating Cooperation: How States Develop Human Capital in Europe* (Ithaca: Cornell University Press, 2003); Mlada Bukovansky, "Embedding or Disembedding Agriculture? Hypocrisy and Legitimacy Contests in the Regime Governing Agricultural Trade", unpublished manuscript, Smith College, April 2004.
28. Reinhard Bendix, *Nation-Building and Citizenship* (Berkeley: University of California Press, 1977), 20–21, 416.
29. For example, Neil Fligstein, *The Architecture of Markets: An Economic Sociology of Twenty-First Century Capitalist Societies* (Princeton: Princeton University Press, 2002), 97.
30. Michael Barnett and Martha Finnemore, *Rules for the World: International Organizations in Global Politics* (Ithaca: Cornell University Press, 2004), 166–70.
31. Leonard Seabrooke, "Legitimacy Gaps and Institutional Change: The International Monetary Fund and Domestic Tax Reforms," unpublished manuscript, International Center for Business and Politics, Copenhagen Business School, September 2004.

erate with values and economic social norms that we have a capacity to influence. Detailing the comparative historical dynamics of legitimation is important because it permits us to understand why domestic political economies and international political economies differ in character over time. Such analyses ask us to interpret and understand the meaning given to economic social action by a range of different actors and, accordingly, how interests are determined not by an atomized economic impulse, but through engagement with the outer world of institutions and society, and the inner world of the self. By augmenting economic constructivism with Weberian economic sociology we are better able to understand the dynamics of legitimacy and, with it, how everyday struggles provide the social sources of institutional change.

Epilogue

The George W. Bush Rentier Shift

While the financial reform nexus under the Clinton administration was able to generate a social source of financial power through strong legitimacy, the signs are that this is now changing. Under the Bush administration sweeping changes to the financial reform nexus are occurring that portend of a rentier shift. Negative state interventions on credit access, property ownership, and tax burdens are redistributing assets and opportunities away from people in lower-income groupings (LIGs) and toward rentiers. There are four key facets to these changes:

i)   how regulatory reforms to financial institutions are undermining the Community Reinvestment Act of 1977 (CRA) and encouraging rentier-type investment behavior;
ii) how the administration seeks to fully privatize the role and purpose of Federal Mortgage Agencies (FMAs);
iii) how tax cuts benefit rentiers, especially if a proposed change to make consumption tax the cornerstone of the U.S. fiscal system takes place; and
iv) how investments to and from the United States reflect a domestic rentier shift.

In aggregate, these changes are radically altering the U.S. financial reform nexus and undermining its legitimacy for LIGs. Underpinning these changes are struggles over how the U.S. economy should work, how individuals should view others in the economy, and what obligations state and society have to protecting LIGs.

Credit Politics: The Sun Shines on Cowboy Financiers

The Bush administration has taken to implementing "regulatory relief" for private financial institutions and weakening the CRA provisions bolstered under Clinton's time in office with great enthusiasm. It began by exploiting a provision in the Financial Modernization Act of 1999 that introduced "sunshine requirements" to permit "small institutions" (those with less than $250 million in assets) relaxed CRA examination conditions. The sunshine for institutions here was a CRA examination only once every four years for institutions with an "outstanding" rating and once every three years for those with a "satisfactory" rating.

In 2004 the Federal Reserve (Fed), the Office of Thrift Supervision (OTS), Office of the Comptroller of the Currency (OCC), and the Federal Deposit Insurance Corporation (FDIC) proposed reclassifying "small institutions" as those with assets less than $500 million. The proposal provoked contestation from groups such as the National Community Reinvestment Coalition (NCRC), the National Fair Housing Alliance, and National People's Action (NPA) who successfully targeted the Fed to stop the reclassification.[1] However, the OTS unilaterally reclassified "small institutions" as those with less than $1 billion in assets, permitting 88 percent of the institutions under its purview to come under more lax rule enforcement. As the OTS primarily regulates savings and loans associations (S&Ls) that specialize in residential mortgages, the change represents a significant violation of the CRA. Unfortunately, the FDIC soon followed by signaling its interest in adopting the reclassification. These changes drew the attention of a campaigning Senator John F. Kerry, who argued that the Bush appointees heading the OTS and FDIC were choosing "favors for special interests over opportunity for millions of average Americans."[2] Should the FDIC decide to adopt the reclassification, 80 percent of the institutions it deals with would also come under "sunshine requirements." Within Congress there is also new Republican-led legislation to pass the "small institutions" reclassification law.[3]

Reforms akin to the deregulation of S&Ls in the early 1980s are also taking place. Particularly important here is the Financial Services Regulatory Relief Act of 2004, which would permit individuals to operate as small investment banks while being taxed as a partnership, allow bank director control of dividend payments, abolish bank's statutory obligation to publicize forthcoming mergers, and legalize the concealment of banks' fee income profits.[4] Such a change would not only encourage the rentier-type investment activity that mushroomed through Texas and California in the early

1. See, for example, testimony of John Taylor, President of the NCRC, to Senate Committee on Banking, Housing, and Urban Affairs, on "Examination of the Gramm-Leach-Bliley Act Five Years After Its Passage," 13 July 2004. See also U.S. Federal Reserve Press Release, 16 July 2004, ⟨www.federalreserve.gov/boarddocs/press/bcreg/2004/20040716/default.htm⟩.
2. "U.S. Set to Alter Rules for Banks Lending to the Poor," *New York Times*, 20 October 2004.
3. Promoting Community Investment Act of 2004. At the time of writing (January 2005), the legislation is in the Subcommittee on Financial Institutions and Consumer Credit.
4. Currently under review with the Senate Committee on Banking, Housing, and Urban Affairs. Voting in the House gave the bill 94 percent support. The first provision is individual classification as a "subchapter S corporation" by the Internal Revenue Service.

1980s, but significantly hobble advocacy groups, such as the NCRC and NPA, who rely on the disclosure of forthcoming mergers to draw attention to banks' poor CRA performance.

Property Politics: Hard Times and Cheap Money

The Bush administration recognizes that the convention of accessing credit for housing through fair housing programs has become a resilient economic social norm, and has promoted programs to increase LIGs' access to tax credits for this purpose.[5] At the same time, it seeks to strip FMAs of their privileges. The two largest, Fannie Mae and Freddie Mac, together hold $3.8 trillion in housing sector assets and are the world's most important issuers of fixed-income securities after the U.S. Treasury. These competing aims have led to dislocations within the U.S. financial reform nexus.

In general, LIGs have been more successful in acquiring mortgages from private financial institutions during a period of low interest rates. However, the rolling back of CRA provisions has also permitted greater rejections. To take an example, for African American LIGs there was a 54 percent increase in loan applications for private financial institutions that were rejected following credit assessment between 2001 and 2003.[6] At the same time, growth in non-owner occupier mortgage loans has been nothing short of remarkable. Between 2001 and 2003, growth in this category for people on more than 120 percent of median income was 40 percent.[7] And while we cannot point to a systematic extraction of rents for landlords, as in the Japanese case in Chapter 6, we certainly should question to what extent FMAs and private financial institutions are embracing landlordism and excluding LIGs from credit access.

As a proportion of total funding in credit markets within the United States, the FMAs rose rapidly during the Clinton years, from 16 percent in 1995 to 26 percent in 2000. By 2003 FMAs' funding went back to below 1998 levels.[8] The reason why is that FMAs have narrowed their client base. After 2000 the FMAs, with the exception of Ginnie Mae, have increasingly catered to institutions providing mortgages for additional homes and for "multifamily residential mortgages" (such as for an apartment block). By 2004 the FMAs were dealing less and less with institutions that lent mortgages to LIGs, prompting the Department of Housing and Urban Develop-

---

5. Such as the *American Dream Tax Credit and the Single-Family Affordable Housing Tax Credit.*
6. Federal Financial Institutions Examination Council, Home Mortgage Disclosure Act Database, National Aggregates, Table 5–2, 2001–03. See ⟨www.ffiec.gov/hmda/⟩.
7. Ibid., Table 5–6, 2001–03.
8. Board of Governors of the Federal Reserve, *Flow of Funds Accounts of the United States, 1995– 2003: Annual Flows and Outstandings* (Washington, D.C.: U.S. Federal Reserve, 9 December 2004), 1, Table F.1.

ment (HUD) to complain that the FMAs were straying from their mission and should "do what is expected of them—helping low- and moderate-income families at least at the same percentage levels as primary market lenders."[9] Clearly reform of the FMAs is needed to ensure that they cater to LIGs as much as or more than private financial institutions. After all, the FMAs' key role in the U.S. financial system has been to deepen and broaden the domestic pool of capital by including groups whose previous attempts to access credit for property ownership were frustrated.

The Bush administration intends to make radical reforms to the FMAs, but not in a manner that would assist them in providing more to LIGs. The administration asserts that the FMAs should be completely privatized and provide a "pass through" service that does not imply access to Treasury capital in case of default. This proposal was no doubt aided by the FMA accounting scandals of 2004 that emerged at the same time as Republicans introduced a number of bills in Congress to remove all privileges going to the FMAs. Completely privatizing the FMAs would, the argument goes, remove their monopoly on the secondary mortgage market and place them on equal footing with private financial institutions. However, the FMAs have become colossal financial institutions precisely because they are not regular financial institutions. Their quasi-public status suggests an implicit *state guarantee* to lenders and borrowers that provides their financial operations with greater legitimacy. Removing their economic social purpose would either result in a diminution of their broad customer base or a diminution of their total business, or both. Neither are confluent with Bush's stated aim of generating a broadly based "ownership society."

Tax Politics: Aggressive Regression

Added to these fundamental changes in credit and property politics, the Bush administration's tax reforms merely add to the problems faced by LIGs. They also run completely counter to the postwar bipartisan consensus on appropriate forms of taxation. From 1960 to 2000 the United States consistently taxed personal income, property, and corporations at a higher level proportional to overall tax revenue than Britain, France, Germany, Japan, and Sweden (with the exception of Japan on corporations).[10] During Bush's first term (2001–05) tax cuts pushed income tax as a percentage of GDP back to 1950s levels (8 percent compared to Clinton's 12 percent), and corporate taxation back to 1940s levels (1.3 percent of GDP in 2003). These changes were enacted through the Tax Reform Acts (TRA) of 2001 and 2003. TRA 2001 pro-

9. HUD Secretary Alphonso Jackson, Department of Housing and Urban Development Press Release, 8 July 2004, ⟨www.hud.gov/news/release.cfm?content=pro4-066.cfm⟩.
10. Leonard Seabrooke, "The Economic Taproot of U.S. Imperialism: The Bush Rentier Shift," *International Politics* 41, 3 (2004): 303–4, Tables 2–5.

vided a 1 percent cut across all income tax rates, and increased tax credits, especially for married couples, as well as upwardly adjusting the Alternative Minimum Tax and limits on investments into Individual Retirement Accounts and "401(k)" accounts for high-income earners.[11]

TRA 2001 also included a major reform to estate taxes, which saw a tax exemption for all estates valued at under $1 million in 2001 (as opposed to Clinton's $700,000), rising to $3.5 million in 2009 before the reversal of all the tax reforms at the start of 2011. TRA 2003 dropped the top marginal rate of income tax from 38.5 percent to 35 percent, as well as cutting capital gains tax from 20 to 15 percent. TRA 2003 also abolished the "double taxation" of dividends on investments from trusts, estates, and personal holding companies on the grounds that it was taxing "sweat equity" and impeding economic growth. In sum, 20 percent of the TRA 2001 has been estimated to benefit only the top 1 percent of income earners for the 2001–05 period, a figure that jumps to 41 percent for 2006–09.[12] Similarly, TRA 2003 provided a 9 percent tax cut for those earning more than $1 million, while providing LIGs with a 0.3 percent tax cut.[13]

The concept of "sweat equity" has become an important framing tool for the Bush administration, since it provides an economic bridge between rentiers and the "Average Joe." The Bush administration has broadened the definition of "sweat equity" beyond the difference between the invested capital and owing capital on a physical asset, like a house, to include energies devoted to financial investment. The conceptual leap for the Bush administration's argument here is that "sweat equity" capital income should not be taxed on the grounds that increased capital costs reduces workers' wages and therefore their capacity to build "sweat equity." What is preferred, then, is a general change from taxing income to taxing consumption to enable individuals to choose how much tax they pay by how much they consume.[14]

In 2003 a president-approved "FairTax" bill was introduced to Congress that would place a flat 23 percent tax on all consumption and remove income taxes. The 2003 *Economic Report of the President* elaborated on this policy, arguing that a shift to consumption tax would allow income tax to be "ripped out by its roots" and would enhance the "well-being" of individual taxpayers by promoting greater freedom of choice.[15] The key point here is the Bush administration's assertion that tax is *not a social obligation but an in-*

11. The Alternative Minimum Tax is a recalculation of taxable income to prevent tax evasion. About 12 percent of Americans were affected by the tax in 2005, and it is expected to affect about 30 percent of taxpayers by 2010.

12. Citizens for Tax Justice, "Year-by-Year Analysis of the Bush Tax Cut Shows Growing Tilt to the Very Rich," 12 June 2002, ⟨www.ctj.org/html/gwbo602.htm⟩.

13. William G. Gale, "The President's Tax Proposal: First Impressions," *Tax Notes* 13 January (2003), 266.

14. *Economic Report of the President* (Washington, D.C.: U.S. Government Printing Office, 2004), 112.

15. *Economic Report of the President* (Washington, D.C.: U.S. Government Printing Office, 2003), 179, 185.

dividual burden. This is a radically different view of taxation from previous administrations and, given that taxation on consumption disproportionately affects LIGs, it will undoubtedly reverse the broadening and deepening of the domestic pool of capital developed during the Clinton years.

Bush and the International Financial Order

The most obvious macroeconomic area of concern for the Bush administration is the deficit. In the closing years of the Clinton administration the fiscal surplus was 2.4 percent of GDP. Under Bush the fiscal deficit was 3.5 percent of GDP in 2003 and began to exceed 4 percent thereafter, with a common expectation that an ongoing deficit of 5.5 percent of GDP will be unsustainable. There has been no clear resolution on how to resolve this issue. The Congressional Budget Office, for example, has suggested that fiscal revenue will increase by 3.6 percent in the next decade to eliminate the deficit, but this depends on the full implementation of the tax reforms described above, along with the continued growth of both credit and property markets often considered to be at bursting point.[16] It is also highly dependent on the severe cutting of social services, an unpopular transformation apparent in Bush's 2005 budget and proposed social security reforms.

Given potential domestic fiscal problems, a key international concern for the Bush administration is how to attract investors to its public debt. In late 2004, Japanese investors held 37 percent of U.S. Treasury securities, with Chinese running second at 10 percent, British third at 8 percent and Caribbean offshore financial centers fourth at 4 percent.[17] Considering the declining value of the U.S. dollar and very low interest rates, the pure commercial incentive for these investors is negligible beyond a possible desire to keep U.S. interest rates low. Even more odd is a switch in foreign investment to the United States from investment in FMAs to U.S. Treasury debt. For example, while foreign investment in FMAs represented just under 15 percent of U.S. credit market liabilities to the rest of the world in 2000, by 2003 the comparative figure was 2 percent.[18] In short, the Bush administration's wildly increased spending has drawn investment from the FMAs and into Treasury debt. We can safely assert that foreign investment in U.S. Treasury debt is a political decision for access to mass consumer markets. Japanese and the Chinese central banks, however, must wonder to what extent the United States can provide the function of an "international consumer of the last resort" with a high consumption tax. Furthermore, a change to consumption tax may lead to a credit crunch and property bub-

16. Congressional Budget Office, "The Budget and Economic Outlook: An Update," September 2004, ⟨www.cbo.gov⟩.
17. U.S. Treasury, Treasury International Capital System A.3, ⟨www.treas.gov/tic/mfh.txt⟩.
18. Board of Governors of the Federal Reserve, *Flow of Funds Accounts of the United States, 1995–2003*, 14, Table F. 107.

ble burst that would narrow the domestic pool of capital and send rentiers looking for investment opportunities overseas.

The comparative historical experience of international rentier investment suggests that when the home economy is flagging, rentiers seek stable profits by investing in "safe risks" overseas. This process is occurring in the United States, but not in a way similar to the English rentiers described in Chapter 7. Rather, it is clear from the available data that U.S. rentiers do not invest in their own government debt or in developing states' debt (foreign holdings of U.S. debt outweigh U.S. holdings of foreign debt by almost five times).[19] The exception here is reverse U.S. investment from Caribbean offshore financial centers back into Treasury debt. Foreign portfolio investment to Bermuda alone has increased nearly four times more than other kinds of U.S. individual foreign investment during Bush's time in office.[20] This represents a classic rentier scenario, whereby the rentier invests in a stable source of "unearned income" created by deficit spending—to pay for tax cuts that directly benefit the same rentier at home—while returns on this "unearned income" are then funneled through an offshore tax haven. U.S. individual investment in foreign equity also reflects what may be considered "safe risks," with investments in (by magnitude) oil and gas, telecommunications, pharmaceuticals, and banking stock.[21] Of course this first type of investment has proved socially divisive in the United States given its association with the use of military force in the Iraq war, and reminds us of LIGs' contestation against rentiers' dreadnoughts in Edwardian England (see Chapter 3).

In addition to investment changes, the United States has been less active than previous decades in attempting to influence international financial regulation. The Bank for International Settlements' Basle Accord II process provides an example. While the United States guided the formation of Basle Accord I, in 2003–04 it wavered on whether or not to participate in the Basle II process. Such inaction is particularly surprising considering that the largest casualty from the Basle II process within the U.S. system is likely to be the small financial institutions that grew rapidly in the late 1990s. The Bush administration is simply not in the game.

Domestic Legitimacy and International Financial Orders

The Bush administration's changes to the U.S. financial reform nexus indicate a rentier shift that is redistributing assets and opportunities away from LIGs. The changes described above signify not only a shift from positive to

19. U.S. Treasury, "Report on U.S. Holdings of Foreign Securities as of December 31, 2001" (Washington, D.C.: U.S. Treasury International Affairs Department, 2003), 7.
20. Ibid., 6.
21. Ibid., 16.

negative state intervention, but the breaking of a postwar consensus upon which the legitimation of the modern U.S. financial system was built. Complete Republican control of Congress will most likely further the rentier shift and narrow the domestic pool of capital as LIGs find themselves frustrated by less credit access, with more trouble obtaining property and with higher tax burdens.

The normative drive that accompanies the reforms detailed above is the propagation of a negative conception of freedom (such as freedom from government through "regulatory relief," as opposed to a positive conception of freedom through government from "community reinvestment") that seeks to alter LIGs' expectations about how the state should intervene in the economy and reinforces an idea of the economic individual atomized from society. A failure to redress this conception embraced by the Bush rentier shift will result in the further narrowing of the U.S.'s social source of financial power with serious implications for financial instability at home and abroad.

The Bush rentier shift has important implications not only for our own time but for comparative historical analyses of the social sources of financial power. It is perhaps no coincidence that the two great financial powers of the nineteenth and twentieth centuries were England and the United States, where forms of social liberalism were strongly developed with a positive conception of freedom. Social liberal ideas spurred social groups to contest the legitimacy of the financial reform nexus and impelled the state to facilitate access to resources necessary for ordinary people to fulfill their normative expectations about how the economy should work. Such state intervention sought to protect citizens, particularly LIGs, against the "unfreedoms" capitalist finance could introduce to society (as noted in the previous chapter). Consequent institutional changes then helped broaden and deepen the domestic pool of capital.

The key policy implication from this book is that the domestic legitimacy of the financial reform nexus for LIGs matters for states' influence on the international financial order. Governments, particularly the Bush administration, should therefore be wary when changing credit and property access and tax burdens. Despite the veil of uncertainty constructed from the war on terror or from "economic crises," LIGs' everyday struggles with tax, credit, and property provide the real battleground for the legitimation of the financial reform nexus. A focus on legitimacy reminds us that institutional change occurs in everyday increments rather than only or primarily in uncertainty. The common people do have a capacity to resist. It is through the "strong slow drilling of hard boards" of everyday political struggle that contests over the legitimacy of institutional change can be renewed.[22]

22. Max Weber, *Gesammelte Politische Schriften* (Tübingen: J. C. B. Mohr, 1988), 560.

Index

Cornell Studies in Political Economy

A series edited by
PETER J. KATZENSTEIN

Milton Keynes UK
Ingram Content Group UK Ltd.
UKHW020645110824
446630UK00003B/13/J

9 780801 443800